Intra-household Resource Allocation: Issues and Methods for Development Policy and Planning

Intra-household Resource Allocation: Issues and Methods for Development Policy and Planning

Papers prepared for the Workshop on Methods of Measuring Intra-household Resource Allocation, Gloucester, Massachusetts, USA, October 1983

Edited by
BEATRICE LORGE ROGERS and NINA P. SCHLOSSMAN

 United Nations University Press

Food and Nutrition Bulletin Supplement 15

This volume arises from the interest of the United Nations University in research contributing to the understanding and support of the central role of women in maintaining household nutrition and health under conditions of poverty. It constitutes a part of the University's Nutrition and Primary Health Care Project, and is based on a workshop funded by USAID that focused on the practical application of methodologies from the disciplines of anthropology, economics, and psychology to the analysis of household resource distribution issues. The objective was information that will help to avoid negative consequences and promote positive effects of development programmes. The book discusses not only measurement of intra-household food and health related behaviours, but also of how the household responds to economic and social changes and interventions.

United Nations University Press
The United Nations University, Toho Seimei Building, 15-1 Shibuya 2-chome,
Shibuya-ku, Tokyo 150, Japan,
Tel.: (03) 499-2811   Telex: J25442   Cable: UNATUNIV TOKYO

Typeset by Asco Trade Typesetting Limited, Hong Kong
Printed by Permanent Typesetting and Printing Co., Ltd, Hong Kong
Cover design by Tsuneo Taniuchi

WHTR-13/UNUP-733
ISBN 92-808-0733-1
United Nations Sales No. E.90.III.A.2
03500 P

Contents

Foreword   vii
Acknowledgements   ix

1. The Internal Dynamics of Households: A Critical Factor in Development Policy
   Beatrice Lorge Rogers   1

I. Conceptual Frameworks

Conceptual Frameworks
Beatrice Lorge Rogers and Nina P. Schlossman   23

2. Programme Interventions, Intra-household Allocation, and the Welfare of Individuals: Economic Models of the Household
   Mark R. Rosenzweig   26
3. Peeking into the Black Box of Economic Models of the Household
   Jere R. Behrman   44
4. Intra-household Allocation of Resources: Perspectives from Anthropology
   Ellen Messer   51
5. Intra-household Allocation of Resources: Perspectives from Psychology
   Patrice L. Engle   63

II. Methodological Approaches to Measurement

Methodological Approaches to Measurement
Beatrice Lorge Rogers and Nina P. Schlossman   83

6. Combining Quantitative and Qualitative Methods in the Study of Intra-household Resource Allocation
   Susan C.M. Scrimshaw   86
7. An Approach to the Study of Women's Productive Roles as a Determinant of Intra-household Allocation Patterns
   Lynn Bennett   99

8. Household Organization and Expenditure in a Time Perspective: Social
   Processes of Change
   Elizabeth Jelín   114

III.   *Measurement of Key Variables*

   Measurement of Key Variables
   Beatrice Lorge Rogers and Nina P. Schlossman   131
9. Multiple Group Membership and Intra-household Resource Allocation
   Peter Heywood   135
10. Time-allocation Research: The Costs and Benefits of Alternative Methods
    Allen Johnson   140
11. Use of Emic Units for Time-use Recall
    Marian Frank Zeitlin   156
12. Data on Food Consumption by High-risk Family Members: Its Utility for
    Identifying Target Households for Food and Nutrition Programmes
    Per Pinstrup-Andersen and Marito Garcia   164
13. Determinants of the Ability of Household Members to Adapt to Social and
    Economic Changes
    Constantina Safilios-Rothschild   176

Conclusions
Beatrice Lorge Rogers and Nina P. Schlossman   185

Appendix   187

Participants   203

Foreword

The papers in this volume were prepared for the Workshop on Methods of Measuring Intra-household Resource Allocation, which took place in October 1983. The workshop was funded by the United States Agency for International Development, Bureau of Policy and Program Co-ordination, Office of Policy Development and Program Review, under grant number OTR-0096-GSS-2268-00 as part of a larger project on ways of incorporating a concern for the internal distribution processes of households into the design of economic development interventions.

The focus on project design and programme planning explains the applied nature of many of the papers in this volume. Wherever possible, the authors discuss applications of their topics in the context of the real-world constraints that donor agencies face on both time and funds. The theoretical issues raised in these papers are vital to the development of methods for measuring and monitoring changes within the household.

The first paper in the volume makes the case for including an analysis of intra-household issues in the design of effective, successful development programmes and as a means of avoiding unanticipated negative consequences. The rest of the papers are grouped in three parts. The first provides a set of conceptual frameworks for the study of the internal dynamics of household resource distribution derived from three major disciplines that have been concerned with these questions: economics, anthropology, and psychology. These papers illustrate the complementary perspectives and methods the three disciplines bring to the study of the household. They effectively show how the insights they provide should be integrated in the programme planning process.

The papers in part II present several approaches to collecting the information needed to analyse household dynamics as part of development planning. As a group, they stress the importance of combining qualitative with quantitative methods, and short-term with long-term perspectives.

The papers in part III discuss specific measurement issues related to estimating key variables of particular interest to planners and scholars concerned with intra-household issues. These variables include the definition of the household, how members allocate time, individual food consumption (as an example of an outcome measure used to assess the need for, and success of, some kinds of welfare-related programmes), and the flexibility of households in adapting to externally induced changes in the economic and social environment.

The Appendix presents in table format one approach to incorporating intra-household issues into the design and evaluation of development programmes.

Acknowledgements

We would like to thank Dr Judy McGuire and Dr Nancy Pielemeier of the Office of Policy and Program Co-ordination of USAID for their assistance, including substantial intellectual input and funding of the original conference.

Dr Stanley Gershoff, Dean of the Tufts University School of Nutrition, was instrumental in funding the activities needed to prepare these papers for publication. Dr Nevin Scrimshaw of the United Nations University arranged for the publication of the volume. Lisa Miller ably co-ordinated the conference at which these papers were first presented. Finally, we wish to express thanks to the people who participated in the conference (listed on page 203), and whose thoughtful comments and insights provided the basis for much of the thinking reflected in this book.

Beatrice Lorge Rogers and
Nina P. Schlossman,
Medford, Massachusetts

1
The Internal Dynamics of Households: A Critical Factor in Development Policy

BEATRICE LORGE ROGERS

Tufts University School of Nutrition, Medford, Massachusetts, USA

INTRODUCTION

Development projects have diverse objectives: the modernization of agriculture, improvement in health and nutritional status, reduction in fertility, and increased levels of literacy and education, to name but a few. The underlying goal of all such projects, however, is the same: to generate self-sustained economic development in order to improve the well-being of the poor in developing countries. The best methods to achieve this goal have been a subject of theoretical argument and empirical exploration for at least 50 years, and, in spite of continuing debate, progress has been made in understanding some of the connections between development projects and development itself.

This progress has added new dimensions to an initially rather simple model of the relationship between a country's aggregate economic activity and the economic well-being of its members. Without denying the importance of national, macro-economic factors, it has more recently been recognized that sectoral relations (e.g. between agriculture and industry) must also be considered; that urban–rural and socio-economic class distinctions must be recognized; and that disadvantaged population groups must be targeted specifically if they are to benefit from the development process. The most recent step in understanding development has been the insight that the process does not stop at the door of the household. If they are to be successful, development projects must take into account the ways in which households (themselves very variable in structure) allocate both goods and responsibilities among their members.

Project objectives, after all, focus on individuals. Health, nutritional status, literacy, even productivity are characteristics of individuals. Income, frequently measured at the level of the household, is a composite of individual members' incomes. Increasing evidence indicates that individual incomes are not simply pooled and then spent to meet household needs in some unified fashion. They are spent at least in part according to the earner's own preference.

The household is certainly an important unit for planning and analysis, but it cannot

1

be the only unit. It serves as a framework for specialization of effort and redistribution of goods, but it can also be a mechanism for limiting access to productive resources and for disproportionately allocating the burdens of work and its returns. While altruism is indeed one motivating force of household members in the allocative process, self-interest is surely another.

THE IMPORTANCE OF HOUSEHOLD DYNAMICS FOR PROJECT SUCCESS

The recognition that households follow allocative rules which may not always protect the most vulnerable members is of great significance for the selection and design of development projects. First, project benefits may be lost between the household and the target individual. It is a well-recognized problem of nutritional supplementation programmes, for example, that substitution of the supplement for home-supplied food often redirects the benefits of the supplement to other, less needy household members. Increasing a household's food supply should increase the food consumption of all members, but if only particular individuals within the household are targeted, patterns of distribution may cause those individuals to receive less than the projected amount. If the patterns are understood beforehand, then quantities can be adjusted or the programme can be redesigned to assure that sufficient food actually reaches the individuals in need.

Similarly, there are numerous cases in which agricultural extension services have been provided to households with the intention of increasing food production for subsistence, but the services were provided to men (or in such a way that only men would make use of them), while it was the women who had the primary responsibility for producing food (UNECA, n.d.; Loose, 1980). If the intra-household allocation of responsibilities had been understood in advance, services could have been planned to reach the appropriate individual, and the projects would have been more effective (Huggard, 1978).

Projects designed to increase household income have sometimes failed to improve indicators of individual well-being (Kennedy and Cogill, 1987), as in cases where the project increased the earnings of one member at the cost of another's, or where the form or the timing of the income was altered. It is not uncommon, particularly in sub-Saharan Africa, to find that husbands and wives have explicit responsibility for different aspects of household maintenance (Guyer, 1980). If women in a given setting are primarily responsible for providing food to the household, then an increase in income to men may not be translated directly into nutritional improvement of at-risk members. This is not to say that women's income is always spent on family well-being and men's income is not. In some cases, men may devote their incomes to investment in productive resources, while women purchase gold or jewellery as a form of savings. One study showed that Bangladeshi women save through hoarding (Alamgir, 1977). These examples emphasize the point that income is often spent differently by different earners. In order to predict the results of increasing household income, planners must understand that all income is *not* treated the same.

Moreover, designing a programme on the assumption that resources are pooled, and that therefore it makes no difference who receives the benefits in the name of the household, results in inequity to those household members who do not actually receive

2

the benefits. After the severe drought in the Sudan and the Sahel in 1975, herds were restored by granting cattle to male "heads of household." This scheme failed to acknowledge that, within the family unit, some cattle are owned by women who separately control their products, and that the women's loss was as serious and as important to rectify as the men's (Cloud, 1978). In the Mwea-Tebere irrigated rice settlement scheme in Kenya, payment for the harvested rice was given entirely to the nominal male head of the household upon delivery of the crop. Even though other household members had contributed a substantial amount of labour, they were unable to obtain payment equal to the value of their own work, because its full value was not recognized (Hanger and Moris, 1973).

Of course, neither households nor their internal patterns of distribution are static. Households adapt to changing circumstances, and if, for instance, the member traditionally responsible for feeding the family can no longer do so, other members will surely take over. Out-migration of male household members seeking urban employment has resulted in women assuming formerly male agricultural tasks. LeVine (1966) has documented this in Kenya and South Africa, and Colvin and colleagues (cited in Chaney and Lewis, 1980) in Mali. In highland Peru, women manage the farms when their husbands are engaged in wage labour elsewhere (Alberti, 1982).

Understanding existing distribution patterns may eventually permit planners to predict how they will change in response to particular interventions. The current state of knowledge in this field is not yet sufficiently advanced for that. At present, it can only be said that households do adapt, but not always rapidly, and not always in the most advantageous ways.

A second implication of intra-household dynamics for project planning is that benefits to some household members may result in burdens to others. Projects should therefore be planned, taking into account their potential secondary effects on household task allocation. Projects which encourage the education of children illustrate these trade-offs. In many if not most developing country settings, school-age children are important contributors of family labour, either in market or in home production (Nag et al., 1978; King-Quizon, 1978). The loss of children's labour time when they go to school results in a greater burden on the remaining household members (Minge-Klevana, 1978; Reynolds, n.d.). How this burden is redistributed will depend on how the children's work was viewed. If the children are seen as "helping their mothers," then the mothers may have to absorb the effects of their absence. This occurred in the Mwea-Tebere irrigated rice resettlement scheme in Kenya, where children were sent away to school as a project benefit (Hanger and Moris, 1973).

Alternatively, the product of children's labour may simply be lost to the household. In a number of societies where women of childbearing age are secluded, their children provide them with access to the market-place. Among the Moslem Hausa of northern Nigeria, for example, children are intermediaries in the sale of processed food produced by women at home (Longhurst, 1980). Here, the loss of children's labour may cause not only an increased workload for the women, but an actual reduction in their personal income. For households which can afford it, the greater returns to children's work after schooling in the long run may be worth the short-run loss, but not all households are free to make that calculation. An education programme will achieve higher participation under these circumstances if an accommodation can be made to fulfil the household's labour needs.

Several agricultural projects have had unanticipated effects on household labour

3

use. In the Gambia, the introduction of irrigation for rice culture permitted an increase in planted area, which augmented the workload of women in weeding and transplanting even though they personally could not own land in the scheme. Eventually, women refused their labour, and the output of rice production actually fell (Dey, 1981). In Sierra Leone, a swamp rice project significantly increased the labour burden of male children relative to the rest of the household (Spencer, 1976). Thus, the introduction of one kind of labour-saving technology increased the burden of another kind of labour. Had planners taken into account the different responsibilities of household members, they could have attempted to alleviate the latter burden as well, either directly or by reducing the labour cost of some other tasks normally done by these individuals.

A programme may even fail completely if it neglects the intra-household dimension. The concern over the loss of children's labour, which may hinder participation in educational efforts, also may be a basic cause of the rejection of family planning by many households. The long-range expectation of support by grown children in old age is often cited as a barrier to voluntary reduction of fertility, but the present or short-run economic contribution of children may be equally important. A less obvious example of the importance of understanding patterns of intra-household exchange is that of the Tolai Cocoa Project in Papua New Guinea (Epstein, 1975). Cocoa growers refused to bring their crop to the local marketing co-operative, even though the co-operative offered higher prices than private traders. Anthropological study found that, because the land which they farmed was inherited through their wives' line, farmers were reluctant to have public written records of the productivity of the land. When the co-operative stopped keeping these records, project participation increased.

A fourth concern for project planners is the danger that economic change may disrupt existing patterns of support among household members and within the extended kinship group or community. In a variety of settings, reciprocal arrangements among household members have been altered by shifts in the economic status of their various tasks. In the Gambia, for example, women's access to household resources was reduced when groundnuts, produced by men, were promoted as a cash crop, so that the perceived relative contribution of women to household income fell (Dey, 1981). In Java, the monetization of agricultural labour reduced the observance of traditional labour-exchange arrangements which guaranteed that the landless would have access to employment in return for a share of the crop (Hart, 1982).

The conclusion to be drawn from these examples is that the success of development projects in any sector depends on an understanding of the sometimes complex economic and social relations among household members. In this context, "success" refers not only to the specific outputs of projects but also to their broader consequences for individual well-being. As we have shown, project benefits may be diluted or lost altogether as they are distributed among household members. Furthermore, projects, even those which achieve their proximate objective, may cause inequitable distribution of burdens and rewards. These secondary effects may create barriers to participation which ultimately result in outright project failure. Negative results can be avoided, and the likelihood of success increased, if the dynamics governing the allocation of resources and responsibilities within households are understood and taken into account in the planning process.

The papers in this volume present some of the recent evidence on how resources and responsibilities are allocated within households, and discuss ways of measuring the

4

processes and the outcomes of intra-household allocation. Although research is still needed to identify the determinants of intra-household allocation patterns, what is already known can be used to improve the design of programmes and projects now being implemented.

INCORPORATING HOUSEHOLD DYNAMICS INTO THE PLANNING PROCESS

All development involves the introduction of some economic or environmental change to achieve certain specified outcomes. Understanding household functioning permits a more accurate evaluation of the likelihood of the outcomes. Behavioural change cannot be forced, but can be induced. It is therefore critical not only to project planning but also to the formation of effective development policy that intra-household dynamics be taken into account.

Four broad areas relating to the household must be considered when setting development goals and selecting or planning projects. These are: (1) the amount of time available to different household members for participation in the project; (2) the allocation of household tasks to different members and the degree to which these tasks are transferable among members; (3) differential access to goods, both for production and for consumption; and (4) differential control over income.

Time Availability

Time is a critical element in development projects. Many types of interventions affect the total amount of time available to the household or propose to alter how time is spent. It was mentioned earlier that family-planning programmes and, to a lesser degree, primary education programmes indirectly lower labour time available to the household by reducing the number of its members or their availability. It has been well documented that the labour burden per person is lower in larger households (Loose, 1980; McSweeney, 1979; Evenson et al., 1979), since (apparently) the amount of extra work involved in maintaining additional household members is smaller than their contribution. A number of studies suggest that the net contribution of labour time which children provide becomes positive as early as age six (e.g. Navera, 1978). Given the other forces which militate against limiting family size in some cultures, such as the dependence of a woman's prestige on the number of her children and the reliance on grown children's support in old age, the poor showing of many family-planning projects does not come as a surprise. Such programmes might achieve better results if the labour constraints on households could be alleviated. Fetching water, for example, is a time-consuming task in many settings, often occupying one household member close to full-time. Piped water or a conveniently located well might reduce the labour burden, creating enough slack in the system so that the loss of a child's labour for education could be absorbed. This illustrates how one apparently unrelated project could enhance the effectiveness of another.

A primary issue in any agricultural or income-generating project is whether the proposed beneficiaries have the time to participate. Examples were cited earlier of projects which failed because the additional time burden they created was unacceptable. The same consideration applies to programmes which directly provide consumption goods such as health care, supplemental food, education and training. As Rosen-zweig discusses in the next chapter, one of the major conceptual contributions of the "new household economics" (Becker, 1965; Lancaster, 1966) is the recognition that consumption of goods entails two kinds of costs – the direct costs of the goods consumed and the time it takes to consume them. Goods which are ostensibly free, therefore, still have a real cost such as that of the time taken to walk to the supplemental feeding site or health clinic, or the time required to attend a training programme.

Task Allocation

Closely related to the question of time availability is the issue of the distribution of tasks among household members. In most cultures, different kinds of work are considered suitable for different household members. These distinctions encompass the sexual division of labour as well as division by age and by status in the household. The rigidity of these distinctions is quite variable, and, with the exception of baby care and cooking, which are always women's tasks, and ploughing and land-clearing, which are usually men's, there is tremendous variability in the allocation of specific tasks between the sexes and ages from one culture to another. Attempts have been made to identify in a generally applicable way the determinants of task allocation to one sex or the other (Brown, 1970; Murdock and Provost, 1973), but these schemes do not have good predictive value, since the division of labour seems to be quite culture-specific. For example, similar tasks were allocated between the sexes differently in three ethnic groups of Nigeria (Tolley, 1978).

Nor is the division of labour immutable. Within certain limits, evidence shows that as circumstances change, so may the division of labour. Cases were already mentioned of women taking over the agricultural tasks of men who had migrated to the cities (LeVine, 1966; Pala, 1978; Alberti, 1982; Reynolds, 1982). It has been argued that women can take over men's tasks more readily than men can adopt those of women (Reynolds, 1982), but changes in task allocation occur in both directions. There are numerous instances of men taking over crops formerly cultivated by women when the introduction of new technology or the development of cash markets made these crops more profitable (Burfisher and Horenstein, 1982). Considerable evidence from settings as diverse as Ethiopia, Bangladesh, and India indicate that the sexual allocation of tasks is less rigid in lower socio-economic groups where such artificial constraints on productive work are an unaffordable luxury (Taddesse, 1982; Alamgir, 1977; Mies, 1982). And certain women, such as widows and the elderly, seem to be exempt from the task limitations imposed on other women (Little, 1987). These issues are addressed in detail by Messer and Safilios-Rothschild in this volume.

What is important, for planning purposes, is that particular tasks are not always transferable among household members and, once transferred, may not revert. Project planners must recognize both the barriers to task reallocation and the dangers inherent in redefining tasks as a result of a project. A number of writers (Abdullah and Zeidenstein, 1975, 1982; Chand et al., 1980; Bryson, 1981; Mitra, 1981; Burfisher and Horenstein, 1982; Acharya and Bennett, 1983) have identified the need to target women specifically in development projects and have suggested that one way to accomplish this is to implement projects which focus on women's activities or women's crops. In certain cases, this approach was tried but was unsuccessful. For instance, a project to promote marketing of rice, cassava, and melons in Nigeria, where these were traditionally subsistence crops grown by women, resulted in the crops being adopted by men (Burfisher and Horenstein, 1982). Apparently it was not the crop, but its subsistence nature, which gave it its identification with women. This shift could have been forestalled, or at least mitigated, if, for example, marketing had been through women's co-operatives. Similarly, the introduction of mechanized rice-hulling in an area of Java caused this task to be taken over by men, depriving women of an important source of cash employment (Stoler, 1977).

The solution is not to withhold labour-saving innovations in areas of women's employment, but rather to introduce them in such a way that they do not shift the allocation of the task away from women. Moreover, work burdens will not necessarily be reallocated equitably. For example, in Laguna, Philippines, when women work in the market up to six hours per day, they do not reduce their work time at home (Folbre, 1984), and men do not increase their contributions to household tasks (King-Quizon, 1978).

Access to Resources

A third major concern in project planning is that household members have unequal access to the goods owned or obtained by the household. The determinants of access to consumption goods are discussed by Engle in this volume. As she points out, the concept of joint ownership by the household, rather than by individuals, is inapplicable in many settings, particularly in Africa (Guyer, 1980). Goods such as food may be distributed within the household according to accepted cultural patterns which do not match planners' preferences. The argument has been made that food, as well as other goods such as health care and education, are allocated within the household according to the perceived economic contribution of the members. The word "perceived" is critical, since much productive work, which contributes to real household income, does not enter the market sector, and thus may not be recognized in the household's structure of entitlements. Examples of this kind of work are food processing and preparation, child care, and household maintenance. This is work which conserves rather than earns income. The services provided are essential to the household and would have to be purchased from outside if they were not provided internally, but since no economic transaction takes place, the value of the service is often not recognized (Abdullah and Zeidenstein, 1975; Hogan and Tienda, 1976).

The generalization that women and children are always disfavoured in food distribution is not supported by the evidence (see, for example, Lipton, 1983). In much of sub-Saharan Africa, where women have well-defined, explicit economic roles (Guyer, 1980), they also appear to receive their fair share of food in the household (Nicol, 1959a, 1959b; McFie, 1976; Kennedy, 1988). Distribution of food within the family, however, often fails to meet the needs of all members when the quantities available are only barely adequate, and there are systematic patterns in some cultures which determine who in the household is most likely to fall short. For example, there is evidence of discrimination against women and girls in food distribution in South Asia, where women's economic roles are more circumscribed (Grewal et al., 1973). A provocative analysis of Indian census data (Rosenzweig and Schultz, 1981) found that differential allocation of resources among children was parallel to their potential economic roles. The survival of girls vis-à-vis boys, taken to reflect the distribution of food and health care, was higher in areas with significant earning opportunities for women, and lower where women had few economic options. Not surprisingly, this relationship was strongest in low-income households, where resource constraints were greatest. A parallel finding from African studies is that females apparently are favoured in house-hold resource distribution in areas where a high brideprice is paid; where no brideprice is paid or a dowry is given, girls did not receive as large a share of the household's food. Other studies in Africa, however, have found that women do consume less than their proportionate share (Schofield, 1974/75).

This discussion underscores the importance of understanding intra-household be-haviour if one is to predict the effects on individuals of policy change and programme implementation. Although much of this evidence is suggestive rather than definitive, it does imply that one policy approach which would encourage equitable distribution of resource flows inside the household is to work toward providing economic opportu-nities in the market sector to both women and men on an equal basis. Alleviating the burden of women's tasks inside the home, though it would provide real benefits, may not have the same effect on women's command over resources as providing work opportunities outside the home, where their economic contribution may be more vis-ible. Certainly, current research indicates that resources provided to a family or house-hold as a unit may not reach the target individual unless distribution patterns are taken into account.

Changes in Income

Finally, those planning development projects and guiding policy must understand the potential effect of altering the form, period, or earner of income. There is considerable evidence that all income which enters a household is not treated identically (Kumar, 1978; Guyer, 1980; Jones, 1983a). A central objective of most development policy is to raise the incomes of the poor, and generally it is recognized that programmes which expand income-earning opportunities are the most likely to generate continued, self-sustaining economic growth. But there are numerous examples of large-scale eco-nomic development projects which had unintended negative effects for some household members because they changed the form in which income was received, the period, or the earner. The Mwea-Tebere irrigated rice resettlement scheme, which disrupted many aspects of the resettled household's economy, also channelled all income through the male household head. Women felt that they had less access to and less control over the income than when they were earning their own income directly (Hanger and Moris, 1973). A plantation development project in Papua New Guinea, which raised incomes substantially but changed the economy from subsistence-based to cash, had a negative nutritional impact on children because households were un-accustomed to using scarce cash to purchase food (Lambert, 1982). Had this problem been anticipated, it could have been avoided, perhaps by incorporating a home food production component into the project.

In many studies, women report that they have much greater control over the income which they directly earn than that which is earned, for example, by their husbands (Ahmad, 1980 [Bangladesh]; Loose, 1980 [Senegal]; Roldan, 1982 [Mexico]). Anec-dotal evidence (Pala, 1978; Tripp, 1981; Nelson, 1979), supported by some empirical research (Guyer, 1980), suggests that the income earned by women is dispro-portionately spent on food and basic household necessities, in comparison with men's income. Few studies make the point, however, that women generally work in the market out of severe economic necessity so it is not surprising that their incomes should be spent on basic needs (Singh, 1977). Kumar (1978) found in Kerala, India, that in households where women worked for wages their incomes were more highly correlated with their children's nutritional status than were total household income or men's wage income. These households, however, were poorer and had less land available to them than did those in which the women were not engaged in wage work. It is to be expected that cash-income increments will have a greater effect on child nutrition in households with the most severe resource constraints.

Moreover, the argument supporting women's spending preference for food does not always take into account how men's income would be spent in the absence of women's income. In an irrigated rice project area of Cameroon, Jones (1983a) found no significant association between the amount of rice retained for home consumption and the sex of the individual controlling the disposition of the crop. Nor was the amount of household expenditure on the sauce ingredients (to supplement the grain staple) significantly different in male- and female-headed households. Married women spent less of their own money on these items than did independent women; their husbands' contributions made up the difference. In contrast to the irrigated rice area, women in the poorest, non-rice-cultivating village in the study bought the bulk of purchased grain for their households during the hungry season, using their own incomes.

Jones (1983b) also found that women preferred to maximize their own incomes rather than the total income of their households, when the two were in conflict. Once again, the important conclusion emerges that income is not entirely fungible. In designing projects and proposing broader sectoral policies to promote development, policy-makers must be alert to the possible consequences of altering the nature of income while attempting to raise it.

Defining the Household

Throughout this discussion, I have relied on an intuitive understanding of what a household actually is. This has been intentional, since the definition of the household is an intractable theoretical problem (Messer, 1983). Given the varied and complex nature of human society, no definition of the household, however general, completely fits all circumstances. One can identify a variety of functions usually associated with the household: co-residence; joint production; shared consumption; kinship links (Bender, 1967). Yet as Heywood points out in part III of this volume, these functions often define different sets of individuals. In many places, the unit of joint production consists of a different set of individuals from the food consumption unit (e.g. Dorjahn, 1977 [Sierra Leone]; Foster, 1978 [Thailand]; Longhurst, 1980 [Nigeria]). Moreover, co-residence may not always be associated with shared production or shared consumption (White, 1980). The definition of co-residence itself may not be clear where many dwelling units form a single compound (cf. Gurney and Omolalu, 1971). Migration of household members also creates ambiguities: a person may leave the household for most of the year but return to contribute labour in certain seasons, share in the product of the household of origin, and contribute remittances for the support of resident household members.

Any fixed definition of the household can create arbitrary and possibly misleading distinctions. For example, in Taiwan, the census defines a nuclear family as part of an extended family household if it receives more than 50 per cent of its income from the extended family. This tends to understate disparities in household income, since the poorest nuclear families have their incomes combined with the larger unit (Greenhalgh, 1982). Yet to exclude the extended family from the definition leaves out an important dimension of sources of support for the members of the nuclear group and vice versa.

Planners and researchers alike must accept the fact that the equivalent of the Western concept of the household does not exist in most places. Guyer's (1980) definition acknowledges the fluid nature of the boundaries separating the household from the community of which it is a part. In her words, "a household is a particularly dense center in a network of exchange relationships." Rather than force a definition on the household which has more exceptions than rules, it makes sense, as Heywood (in this volume) suggests, to define the household unit according to the particular dimension of interest, whether it be sharing of production responsibilities, common uses of income, co-residence, or the common cooking pot. Adopting a definition of the household which is inappropriate to the culture being studied may result in erroneous conclusions about household processes. For example, in some cultures, women traditionally return to their natal home to bear their first child, and remain there for several months after the birth. Resources which raise the income of the woman's affinal family would therefore have no effect on the welfare of the mother and her newborn in these early months. It would, however, be a mistake to conclude that the head of the affinal household was somehow withholding resources from his wife and child; rather, the wife is, temporarily, a member of a different household whose resources affect her level of living.

There is no doubt that organization into households is a vital survival mechanism for individuals. Where traditional households (co-residential kinship groups of various kinds) do not exist, people commonly establish reciprocal relationships with "fictive kin" who serve similar functions of mutual support and specialization of household maintenance tasks (Nieves, 1979). Regardless of how it is defined, the household is definitely not a homogeneous unit in which all members share a common set of preferences. It can better be seen as a group of people bound by an implicit contract which specifies the rights and obligations of each member. As in conventional contracts, the balance of rights and obligations is determined in part by the alternatives available to each member and in part by their relative power. Thus Jones (1983a) found that married women in Cameroon provided their husbands with labour at below-market wage rates. Although these women could not completely refuse to work out of fear of being beaten, they worked less for their husbands than did wives who were paid a higher wage. Moreover, they spent the balance of their time working on crops which were less profitable, but whose profit they personally controlled. Similarly, within the Moslem Hausa conjugal unit in northern Nigeria (Longhurst, 1980), labour and goods are often exchanged for cash, rather than pooled and redistributed according to need. Jelín, in this volume, describes an example of how the consumption preferences of individuals within households conflict with one another.

A cultural component is inherent in the nature of what might be called the household contract. A strong tradition exists in Africa of separate economic spheres of activity for men and women, with considerable independence for each (Guyer, 1980). But even in a traditionally patriarchal Asian society such as Bangladesh, economic forces affect the balance of decision-making power in the household. Women who bring in wage income have a greater influence on how the income is spent than do those who work only in the home (Alamgir, 1977). That traditional patterns are in fact

10

mutable is significant for development policy. It demonstrates that cultural factors are not an absolute constraint on behaviour, and that economic forces can generate lasting change and progress. This underscores the importance of identifying patterns of household behaviour because those patterns are indeed subject to outside influence. Jelín, in this volume, details some of the negative consequences these influences have if they are not explicitly taken into account in development policy.

METHODOLOGICAL ISSUES IN THE STUDY OF INTRA-HOUSEHOLD DYNAMICS

The study of internal household dynamics poses difficulties of definition, access, and measurement. Defining the household for study or for programme/project planning is already a difficult task. Households are private institutions, and their interactions and relationships may be considered too personal to discuss. Moreover, there is still much to be learned about what needs to be measured and how to measure it. Most of the empirical research on these issues has been carried out in the context of long-term research projects and doctoral dissertations where the cost of time-consuming data collection methods was not a deterrent to their use. Approaches are needed which can provide at least some guidance to project planners within a practical time horizon. One such approach is presented in the Appendix to this volume.

As a start, certain information may be obtained from the analysis of secondary data such as census information, household income and expenditure surveys (if they contain demographic information), and consumption and nutrition surveys. Valuable information can also be located in the ethnographic literature available on the area. There are few instances of planning for development in a location where no prior research has been done.

This is not to suggest that data collection as part of the planning process is superfluous, but any project should be evaluated in terms of its potential rate of return for the effort and resources expended. As this paper has demonstrated, knowledge of intra-household dynamics is vital to an accurate assessment of project outputs. It is therefore crucial to identify the most efficient ways of obtaining such knowledge. The issues which need to be addressed in this context are the following:

1. Defining the unit of analysis.
2. Measuring individual income and expenditure – that is, resource flows among and within households.
3. Measuring time use and task allocation.
4. Measuring individual access to household resources, including productive assets, food, education, and other human capital investments.
5. Measuring the distribution of power and decision-making responsibility.

Defining the Unit of Analysis

The difficulty of defining precisely what a household is has already been discussed. Aside from this theoretical question, the practical problem exists that household composition and structure are highly variable over time. One study of household economy found that, over a one-and-a-half-year period, 20 per cent of the sample Embu households in Kenya were disrupted in some way (Haugerud, 1981). In a study of food consumption in Zambia, household structure was charted anew in each monthly round of data collection because variations in composition were so great (Kumar, 1982). Households adapt by changing their structure (Nieves, 1979; Jelín, n.d.), so that information on the flexibility of household units over time is an important indicator of their ability to cope with economic stress and change (cf. Jelín, this volume).

In addition, individuals may belong to several different households at one time (Loufti, 1980), as when they receive support from both their natal and affinal families. While people cannot be studied outside the context in which they live, an effective way of getting around this problem is to take the individual as the point of departure, and to analyse the household or other support network to which he or she belongs as a characteristic (Watts and Skidmore, 1976). Heywood discusses a practical application of this approach in part III of this volume.

Income and Expenditure

Most income and expenditure surveys measure all income (cash and kind) flowing into the household and the household's total expenditure or consumption in a given reference period. It is still unusual to find a survey which distinguishes income by separate earner (exceptions are Kumar, 1978; Guyer, 1980; Jones, 1983b; Kennedy and Cogill, 1987; Rogers and Swindale, 1988) or expenditure by individual. Yet it is well recognized that, to obtain accurate income data, each earner must be questioned and each source of income separately identified: household members often lie to each other about the amount of their income or simply keep it secret. While useful for some purposes, aggregate household income does not provide the information needed to study intra-household processes. In many cases, this data is obtained in household interviews, and simply needs to be preserved in disaggregated form so that it can be used in later analyses.

Obtaining details about individual income flows requires making the trade-off of a smaller sample size. For planning purposes this does not pose a problem: the statistical accuracy preserved in quantity measures of large-scale surveys is likely to be less important than capturing the nature and approximate relative size of resource flows in and out of households and among their members.

Data from large-scale surveys may in some cases be used to infer patterns of intra-household resource allocation. An example of one such innovative analysis is the Rosenzweig and Schultz (1981) study which used census data on male-to-female ratios and additional information of female employment opportunities by region to infer something about the determinants of investment in child health and survival. Many countries use household-level income and expenditure surveys to establish the basis for a consumer price index. These might also be used to compare the spending patterns of households of varying composition, and then to make some educated guesses about the consumption patterns of given categories of individuals. This type of analysis must be viewed in most cases as indicative rather than conclusive, because it is often impossible to distinguish between equally plausible explanations of an outcome. For example, Hanger and Moris (1973) attribute reduced expenditure on food in the Mwea-Tebere rice project, with no reduction in income, to the shift in income earner. An alternative explanation might be the shift from a steady flow of small amounts of income to an annual, lump-sum payment. The observation that spending patterns and task allocation are different in households where women work may be explained by women's greater power and influence in such households, or simply by the difference in the implicit cost of women's time once they have entered the labour force. This confusion confirms the real need for undertaking studies which are explicitly designed to investigate intra-household questions.

Time Use and Task Allocation

The literature amply illustrates the danger of relying on recall and self-report to obtain information on time use. Studies which have compared recall with direct observation have found substantial differences between the two methods. One study in Upper Volta found that 44 per cent of women's work activities measured by direct observation were missed in a recall questionnaire (McSweeney, 1979). This is even greater than the 30 per cent difference measured between a 24-hour and a one-month time-use recall questionnaire in Java (Sajogyo et al., 1979). In the Philippines, King-Quizon (1978) found that children's market work time was three times as great when measured by direct observation than by recall. Relying on recall data to measure time use raises several problems. First of all, people simply may not know how much time they spend at a given task. Even in cultures that are not ruled by the clock as ours is, it is possible to construct appropriate chronometric references, as Zeitlin explains in part III of this volume. Furthermore, people may not define their tasks in the same way as the researcher; some activities done by one group may simply not be recognized as work by another. For instance, the women lacemakers in Narsapur, India, spend six to eight hours a day at the task, yet their husbands report this as leisure time, because it is not perceived as work (Mies, 1982).

Johnson's paper in this volume reviews the various methods for measuring time allocation. Time use can be directly observed by following a small sample of individuals continuously during a day or a sample of days; by observing a random sample of individuals during randomly selected 15-minute periods (Johnson, 1975); or by participant observation over some period of time (24 hours minimum). The method of spot-checking at random moments has the advantage of minimally disrupting normal activities and of providing a systematic body of observations. Pre-defined categories are not used, and multiple activities can be recorded. However, these random moments do not provide a sense of the organization and sequencing of activities, which may be important factors in how time is used and constrained. Therefore, this method should be combined with the observation of whole tasks (see Appendix, table A) or a time-use record that accommodates simultaneous and frequently interrupted tasks and maintains their temporal relationships (cf. Schlossman, 1986).

Access to Resources

The special case of intra-family food distribution has received considerable attention (Horowitz, 1980; Carloni, 1981; Nutrition Economics Group, 1982). The importance of individual-level measures has long been recognized, and various data-collection methods have been tested. The food question is complex because, unlike education and other resources, food consumption has meaning only in relation to nutrient need. Chaudhury (1983) suggests that one explanation for the commonly held notion that women receive less than their fair share of household food is that careful controls for activity level and body weight have not been used in data analysis. Making such adjustments, his study in one village in Bangladesh found no evidence of sex discrimination in food distribution in most age-groups. The question of whether the recommended nutrient intake used to determine dietary adequacy levels (WHO/FAO, 1985) may be set too high adds another dimension of uncertainty.

It is easier to measure outcomes (e.g. weight gain or loss, or nutritional status) than food consumption directly, but such measures do not distinguish patterns of food allocation from differences in energy expenditure, or in morbidity which affects growth. For purposes of simply indicating patterns of distribution, short-cut methods may be adequate. Check-lists and food frequencies have been used to indicate overall dietary quality, but once again methods designed specifically to measure intra-household distribution of food have not been widely used. Pinstrup-Andersen and Garcia, in part III of this volume, show clearly that such methods are indispensible, as household-level measures are inaccurate indicators of individual food intakes.

Power and Decision-making within the Household

The measurement of decision-making power within the household poses serious con-ceptual problems. First, genuine differences of opinion are likely to exist among household members as to who makes what decisions (Safilios-Rothschild, 1969). Second, people may not admit the true allocation of influence. Alamgir (1977) sug-gests that the female contribution to household decision-making is greater than either party will publicly acknowledge. A third consideration is that decisions take place in a context which limits alternatives. Studies from many countries indicate that women and men make decisions which pertain to their own spheres of activity (Laird, 1979 [Paraguay]; Cloud, 1978 [Sahel]; Alamgir, 1977 [Bangladesh]), but presumably in the female sphere some of these decisions are fairly limited in scope: not what type of crop to plant, but how much to plant. Roldan (1988) makes the important point that man-agement of household finances need not imply control over them. In an environment of severe resource constraint, she points out that there are no decisions to be made; expenditure patterns are dictated by survival needs.

The best way to observe the allocation of decision-making may be to look at the results, that is, to look at investment and consumption decisions among households of a given type: female- versus male-headed, households where women do or do not work outside the home for pay. The only other approach is to use psychological methods or measurements which are not well suited to project planning.

Participant Observation Methods

Several researchers have argued that it is essential to have a fundamental understand-ing of a culture, such as can only be obtained by living in it, before more specific research questions can be addressed or interventions developed (e.g. Haugerud, 1979). Certainly, project experience has demonstrated the danger of treating, as it were, one symptom rather than the whole patient. One can view household dynamics as the fundamental and complex expression of a culture, requiring an integrated study of its various dimensions.

Epstein (1975) has suggested that the aid agencies make greater use of the relatively cheap resource of anthrolopogical studies, and argues that ordinarily there is sufficient lead time for such studies to be carried out in an area which has been targeted for aid before specific projects are planned. An effort should at least be made to seek out those who have already worked in the target area and to review the work which has been done in the light of the specific questions which pertain to household dynamics. In this way, specific knowledge gaps can be identified, and resources can be most efficiently concentrated on obtaining the missing pieces of information. An awareness of the need for this information is probably the most important first step. The Appendix contains an approach to obtaining the information on intra-household dynamics needed for effective development planning.

DIRECTIONS FOR FUTURE RESEARCH

The study of household dynamics in relation to development policy is a relatively new field. There are still a number of important empirical questions to be answered. Among these, perhaps most relevant to economic development, are questions of the effect of changing income-earning opportunities on the behaviour and well-being of household members. This relates to the ways in which the form, period, and reliability of income, as well as who earns it, influence how it is spent, and how these alter household decisions about consumption, investment, and fertility. Another important question underlying sound development policy is the balance between market work, home production, and the care of children. A third area of exploration is how to influence patterns of control over productive resources, especially as technological or marketing interventions alter their productivity and value.

As vital as these empirical questions are, it is perhaps even more important to identify timely and low-cost ways of obtaining information on development programmes. Such information has seldom been sought outside an academic or research context, and, as a result, the development of innovative and efficient data-collection methods has not been a priority. Now that the relevance of these questions is being recognized by the aid community, the development of systematic, practical approaches to their resolution should be placed high on the policy agenda. This volume is offered as a contribution to this process.

REFERENCES

Abdullah, T.A., and S. Zeidenstein. 1975. Socio-economic Implications of High-yielding Variety Rice Production on Rural Women of Bangladesh. Presented at the Integrated Rural Development Programme Seminar, Dacca, April 1975.
——. 1982. *Village Women of Bangladesh: Prospects for Change*. ILO/WEP Women in Development Series, vol. 14. Pergamon Press, New York.
Acharya, M., and L. Bennett. 1983. *Women and the Subsistence Sector: Economic Participation and Household Decision-making in Nepal*. World Bank Staff Working Paper 526. World Bank, Washington, D.C.
Ahmad, P. 1980. *Income Earning as Related to the Changing Status of Village Women in Bangladesh: A Case Study*. Women for Women Study and Research Group, Dacca.
Alamgir, S.F. 1977. *Profile of Bangladeshi Women: Selected Aspects of Women's Roles and Status in Bangladesh*. United States Agency for International Development, Mission to Bangladesh.
Alberti, A. 1982. Some Observations on the Productive Role of Women and Development Efforts in the Andes. Prepared for the Women in International Development Workshop,

Women, Work and Public Policy, Center for International Studies, Massachusetts Institute of Technology, Cambridge, Mass., 26 March.

Becker, G.S. 1965. A Theory of the Allocation of Time. *Econ. J.*, 75: 493–518.

Bender, B.D. 1967. A Refinement of the Concept of the Household: Families, Co-residence, and Domestic Functions. *Am. Anthropologist*, 69: 493–504.

Brown, J. 1970. A Note on the Division of Labor by Sex. *Am. Anthropologist*, 72: 1073–1078.

Bryson, J.C. 1981. Women and Agriculture in Sub-Saharan Africa: Implications for Development (An Exploratory Study). In: N. Nelson, *African Women in the Development Process*. F. Cass and Co., Totowa, N.J.

Burfisher, M., and N. Horenstein. 1982. *The Differential Impact of an Agricultural Development Project on Women and Men*. Staff Report AGES 820930. International Economics Division, Economic Research Service, US Department of Agriculture, Washington, D.C.

Carloni, A.S. 1981. Sex Disparities in the Distribution of Food within Rural Households. *Food Nutr.*, 7(1): 3–12.

Chand, M., D. Jain, R. Kalyandsundaram, and H. Singh. 1980. *Income-generating Activities for Women: Some Case Studies*. Indian Cooperative Union, New Delhi.

Chaudhury, R.H. 1983. Determinants of Intrafamilial Distribution of Food and Nutrient Intake in a Rural Area of Bangladesh. Mimeo. Bangladesh Institute of Development Economics, Dacca.

Cloud, K. 1978. *Sex Roles in Food Production and Distribution Systems in the Sahel*. Prepared for Women in International Development, International Conference on Women and Food, University of Arizona, Tucson. USAID/Office of Women in Development, Washington, D.C.

Colvin, L.G., B. Cheikh, B. Boubacar, J. Faye, A. Hamer, M. Soumah, and F. Sow. 1980. The Uprooted in the Western Sahel: Migrants' Quest for Cash in the Senegambia. In: E. Chaney and M. Lewis, *Women, Migration, and the Decline of Smallholder Agriculture*. USAID/Office of Women in Development, Washington, D.C.

Dey, J. 1981. Gambian Women: Unequal Partners in Rice Development Projects? *J. Devel. Stud.*, 17(1): 109–122.

Dorjahn, V. 1977. Temne Household Size and Composition: Rural Changes over Time and Rural–Urban Differences. *Ethnology*, 16(2): 105–127.

Epstein, T.S. 1975. The Ideal Marriage between the Economist's Macroapproach and the Anthropologist's Microapproach to Development Studies. *Econ. Devel. Cult. Change*, 24(1): 29–46.

Evenson, R., B. Popkin, and E. King-Quizon. 1979. Nutrition, Work, and Demographic Behavior in Rural Philippine Households. Economic Growth Center Discussion Paper 308. Yale University, New Haven, Conn.

Folbre, N. 1984. Household Production in the Philippines: A Non-neoclassical Approach. *Econ. Devel. Cult. Change*, 32: 303–430.

Foster, B.L. 1978. Socioeconomic Consequences of Stem Family Composition in a Thai village. *Ethnology*, 17(2): 139–156.

Greenhalgh, S. 1982. Income Units: The Ethnographic Alternative to Standardization. *Popul. Devel. Rev.*, 8 (Suppl): 70–91.

Grewal, T., T. Gopaldas, and V.J. Garde. 1973. Etiology of Malnutrition in Rural Indian Preschool Children (Madhya Pradesh). *Environ. Child Health*, 19(3): 265–270.

Gurney, I.M., and A. Omolalu. 1971. A Nutritional Survey in Southwestern Nigeria: The Anthropometric and Clinical Findings. *J. Trop. Ped.*, 17(2): 50–61.

Guyer, J. 1980. Household Budgets and Women's Incomes. Working Paper 28, African Studies Center. Boston University, Boston, Mass.

Hanger, J., and J. Moris. 1973. Women and the Household Economy. In: Chambers and Moris, eds., *Mwea: An Irrigated Rice Settlement in Central Kenya*, pp. 209–244. Weltforum-Verlag, Afrika Studien, Munich.

Hart, G. 1982. Research seminar delivered at Tufts University School of Nutrition, Medford, Mass., Autumn 1982.

Haugerud, A. 1979. Methodological Issues in a Study of Resource Allocation Decisions among Embu Farmers. Working Paper 357. Institute for Development Studies. University of Nairobi, Nairobi.

———. 1981. Economic Differentiation among Peasant Households: A Comparison of Embu Coffee and Cotton Zones. Working Paper 383. Institute for Development Studies. University of Nairobi, Nairobi.

Hogan, J., and J. Tienda. 1976. *Zinacanteco Women: Prediction for Change in a Mexican Village*. Land Tenure Center, Madison, Wis.

Horowitz, G. 1980. Intrafamily Distribution of Food and Other Resources. Report to the Nutrition Economics Group, United States Department of Agriculture, International Development Staff, Washington, D.C., July.

Huggard, M. 1978. *The Rural Woman as Food Producer: An Assessment of the Resolution on Women and Food from the World Food Conference, 1974*. Prepared for Women in International Development, International Conference on Women and Food, University of Arizona, Tucson. USAID/Office of Women in Development, Washington, D.C.

Jelín, E. N.d. *Daily Lives of Urban Women: Needs, Resources, and Women's Work*. Centro de Estudios de Estado y Sociedad, Buenos Aires.

Johnson, A. 1975. Time Allocation in a Machiguenga Community. *Ethnology*, 14(2): 301–310.

Jones, C. 1983a. The Impact of the SEMRY I Irrigated Rice Project on the Organization of Production and Consumption at the Intrahousehold Level. Prepared for USAID/PPC, Washington, D.C.

Jones, C. 1983b. The Mobilization of Women's Labor for Cash Crop Production: A Game Theoretic Approach. *Am. J. Agric. Econ.*, 65(5): 1049–1054.

Kennedy, E., and B. Cogill. 1987. Income and Nutritional Effects of the Commercialization of Agriculture in Southwestern Kenya. Research Report 63. International Food Policy Research Institute, Washington D.C.

King-Quizon, E. 1978. Time Allocation and Home Production in Rural Philippine Households. *Phil. Econ. J.*, 17(1–2): 185–202.

Kumar, S. 1978. Role of the Household Economy in Child Nutrition at Low Incomes: A Case Study in Kerala. Occasional Paper 95, Department of Agricultural Economics. Cornell University, Ithaca, N.Y.

——. 1982. Personal communication, International Food Policy Research Institute, Washington, D.C.

Laird, J.F. 1979. *Rural Women in Paraguay: The Socioeconomic Dimension*. USAID/Office of Women in Development, Washington, D.C.

Lambert, J. 1982. The Relationship between Cash Crop Production and Nutritional Status in Papua New Guinea. History of Agriculture. Working Paper 38. University of Papua New Guinea, Port Moresby. Cited in: J. Lambert, Effect of Urbanization and Western Foods. *Food Nutr. Bull.*, 4(3): 11–13.

Lancaster, K.J. 1966. A New Approach to Consumer Theory. *J. Pol. Econ.*, 74: 132–157.

LeVine, R.A. 1966. Sex Roles and Economic Change in Africa. *Ethnology*, 5(2): 186–192.

Lipton, M. 1983. Poverty, Undernutrition, and Hunger. Staff Working Paper 597. World Bank, Washington, D.C.

Little, P.D. 1987. Women as Ol Payian (Elder): The Status of Widows among Il Chamus (Njemps) of Kenya. *Ethnos*, 52(I–II): 81–102.

Longhurst, R. 1980. Rural Development Planning and the Sexual Division of Labour: A Case Study of a Moslem Hausa Village in Northern Nigeria. World Employment Programme Research Working Paper WEP10/WP10, Rural Employment Policy Research Programme, ILO, Geneva.

Loose, E. 1980. Women's Time Budgeting in Rural Senegal. Prepared for the Workshop on Sahelian Agriculture, Department of Agricultural Economics, Purdue University.

Loufti, M. 1980. *Rural Women: Unequal Partners in Development*. A World Employment Programme Study. ILO, Geneva.

McFie, J. 1967. Nutrient Intakes of Urban Dwellers in Lagos, Nigeria. *Br. J. Nutr.*, 21: 257–268.

McSweeney, B.G. 1979. Collection and Analysis of Data on Rural Women's Time Use. *Stud. Fam. Plan.*, 10(11/12): 379–383.

Messer, E. 1983. The Household Focus in Nutritional Anthropology: An Overview. *Food Nutr. Bull.*, 5(4): 2–12.

Mies, M. 1982. The Dynamics of the Sexual Division of Labor and Integration of Rural Women into the World Market. In: L. Beneria, ed., *Women and Development*. Praeger, New York.

Minge-Klevana, W. 1978. Household Economy during the Peasant-to-worker Transition in the Swiss Alps. *Ethnology*, 17: 183–196.

Mitra, A. 1981. Participation of Women in Socio-economic Development: Indicators and Tools for Development Planning. The Case of India. In: *Women and Development: Indicators of Their Changing Roles*. Unesco, Paris.

Murdock, G.P., and C. Provost. 1973. Factors in the Division of Labor by Sex: A Cross-sectional Analysis. *Ethnology*, 12: 203–255.

Nag, M., B. White, and R.C. Peet. 1978. An Anthropological Approach to the Study of the Economic Value of Children in Java and Nepal. *Curr. Anthropol.*, 19: 293–306.

Navera, E.R. 1978. The Allocation of Household Time Associated with Children in Rural Households in Laguna, Philippines. *Phil. Econ. J.*, 17(1–2): 203–223.

Nelson, N. 1979. Productive and Income-generating Activities for Third World Women. Knowledge Network on Women, Paper No. 3. UNICEF, New York.

Nicol, B.M. 1959a. The Calorie Requirements of Nigerian Peasant Farmers. *Br. J. Nutr.*, 13(3): 293–306.

——. 1959b. The Protein Requirements of Nigerian Peasant Farmers. *Br. J. Nutr.*, 13(3): 307–320.

Nieves, I. 1979. Household Arrangements and Multiple Jobs in San Salvador. *Signs*, 5(1): 134–142.

Nutrition Economics Group, USDA. 1982. *Intrafamily Food Distribution: Review of the Literature and Policy Implications.* USDA/OICD, Washington, D.C.

Pala, A. 1978. Women's Access to Land and Their Role in Agriculture and Decision-making on the Farm: Experiences of the Joluo of Kenya. Discussion Paper 263. Institute of Development Studies, University of Nairobi, Nairobi.

Reynolds, D.R. 1982. The Household Divided: Competition for Cash between Husbands and Wives in West Pokot, Kenya. Presented at the 81st Annual Meeting, American Anthropological Association, Washington, D.C., December.

Reynolds, D.R. N.d. Appraisal of Rural Women in Tanzania. Mimeo. USAID/REDSO, Washington, D.C.

Rogers, B., and A. Swindale. 1988. Determinants of Food Consumption in the Dominican Republic. Report prepared for USAID Bureau of Science and Technology, Office of Nutrition.

Roldan, M. 1988. Intrahousehold Patterns of Money Allocation and Women's Subordination. In: D. Dwyer and J. Bruce, eds., *A Home Divided: Women and Income in the Third World.* Stanford University Press, Stanford, Calif.

Rosenzweig, M.R., and T.P. Schultz. 1982. Market Opportunities, Genetic Endowments and Intrafamily Resource Distribution: Child Survival in Rural India. *Am. Econ. Rev.*, 72(4): 803–815.

Safilios-Rothschild, C. 1969. Family Sociology or Wives' Sociology? A Cross-cultural Examination of Decision-making. *J. Marr. Fam.*, 31: 290–301.

Sajogyo, P., L. Endang, S. Surkati, W. Winati, K. Suryanata, and B. White. 1979. Studying Rural Women in West Java. *Stud. Fam. Plan.*, 10 (11/12): 364–370.

Schlossman, N.P. 1986. Work Resumption, Breast-feeding, and Time Allocation of Mothers in Boston, Mass.: The First Half-year Postpartum. Unpublished doctoral dissertation, Tufts University School of Nutrition, Medford, Mass.

Schofield, S. 1974/5. Seasonal Factors Affecting Nutrition in Different Age Groups and Especially Preschool Children. *J. Devel. Stud.*, 11: 22–40.

Singh, A.M. 1977. Women and the Family: Coping with Poverty in the Bastis of Delhi. *Soc. Action*, 27: 3.

Spencer, D. 1976. African Women in Agricultural Development: A Case Study in Sierra Leone. Overseas Liaison Committee Paper 9. American Council on Education, Washington, D.C.

Stoler, A. 1977. Class Structure and Female Autonomy in Rural Java. *Signs*, 3(1): 74–89.

Taddesse, Z. 1982. The Impact of Land Reform on Women: The Case of Ethiopia. In: L. Beneria, ed., *Women and Development.* Praeger, New York.

Tolley, D.M. 1978. Cultural Aspects of Regional Development among Nigerian Women. Prepared for the Annual Meeting of the Society for Applied Anthropology, Merida, 2–9 April.

Tripp, R.B. 1981. Farmers and Traders: Some Economic Determinants of Nutritional Status in Northern Ghana. *J. Trop. Ped.*, 27(1): 15–22.

United Nations Economic Commission for Africa. N.d. *The Role of Women in Population Dynamics Related to Food and Agriculture and Rural Development in Africa.* UNECA/FAO Women's Programme Unit, Addis Ababa.

Watts, H.W., and F. Skidmore. 1978. Household Structure: Necessary Changes in Categorization and Data Collection. Prepared for the Conference on Issues in Federal Statistical Needs Relating to Women, Bethesda, Md., 27–28 April.

White, B.N.F. 1980. Rural Household Studies in Anthropological Perspective. In: H.-P. Binswanger, R.E. Evenson, C.A. Florencio, and B.N.F. White, eds., *Rural Household Studies in Asia*. Singapore University Press, Singapore.

World Health Organization/Food and Agriculture Organization. 1985. *Energy and Protein Requirements*. Technical Report Series, 724. World Health Organization, Geneva.

I. Conceptual Frameworks

Conceptual Frameworks

BEATRICE LORGE ROGERS

Tufts University School of Nutrition, Medford, Massachusetts, USA

NINA P. SCHLOSSMAN

Office of Nutrition, US Agency for International Development, Washington, D.C., USA

The papers in part I present three frameworks for studying the household, derived from the disciplines of economics, anthropology, and psychology. Rosenzweig, in his paper, stresses the importance of constructing a model of the household which contains measurable variables, and which leads to the development of testable hypotheses about the determinants of different patterns of intra-household allocation. His economic model of the household rests on the concept of a "unified household preference function," a model of household behaviour that suggests that the household, at least from the outside observer's point of view, allocates resources among its members according to some jointly held set of allocative rules.

Both Messer and Engle criticize the unified household model as a misrepresentation of reality: they argue that allocation rules are the result of conflict and conflict resolution based on different members' power and influence within the household. In fact, the unified household model does acknowledge the importance of the varying characteristics of each member. Moreover, it does not suggest that the behavioural outcome, a set of implicit rules for the allocation of resources, is reached without conflict. The model simply does not address the interpersonal dynamics by which the household preference function emerges. It does, however, include individual-level variables which have been identified as important determinants of household preferences, provided they are measurable characteristics (such as earning power). Rosenzweig acknowledges that the idea of a joint household welfare function "does violence to reality," but suggests that the conflict resolution model must be shown to predict distinct outcomes before it can prove its value empirically.

Behrman's comment on Rosenzweig's economic model introduces the idea, developed further by Engle, that it would be useful to identify the allocative rules for different types of households and individuals, and what determines the choice of a rule. Behrman distinguishes allocation based on equity (each member is entitled to a fair share of any resource), equal outcome (resources are distributed in such a way as to equalize the welfare of members, so that the least endowed member might receive the most), fair return (each member is entitled to resources in proportion to his/her material contribution to the household), and maximization (members most likely to benefit from a resource are given the largest share). This latter rule may produce the greatest inequality among members, while maximizing returns to the household as a whole. Moreover, different rules may be followed for different resources (e.g. health care may be allocated equally among children while only the brightest child might be sent to school), and households facing different kinds of constraints may follow different rules. For example, households under severe resource constraints may try to maximize the household's resources at a cost to the welfare of some members, while households with relatively abundant resources may follow an equal-share or equal-outcome strategy.

Messer, writing from the perspective of anthropology, stresses the importance of understanding household behaviour from the point of view of the people being studied (the emic perspective), as well as in the outsider's, objectively measurable terms (the etic perspective). Messer and then Engle argue that the subjective meanings inherent in behaviour must be taken into account in project planning because they affect the ways in which households and individuals respond to a changed environment. They hold that knowledge of how the local population perceives a given activity or resource will be invaluable in predicting whether people will accept the changes effected by a project, and whether new resources will be used in the manner anticipated by its planners.

Messer further cautions that cultural rules and practices, and culturally determined systems of rights and obligations, condition the acceptance (or rejection) of new forms of behaviour and new relationships resulting from project-induced changes. The culture is the context into which programmes are introduced. Programmes which distort existing patterns (e.g. introducing a new technology which results in devaluation of the older generation's knowledge and skills) may engender resistance or, worse, may disrupt the culture in profound, unanticipated ways.

The economic approach to analysis typically depends on a model of behaviour that has already been formulated. The ethnographic method is less structured, more open-ended. This approach, commonly used by anthropologists, is therefore particularly well-suited to identifying variables whose importance might not have been revealed without a sensitivity to the culture. Cultural constraints on behaviour are, in fact, concrete and measurable variables. Once their existence has been documented, it is possible to incorporate them into a more formal model such as Rosenzweig's. For example, certain categories of people (the elderly, women, children) may be prohibited from engaging in specific types of labour. Returns to human capital such as education may also differ among groups. These cultural variables can be modelled by introducing, for instance, separate imputed wage rates for males and females of equal skill level, or by distinguishing several categories of market labour time. The anthropological approach clearly does not conflict with the economic, but complements it by focusing attention on important variables which may have been missed in a purely economic framework. Including these variables ensures a more accurate and complete model of household behaviour.

Engle emphasizes that the important contribution of psychology is the recognition of individual psychological characteristics as determinants of behaviour. She posits that personality may be a significant factor in both control over resource allocation and access to consumption goods. One empirical application of this perception is that personality characteristics themselves may be affected by externally introduced changes. If, for instance, women are given income-earning opportunities outside the home, they may develop greater self-esteem, which in turn may increase their ability and willingness to influence allocation decisions.

Engle stresses the conflict-resolution model rather than the unified household model of intra-household allocation, noting that household priorities may be influenced by individual members in a variety of ways. Members with the power to enforce their preferences may coerce, but household members without authority can still exercise influence through their own special knowledge and expertise, by persuasion, or by quiet resistance. Engle also distinguishes between the power to influence allocation decisions and the access to consumption goods and productive resources.

Both Messer and Engle discuss the widely held notion that resources under the control of women are more likely to be used to enhance child welfare (through the purchase of food, health care, and other basic needs) than are resources controlled by men. Engle offers a psychological explanation for this phenomenon, based on the closer relationship and greater degree of bonding between mothers and their children than between fathers and children. She cautions, however, that this theory has not yet been empirically tested in a rigorous manner.

These papers taken together underscore the need for integrating a wide variety of types of information in order to achieve a complete understanding of patterns of intra-household resource allocation. Rosenzweig emphasizes that models of the household are only useful if they help to predict behaviour. If two alternative explanations of an observed phenomenon are equally plausible and cannot be distinguished in practice, then, he suggests, it does not matter for planning purposes which one is in operation.

Both Engle and Messer suggest, to the contrary, that comprehending the subjective perceptions of a target population is essential precisely because these perceptions do affect behaviour. Moreover, cultural perceptions of mutual obligations may result in dispersion of some programme benefits beyond the target household or individual for which or whom it was intended. The psychological consequences of changing accepted lines of authority in the household may lead to resistance, conflict, or even violence. The outsider's (etic) perception of efficiency in the use of a resource may conflict with the native's (emic) perception of individual rights to its use. In such cases, it is essential to know both perspectives in order to assess the desirability and the likely adoption of a change.

The economic and material, the cultural, and the psychodynamic perspectives each furnish elements instrumental to the analysis of intra-household allocation processes. Operational definitions of psychological and cultural constructs may be difficult to derive, but recognizing their importance in shaping intra-household behaviour is the first step in solving the measurement problem. The very different approaches implied by these papers are not irreconcilable. On the contrary, they complement each other in developing a complete understanding of current intra-household allocation practices, and of the likely directions for change.

2
Programme Interventions, Intra-household Allocation, and the Welfare of Individuals: Economic Models of the Household

MARK R. ROSENZWEIG

Department of Economics, University of Minnesota, St Paul, Minnesota, USA

Many policy initiatives and programmes have as their objective the improvement of the welfare of individuals. Such policies and programmes alter the environment in which agents make decisions, thereby affecting resource allocations, and/or directly transfer resources across groups or individuals. Almost all individuals, however, reside within multi-member entities, families, or households;[1] moreover, many of the most important components of well-being, such as health and education, are principally determined within households. To the extent that the household or the family is the ultimate decision-making unit, it is necessary to understand how households allocate resources among their individual members and across household activities in order to predict how policies will affect individuals. The household is thus an important intermediary between aggregate policies, local programmes, and the individual.

In this essay, I will review what economic models of the household have to say about the effects of various policy-relevant interventions on the intra-household distribution of resources, and thus on the welfare of individuals. I also review empirical evidence, informed by such models, on these issues. To focus the discussion, I will pay particular attention to the within-family allocation of two household resources – time and food – and to three individual-specific outcomes – schooling, earnings (labour supply), and health status. Policies and/or programmes considered are: direct food or nutritional supplements provided to individuals, female employment-creation schemes, interventions that have as direct or indirect consequences the alteration of relative food prices, and subventions of health services or schooling.

Most of the discussion will be devoted to household models that (1) assume that the size and composition of family members (with the exception of the number of children) are exogenously determined and (2) treat the household as if it were maximizing a single welfare function. Clearly these assumptions do violence to reality. However, these models are the most developed, have seen the most rigorous empirical applications, and, most importantly, provide a clear foundation with which to begin to develop a more comprehensive model of family behaviour. Moreover, most policies and programmes effect marginal changes in the environment that are not likely to alter

26

significantly the structure of households. For predicting the consequences of such policies, as listed above, the models appear useful. For predicting the long-term consequences of economic development, more attention would need to be paid to understanding the determinants of the size and composition of families and/or households and the processes of household decision-making (Pollak, 1985; Rosenzweig, 1988; Safilios-Rothschild, this volume).

Whatever the limitations of existing economic models of household behaviour, they do represent a comprehensive framework for describing and predicting important aspects of intra-household resource allocations. Policy evaluation, data collection, and data analysis cannot be executed well in the absence of an organizing framework. Collections of "precautions," "insights," and/or examples are surely not sufficient for discerning what data to collect, what statistical techniques to use in order to learn something from the data that inform policy, or what consequences to expect from policy interventions.

The first part presents a prototypical economic model of the household, incorporating multiple family members with differing characteristics, household production, labour-market relations, and time and income constraints. The equilibrium of the household is described in terms of the optimal intra-household allocation of goods across individuals and household activities. The second part assesses the effects of in-kind or pecuniary income transfers to the household on the intra-household distribution of resources as implied by the model. The third part investigates the consequences of employment-creation programmes and of alterations in relative food prices on household time allocation and on the distribution of household human capital investments (schooling or health). Datasets describing household behaviour in India, the Philippines, and Indonesia provide empirical examples. The fourth part discusses the implications of intra-household allocative behaviour for discerning how household resources affect such individual outcomes as health and earnings potential when certain traits of individual household members are not measured. The final section briefly recommends future research directions and identifies priorities in data collection for policy-relevant research, as implied by the economic framework.

THE EQUILIBRIUM OF THE HOUSEHOLD

The economic model of the household has three central features: (1) the household welfare function, describing how the household decision-makers value the outcomes of the allocation of household resources; (2) the household technology, describing how income allocations – goods and time – affect outcomes valued by the household, such as health, earnings potential, and a clean house; and (3) the household budget constraint, describing the total resources of time and goods the household can command. No allocation of resources can violate this constraint.

Consider a household with n members. Each member i consumes food x^i, spends some time in leisure T^i, has a stock of human capital H^i (e.g. health, earnings potential), and receives a wage rate W^i in the labour market. The amount of human capital for individual i is determined by the food he or she consumes, other goods Z^i (e.g. schooling or medical services), and the time he/she and other family members allocate to given activities $t_j, j = 1, \ldots, n$. Each individual i also has an exogenously given set of characteristics μ^i (personal ability, gender, etc.) that possibly affect the productivity of inputs. The relationship between household or individual inputs, person-specific characteristics, and the human capital for each family member is given by the production function:

$$H^i = \Psi(X^i; Z^i; t_l^i, \ldots, t_l^n; \mu^i) \tag{1}$$

The wage paid to each family member i also may depend on his/her human capital H^i and on personal characteristics μ^i, such that:

$$W^i = r^i H^i \tag{2}$$

where $r^i = r(\mu^i)$.[2]

Household resources may also be used to produce a set of commodities G, consumed jointly by all household members, including household sanitation, cleanliness, or meals. Such household "public" goods employ the time of individual family members as well as purchased goods Y; i.e.

$$G = G(Y; t_G^l, \ldots, t_G^n), \tag{3}$$

but all household members benefit equally from the production of those goods.

The household decision-makers care about individual food consumption, the level of human capital, the amount of leisure time, and the earnings potential of every household member and the level of the public good G.[3] The household welfare function is thus:

$$U = U(X^l, \ldots, X^n; H^l, \ldots, H^n; T^l, \ldots, T^n; W^l, \ldots, W^n; G) \tag{4}$$

If each family member i has Ω amount of time to allocate among all household production activities T_H^i, work T_W^i, and leisure T^i, then the household budget constraint is:

$$\sum_{i=1}^{n} \Omega W^i + \sum_{i=1}^{n} V^i = \sum_{i=1}^{n} (T_H^i + T^i) W^i + p_x \sum_{i=1}^{n} X^i + P \sum_{i=1}^{n} Z^i + p_y Y \tag{5}$$

where p_x is the price of food, p_z and p_y are the prices of other goods, and V^i is the wealth income of each member i.

This model ignores financial bequests from parents to children that are the focus of attention in Becker and Tomes (1979) and in Behrman et al. (1982), but incorporates the pecuniary contribution of children to family income, as in Rosenzweig and Schultz (1982). However, the implications of the model are retained even if parents make bequests or financial transfers and care about the total income of each family member, as long as they also care, as here, about the health, earnings potential, and/or food consumption of each member.

The household is assumed to allocate all resources across activities and individuals in order to maximize the welfare function (4), subject to the technology (1) and (3), earnings function (2), and budget constraints (5). For given prices and the set of endowments μ of all family members, the optimal allocation of food, for example, across any two family members i and j is given by:

$$\lambda^{-1} \frac{\partial U}{\partial X^i} + \frac{\partial H^i}{\partial X^i} \left[\lambda^{-1} \frac{\partial U}{\partial H^i} + r^i \left(T_W^i + \lambda^{-1} \frac{\partial U}{\partial W^i} \right) \right]$$

$$= \lambda^{-1} \frac{\partial U}{\partial X^j} + \frac{\partial H^j}{\partial X^j} \left[\lambda^{-1} \frac{\partial U}{\partial H^j} + r^j \left(T_W^j + \lambda^{-1} \frac{\partial U}{\partial H^j} \right) \right] = p_x \qquad (6)$$

where λ is the marginal utility of wealth.

Expression (6), while formidable in appearance, merely says that the *marginal* returns to food allocated to each individual in terms of family welfare dU and earnings $T_W^i dW^i$ be equal for each individual and equal to the (marginal) cost per unit of food (the food price p_x). Food will thus be allocated equally among family members only if exogenous endowments or characteristics μ^i are the same for all members. Differences in market returns r^i to human capital, in endowment levels μ, in returns to human capital inputs $\partial H^i / \partial X^i$, or in employment T_W^i among family members will lead to an unequal intra-family distribution of resources. Rosenzweig and Schultz (1982) used a simplified version of this model and showed that where opportunities for female employment and earnings were exogenously higher, female infants in India had higher survival probabilities and, by inference, received a larger share of household resources.

INDIVIDUAL-SPECIFIC TRANSFERS AND INDIVIDUAL WELFARE

Any change in the constraints, technology, or prices facing the household will induce the household to reallocate resources in order to conform to the optimizing allocation, of which expression (6) is one condition. More direct interventions will also lead to reallocations. Consider a programme that provides food at no cost to an individual i, such as in a school-lunch programme. Given the usual neo-classical properties of the welfare function (diminishing marginal utility), such an intervention will lower the left-hand side of (6) relative to the two right-hand side expressions (individual i will be more well-off than any other individual j *compared to his/her condition before the intervention*); the family will thus attempt to correct this imbalance and increase *family* welfare by reducing family-controlled resources given to individual i and redistributing those resources to other members j, in order to maintain the equalities in (6). If family resources are perfect substitutes for the resource provided in the programme, the person-specific subsidy will thus be no more successful in raising individual i's food consumption, health, or welfare compared to other family members than would a programme providing an equivalent amount of money to the family as a whole.

In the neo-classical model of the household, in which all resources are essentially pooled and reallocated to individuals, it thus does not make any difference to whom income subsidies are given or, for the most part, whether such subsidies are in cash or in kind. The effect on the intra-family consumption of resources will be the same and will correspond to that of a general income effect. This strong prediction – the irrelevance of the source of *income* transfers (as opposed to earnings) – is in sharp contrast to models that emphasize conflict among family members and depict the household allocation of resources as the outcome of a bargaining process (cf. Engle, Safilios-Rothschild, this volume). In such models, a rise in assets owned or resources received by an individual i from extra-family resources increases that person's relative bargaining position or power (McElroy and Horney, 1981; Folbre, 1984). Such models, while more realistic, have not provided clear directions, however, as to how intra-household allocations *will* differ when some individual attains more bargaining strength (Rosenzweig and Schultz, 1984); nor has there been any clear empirical rejection of the implications of the unified household model. Whichever model is adopted, unless each individual in the family has full control over all resources (not true even in household bargaining models), person-specific transfer programmes which provide resources to an individual may not succeed in effecting a significant net redistribution of resources to that individual because of family redistribution rules over which policy-makers have no direct control.

PERSON-SPECIFIC PRICES AND GOODS-SPECIFIC PRICES

The family not only allocates consumption goods across its members, but determines (a) the time each individual spends in household production, leisure, and earnings activities and (b) the allocation of inputs among production activities. The human capital (health, earnings potential), consumption, and time allocation for each family member thus depends on the prices of all goods, the wage rates of every family member (or the returns to human capital r^i of each family member), the endowments and/ or characteristics of every family member, and total family income. Solution of the model yields a set of person- and activity-specific "demand" equations for consumption, input, and outcome variables:

$$\begin{matrix} X^i \\ H^i \\ T^i_W \\ Z^i \end{matrix} = D^{ki}(p_x, p_z, p_y; r^i, \ldots, r^n; \mu^i, \ldots, \mu^n; V) \qquad (7)$$

where $V = \sum_{i=1}^{n} V^i$. Policy or programme interventions that alter one of the right-hand side variables in the "demand" equations will thus generally change the intra-family distribution of all resources and outcomes.

Two kinds of "prices" are worth distinguishing. First, there are prices which are specific to goods but not to individuals. A food subsidy/farm policy that induces a change in the price of wheat, for example, affects the relative desirability of wheat compared to other foods and goods for the household but not differentially for individuals within the household. Conversely, there are prices which are specific to individuals but not to activities. A change in the return to human capital (or the wage rate for individual i) affects the relative returns to allocating time to the labour market versus household production/maintenance among family members, but not the relative costs of the different household activities to which each person i allocates his/her time. As a consequence, the model, with few additional restrictions, provides predictions with respect to how changes in goods-specific prices affect the aggregate composition of goods consumed at the household level, but not how these goods are reallocated among family members. The model also provides predictions as to how a change in the value of time (a person-specific price) of any individual family member influences the time allocation of family members across market and non-market activities, but not how the members will allocate their time across household activities. These predictions and their policy implications are discussed in the next two sections.

Wage Rates, the Value of Time, and Time Allocation: Investments in Schooling

As noted, in the unified household model it does not matter in terms of resource allocation to whom in the family income is provided. The source of family income change, however, is critically important. If the source of income growth is an increase in the return on a particular family member's time, for example an increase in the wage rate for member i, then that will induce the family to reallocate resources within and across household activities. In particular, the household will tend to devote less of its resources – time and goods – to activities "intensive" in the time of the family member i, whose opportunity cost of time has risen. Moreover, within activities, goods and other family members' time will substitute for member i's now higher-priced time.

Some projects are designed mainly to increase jobs, and many others have employment consequences, even if they are initiated to accomplish other goals. An employment-creation scheme or any project which increases the demand for labour will thus induce within-household reallocations, particularly if the programme raises the labour-market returns of one group relative to another. If the closest substitutes for an individual's time in household activities are other household members' time, then the principal reallocation will occur with respect to the household's pattern of time allocations.

To illustrate the importance of the source of income growth, consider two schemes: a job-creation programme that increases the labour demand for unskilled, adult women relative to others, and one that augments the demand for skilled women. The first programme raises the value of time of adult women W but not the return to investments in human capital r in the model. If the income effects of such a programme are small, adult women will increase their time allocated to market work and other family members may work less in the market, substituting their time in household activities for that of adult women. Who works less and what the new allocation of family members' time is among activities will depend on household preferences (4) and on the substitutability of different members' time and goods in these activities (1) and (3). If, for example, the time of daughters is considered a better substitute for the time of the mother in home production activities, it is possible that the first (unskilled jobs) programme will reduce the time girls spend in the labour market (and thus their work experience) and in school, while increasing the employment of adult women. Wage rates of women in the longer run may thus decline relative to men as a consequence of the lesser experience and schooling of the next generation of women, because of intra-household allocative responses. These intergenerational effects are elaborated in Rosenzweig (1982).

The second, skill-based, employment scheme has two effects. First, the opportunity cost of adult women is increased, thereby inducing the possible time-allocative effects just discussed. Second, and possibly offsetting these, is the incentive for investments in skills, particularly for girls, induced by the rise in the return on the human capital of women caused by the programme. The within-household cross-wage effects of the job-creation schemes thus depend on: (1) how the jobs affect the relative time costs of family members and the incentives they create for human capital investment; (2) the technology of household production, i.e. substitution possibilities; and (3) household preference orderings.

How important are these "cross-wage" effects on the allocation of family members' time? Many studies of the labour supply of married women in the United States confirm the importance of these effects for labour supply (Ashenfelter and Heckman, 1974). There has as yet been little empirical work on how, for example, mothers, fathers, sons, and daughters interact. Tables 1 and 2 report matrices of estimated "own" and cross-wage effects by sex on children's time in the labour market and in school. The results of table 1 were obtained from regressions run on a 1971 national probability sample of 979 rural Indian households with children; a full report of the

Table 1. Matrix of family wage effects on activities of mother, daughters, and sons in rural households, India[a]

	Labour-force participation			Schooling attendance index[c]	
	Mother	Daughters	Sons	Daughters	Sons
Log of child's wage in district	−0.159 (2.31)[b]	0.454 (0.92)	0.748 (1.45)	−0.486 (2.54)	−0.376 (1.84)
Log of mother's wage (predicted)	0.046 (0.68)	−0.696 (1.44)	0.053 (0.10)	−0.118 (0.63)	−0.375 (1.86)
Log of father's wage (predicted)	−0.184 (3.90)	−0.087 (0.26)	−1.00 (2.82)	0.748 (5.64)	0.929 (6.65)
Landholdings (x 10⁻²)	−0.203 (1.52)	−0.888 (0.93)	−0.909 (0.90)	0.585 (1.48)	1.64 (4.41)

a. For a list of all included variables, estimation procedures, variable construction, and data description, see Rosenzweig (1981).
b. Absolute values of t-ratios beneath regression coefficients.
c. Age-standardized index of attendance.
Source: NCAER-ARIS.

Table 2. Matrix of family wage and schooling effects on activities of daughters and sons, Philippines[a]

	Hours per week in labour market		Schooling attendance index[c]	
	Daughters	Sons	Daughters	Sons
Child's wage	−0.011 (3.67)[b]	−0.008 (1.64)	−0.001 (1.61)	−0.001 (1.50)
Mother's schooling attainment	−0.054 (1.97)	−0.009 (0.54)	0.020 (5.98)	0.025 (6.99)
Father's wage	−0.004 (0.68)	−0.003 (0.78)	0.002 (2.76)	0.002 (2.48)

a. For a list of all included variables, estimation procedures, variable construction, and data description, see Rosenzweig (1978).
b. Absolute values of t-ratios beneath regression coefficients.
c. Age-standardized.
Source: National Demographic Survey, 1968.

study and details of estimation can be found in Rosenzweig (1981). The results indicate that a rise in the value of one person's time significantly affects the time allocation of other family members. In particular, where adult female wage rates were high, both sons and daughters were evidently less likely to be attending school, and daughters, but not sons, were less likely to be employed in the labour market. In contrast, where adult male wage rates were high, for given levels of female and child wages, children were significantly more likely to be attending school and were less likely to be working in the labour market.

The matrix of wage-rate effects from Indian data suggest, moreover, that the times of mothers and female children appear to be closer substitutes in the household than those of mothers and male children, but the opposite is true for fathers' time. A 10 per cent rise in the adult female wage is associated with an 8 per cent fall in daughters' labour-market participation (rise in home time), with little effect on that of sons; while a similar rise in the adult male wage lowers the market participation of sons (raises non-market time) by 9 per cent, with only a small drop for female children. The results thus suggest that attempts to encourage the employment of adult women in agriculture, where most employment is concentrated in India, would increase the time spent by children, particularly girls, in the home by lowering both their participation in earnings activities (girls) and their time in school (boys). The results also indicate, however, that, symmetrically, increases in employment opportunities for children that result in higher child wage rates lower the labour-market participation rates of their mothers. By increasing the cost of children's time, they also lower children's time in school. The symmetry of cross-child and maternal wage effects on labour supply is an important implication of the economic theory of the household.

Table 2 shows parallel estimates from a 1968 national probability sample of 1,829 Filipino households (rural and urban) containing women aged 35–49 (cf. Rosenzweig, 1978).

Some patterns of cross "wage" effects found in the Indian data are replicated in the Philippines sample, although this study utilized the mother's schooling attainment instead of the mother's wage. First, where adult male wages are high, so are the school attendance rates of children. Second, in families where the mother is more educated, market work by daughters is significantly lower, while that of sons is only marginally affected. Since better-educated Filipino women are more likely to work (Rosenzweig, 1976), this result suggests again that daughters' non-market time may be more substitutable (than sons' would be) for that of mothers. Third, when child wage rates are high, school attendance rates are low. The only significant discrepancy between the Indian and Philippine results is the positive and significant association found in the Philippine data between the mother's schooling attainment and the school attendance rate of the children. This suggests that schooling attainment, in addition to being a correlate of the wage, may also reflect parental preferences for schooling.[4]

The empirical results from India and the Philippines illustrate the importance not only of changes in income level, but also of the means by which these changes take place. Different means of changing income may result in different patterns of household resource allocation. The implications for data collection and data analyses are clear: information should be obtained on the wage rate of every family member who works. Conversely, information on "total family income" is of little value for testing models or for policy evaluation. Estimates of the effects of variations in total family income on whatever measure the researcher and/or policy-maker is interested in are not very useful for two reasons. First, such measures obscure the fact that pure income transfers have different effects from wage rate changes which alter the value of individuals' time. Income transfers and wage rate changes represent two distinct policy levers. Second, variations in total family income reflect intra-household differences in the allocation of time to the market by family members as well as wage rates. Since time allocation is an important variable, subject to family decision-making, variations in total family income will reflect household preferences as well as market returns on work. Estimates of "family" income effects will, therefore, not correspond to true income effects induced by income transfers; they will be contaminated by household preferences. Note that, for the same reasons, the *earnings* of family members are endogenous variables in the model, since the earnings of any family member i are just $W^i T_W^i$, where, in (7), T_W^i is a choice variable unless work time is constrained in some way. Of course, estimates of all relationships obtained from multivariate analyses employing such endogenous variables as family income and/or earnings as "control variables" or covariates are biased, unless very special conditions are met.

Additional complications arise when some members of households do not participate in the labour market. The value of time of such "non-working" individuals is not then equal to the market wage but is instead a function of all parameters characterizing the household, and is endogenously determined. An increase in income to the household (through transfers, for example) will generally raise the value of the time of all of the household's non-market participants (Willis, 1973; Gronau, 1973), leading to reallocations of time and goods. Thus, the consequences of an income increase will not only depend on the source of income but on the extent of labour-market participation by family members. In the exetreme case where no family members work for a constant wage rate, it is then very difficult to predict the consequences of interventions without knowledge of the family objective function (4) and the household technology (1) and (3). Estimation of the fundamental parameters characterizing these essential features of the household is difficult at best, and there have been few attempts to estimate, in particular, household technology parameters. I will discuss issues associated with the estimation of household production relations, as they pertain to intra-household allocation, in the fourth part.

Food Prices, Household Food Consumption, Nutritional Status, and Health

The increased attention governments of many developing countries are paying to the "basic needs" of their populations has motivated a number of econometric investigations into the nutritional consequences of food price variation (Pinstrup-Andersen et al., 1976; Alderman and Timmer, 1980; Pitt, 1983; Strauss, 1983). Many policies adopted by developing countries (tariffs, support prices, ceilings, export taxes) and development agencies (food aid) serve to alter the price structure consumers and food producers face. Knowledge of how changes in food prices affect the distribution of food, the nutritional status, and health of the population is crucial to effective policy-setting. Yet, equations estimating the household expenditure system in these studies utilize foods (sometimes converted into nutrients) aggregated over all household members; they do not estimate the individual-specific food demand or health equations (7). Since the price structure pertaining to goods (foods) is the same for each household member i, as noted, such aggregation is permissible (Hick's Composite Good Theorem), and the usual restrictions of demand theory (symmetry, negative own compensated price effects) apply to the household aggregations. Because no such restrictions hold for the individual-specific health or food consumption reduced forms (7), few inferences can be made from these estimates of aggregate household food demand equations about the effects of changes in food prices on the consumption of *individual* family members in those households. That is, when aggregate calorie availability in the household goes up, one cannot infer who in the household consumes those calories or whether such calorie consumption is beneficial. Moreover, in the absence of information on the health technology in (1), little can be said from aggregated food-consumption studies about the impact of food price changes on health. Using such household-level food-demand estimates for establishing policy or for designing interventions may be misleading (cf. Pinstrup-Andersen and Garcia in this volume).

The theoretical ambiguity with respect to the effects of a particular food price change on the level and pattern of nutrient consumption at the household level, arising from theoretically unsigned cross-price effects, is well known. Additional ambiguities arise with respect to the effect of changes in individual food prices on the health status of family members. These are due to a lack of information on how the household distributes food and other resources among its members and on how various foods differentially affect the health of individuals. Consider the simple model in the first section, modified to include more than one food type so that there are aggregate cross-price effects. The reduced form effect of a change in the price of food on the health of individual i, when there are m foods, is given by:

$$\frac{dH^i}{dp_k} = \sum_{l=1}^{m} \frac{\partial H^i}{\partial X^i_l} \frac{dX^i_l}{dp_k} \tag{8}$$

and the effects of a change in food price k on the *household's* aggregate consumption of each food is given by:

$$\frac{d\left(\sum_{i=1}^{m} X^i_l\right)}{dp_k} = \sum_{i=1}^{n} \frac{dX^i_l}{dp_k}, \quad 1 = 1, \ldots, m. \tag{9}$$

Thus, knowledge of the effects of food price changes on household consumption of all foods in (9) cannot be used to predict how that food price, if altered, would affect anyone's health, the magnitude of (8), without the knowledge of how each food X_l affects health (the production function (1) for each individual), and/or of the individual-specific consumption price effects dX^i_l/dp_k, from (7).

Since reliable data on individual-specific food intakes are expensive to obtain, few surveys have collected this information (cf. Pinstrup-Andersen and Garcia, this volume). More common, and less expensive to obtain, are measures of health for individuals. With the latter, estimates of the health reduced-form equation (7) may be estimated, given suitable price variablity. While such reduced-form estimates do not provide information on how the consumption of food items directly affects health (the health technology), they do yield information on how changes in the prices of foods, medical services, and other goods result in changes in the health or nutritional status of individuals. If that is what policy-makers want to know, then collection of health information for individuals and comprehensive price information is sufficient; collection of such information is surely less costly than is the measurement of a household's

35

complete diet and especially of individual food consumption. While there may be good reasons to want to know how households alter their demand for, say, wheat when commodity prices change, this information is not very useful in predicting how the health status of individuals is affected. Moreover, it is a poor choice of a measure to use in the (health) project identification stage.

In Pitt and Rosenzweig (1985), estimates of food price effects on the aggregate household consumption of foods converted into nine nutrients were obtained and compared to estimates of how variations in the same food prices affected the incidence of illness among heads of households and their wives (all heads were males), based on a probability sample of 2,847 farm households in Indonesia. Table 3 excerpts those findings: the effects of four food prices (out of ten) on the nine nutrients and on individual illness probabilities. Only one of the four food prices is unambiguously and negatively associated with the aggregate consumption of all nutrients in the household. An increase in the price of fruits actually increases the consumption of all nutrients except vitamin C, although an increase in the vegetable price appears to significantly lower nutrient consumption for four nutrients. Alterations in the price of sugar appear not to significantly affect the aggregate household consumption of any one nutrient.

The estimated effects of the food price changes on the illness of individuals in the household, provided in the last two columns of table 3, reveal a very different picture of the importance of those food prices for health status, showing a distribution pattern that could not have been anticipated from the nutrient "availability" findings. First, while a fall in the milk price evidently significantly lowers the consumption of all nutrients, variations in milk prices are unrelated to the actual incidence of illness among either farm heads or their wives; the reductions in nutrient consumption may fall predominantly on other household members. Second, while vegetable prices are significantly and negatively associated with the incidence of illness for the male heads of households, rises in vegetable prices do not appear to increase the incidence of illness for farm wives. This uneven distribution of the health effects of vegetable prices is statistically significant (Pitt and Rosenzweig, 1985). Similarly, increases in the price of fruit appear to raise marginally the incidence of illness for farm wives, but not for male farm heads. This differential is not statistically significant, however. Finally, despite the sugar price exhibiting no statistically significant association with household-level nutrient consumption, higher sugar prices are significantly associated with lower illness probabilities among farm heads, but not among farm wives.

HETEROGENEITY AND HOUSEHOLD BEHAVIOUR: DISCERNING THE CONSEQUENCES OF INTRA-HOUSEHOLD RESOURCE ALLOCATIONS

The findings presented in tables 1 to 3 are of value to policy-makers. While certainly not conclusive regarding the effects of changes in wage rates on schooling and non-market time and of the effects of changes in food prices on health, they do confirm the value of estimating the person-specific "demand equations" (7) and the importance of data sets containing variability in wage rates, prices, and measures of outcomes of interest to policy-makers. These reduced-form estimates, however, are only relevant to the populations studied; in particular, they are conditional on the specific technological relationships characterizing household production (and agricultural production)

Table 3. Food price effects, aggregate household nutrient consumption, and the incidence of illness among household heads and their wives, Indonesia[a]

Food price	Household nutrient consumption									Illness probability	
	Calories	Protein	Fat	Carbo-hydrates	Calcium	Phos-phorus	Iron	Vitamin A	Vitamin C	Head	Wife
Milk	-0.0968	-0.0788	-0.0375	-0.1070	-0.0971	-0.0864	-0.1250	-0.1800	-0.2220	0.0162	-0.0217
	(2.75)[b]	(2.16)	(0.84)	(2.88)	(2.14)	(2.57)	(3.18)	(2.90)	(3.78)	(0.81)	(0.97)
Vegetables	-0.00068	0.00226	0.0340	-0.00916	-0.104	0.0152	-0.0685	-0.1970	-0.2070	0.1680	-0.0930
	(0.03)	(0.93)	(1.15)	(0.38)	(3.47)	(0.69)	(2.63)	(4.80)	(5.34)	(2.27)	(0.81)
Fruits	0.0470	0.0294	0.0727	0.0457	0.0487	0.0293	0.0604	0.0113	-0.0645	0.0821	0.1180
	(2.11)	(1.27)	(2.57)	(1.96)	(1.70)	(1.38)	(2.42)	(0.29)	(1.74)	(0.88)	(1.24)
Sugar	0.109	0.0698	-0.1090	0.1380	0.0528	0.0725	-0.1090	-0.0229	-0.1320	-0.4890	-0.1720
	(0.68)	(0.95)	(0.48)	(0.75)	(1.14)	(0.35)	(0.66)	(0.84)	(1.20)	(0.69)	(1.94)
Estimation procedure	2SLS	2SLS	2SLS	2SLS	2SLS	2SLS	2SLS	2SLS	2SLS	MLProbit	MLProbit

a. For a list of all included variables and description of data, see Pitt and Rosenzweig (1985).
b. Absolute values of asymptotic t-values beneath coefficients.
Source: National Socio-economic Survey, 1978.

in those populations. Moreover, it is obviously useful to understand *how* price changes alter health – how the intra-family distribution of food and other inputs varies across individuals and how these resources directly affect health. To better anticipate how the allocation of time and goods within the household will respond to price and wage changes induced by new programmes or policies, and how foods and other inputs directly alter health or other outcomes, requires knowledge of the technological substitution possibilities in, and other characteristics of, household production, depicted in relation (1) of the household model.

Knowledge of the "technological" relationships between family resources and such outcomes as the health and earnings potential of children is valuable not only for improving understanding of the constraints conditioning household behaviour but also for educational interventions aimed at helping households better to allocate resources (when and if their understanding of such relationships is deficient). Information about which foods or other household resources are most "productive" with respect to health, how the timing of childbearing and family size directly affect the survival of children, and how investments in schooling affect the returns on market and non-market activities must come from estimates of the effects of household allocations on such outcomes. Indeed, the estimation of the effects of household resources on the survival, health, and well-being of children has been a central concern in the demographic, economic, and medical literatures (cf. Heller and Drake, 1979; Olsen and Wolpin, 1983; DaVanzo et al., 1983). One of the potential problems in obtaining estimates of the effects of such household-controlled inputs as breast-feeding, foods, schooling, and the use of medical services on measures of child health or indicators of earnings potential, however, is the existence of factors known to or affecting parents but unobserved by the researcher. Variations in such unobserved factors (heterogeneity) across households and across individuals *within households* in the sample population may result in misleading estimates of the causal relationships between parental choices and observed outcomes. Yet few studies have been attentive to this problem (cf. Engle, this volume).

There are two distinct sources of heterogeneity, with different implications for statistical treatment. First, there may be across-household variation in the environment in which allocative decisions are made – mosquito infestation, sanitary conditions – or in the inherent healthiness or abilities of parents, some of which is transmitted genetically to offspring. If parents take into consideration these household factors in their allocative decisions – for example, if households in healthier environments use fewer medical services – then the observed association between variations in family inputs and measures of outcomes will not correctly measure their consequences for those outcomes.

A second source of heterogeneity arises from variations in the inherent qualities of individuals within a family. As is indicated in the resource allocation "rule" (6), differences among individuals in healthiness or skills (μ^i in the model (1)) will generally influence resource allocations across family members.[5] Yet little empirical evidence exists on how resources are allocated across family members as a function of their "endowments." Moreover, without the imposition of additional structure on the household model, it is impossible to know a priori whether more-endowed or less-endowed individuals will receive higher levels of household resources (cf. Engle, this volume). Therefore it is difficult to anticipate how estimates of resource effects which

38

do not take into account intra-family heterogeneity and allocative behaviour will be biased.

To see the trade-offs implicit in the household model, consider a household containing two children with unequal abilities; specifically, assume that one child is characterized by a higher return on schooling than another (a higher r^i in relation (2) of the model). If parents provide schooling equally across the children, their offsprings' earnings will be unequal; if parents provide more schooling to the more able child (until marginal returns are equalized), average and total child earnings will be maximized, but earnings inequality will be exacerbated compared to the equal-input allocation rule. If the parents equalize outcomes (earnings in this case), the less-endowed child receives more schooling. The average and thus total earnings of the offspring will be reduced compared to the equal-input or earnings-maximizing allocative rules.

In the absence of transfers among siblings when they become adults, or with parents caring about individual earnings potential (rather than just the total income of their offspring) as in (3), the household faces a trade-off between equality and efficiency in the intra-family distribution of its resources. How it resolves this trade-off will determine the sign and magnitude of the biases in estimates of the effects of household resources. If, for example, more (less) food is allocated to healthier children or more (less) schooling is allocated to higher-ability children, then associations between food intake and health or schooling and earnings will overstate (understate) the true causal effects of these inputs. Behrman and colleagues (1982) show empirically, based on United States data and a particular configuration of the household model, that parents do not allocate schooling resources across children to maximize average children's earnings; parents are inequality-averse (cf. Behrman, next chapter).

The association between the endowments of individuals and the resources they receive from the family depends on both the characteristics of the technology and the household welfare function. In the schooling case, it was assumed that individuals with higher ability received higher market earnings for given invested skills. However, medical services may be most productive when allocated to less healthy individuals. In that case, there is no trade-off between outcome (health status) equality and efficiency. Moreover, estimates of the efficacy of medical service use inattentive to allocative rules and heterogeneity will then be too low, as found by Rosenzweig and Schultz (1983) in our study of the consequences of pre-natal care for birth-weight outcomes.

One relatively straightforward estimation procedure that can be (and has been) used to eliminate the biases caused by intra- and inter-family heterogeneity relies on the input demand equations (7). The right-hand-side variables in (7) are natural instruments for identifying the technology of production, since variations in prices and in the exogenous determinants of market wage rates are presumably uncorrelated with family endowments (in the absence of significant selective migration), and influence outcomes only by affecting the intra-family distribution of resources. Consistent estimates of the relationships between family resource distributions and outcomes can therefore be obtained by estimating the demand equations first, and then estimating the production functions using predicted allocations based on the demand estimates.

How important are these sources of bias? Rosenzweig and Wolpin (1988) compared estimates of the effects of various household control variables – the timing, spacing, and number of children; the use of inoculations; breast-feeding; and food consumption – on the age-standardized weight of children within six months of their birth, using different estimation procedures. In order to isolate within-household and across-household sources of heterogeneity we used information from households that had at least two children born within a seven-year period, taken from a probability sample of 104 households in Candelaria, Colombia. Table 4 reproduces estimates of the parameters of the normalized child-weight equations obtained from procedures that (1) ignored all forms of heterogeneity (OLS); (2) took into account only heterogeneity across families (family fixed effect or FFE); and (3) took into account both intra- and inter-family heterogeneity (two-stage least squares or TSLS) using parental schooling, programmes, and occupation as instruments.

The FFE method, which "corrects" for inter-family heterogeneity, and the TSLS method, which additionally avoids biases associated with intra-family heterogeneity, yield different results. These also differ from results obtained using the OLS procedure. In particular, while the OLS estimates suggest that breast-fed children experience (marginally significantly) greater weight gain, the breast-feeding coefficients are neither positive nor significant when estimated with either FFE or TSLS methods. This result does not necessarily imply that breast-feeding is ineffective (since the effect of breast-feeding depends on its duration and intensity, and breast-feeding may enhance child survival).

Rather, the estimates suggest that inattention to heterogeneity may lead to an overstatement of the effects of breast-feeding incidence on children's weight. Conversely, the effects of household food consumption per capita, and to a lesser extent of inoculations, appear to be understated using either OLS or FFE methods, which ignore intrahousehold heterogeneity. Neglect of heterogeneity across and within households also appears to lead to an overestimate of the persistent effects of birth order and birth intervals on post-birth weight. While many of the individual coefficients are not measured with much precision, heterogeneity both within and across the sample house-

Table 4. Household resource allocations and the log of weight-for-age: children in Candelaria, Colombia[a]

Estimation procedure	OLS	FFE	TSLS
Breast-fed[b]	0.0316	−0.0106	−0.0358
	(1.12)[d]	(0.24)[e]	(0.35)
Inoculated[b]	0.0259	0.0364	0.0598
	(1.22)	(1.29)	(1.15)
Food per capita[b,c]	0.0284	0.0119	0.1330
	(1.23)	(0.28)	(1.69)
Birth order[b,c]	−0.0726	−0.0853	−0.0230
	(2.96)	(1.13)	(0.21)
Prior interval length[b,c]	0.0306	0.0311	0.0225
	(2.14)	(1.73)	(0.92)
Maternal age at birth[b,c]	0.0460	0.1470	−0.4880
	(0.69)	(0.45)	(1.03)
Selection correlation	−0.2650	—	—
variable)	(1.72)		
n	238	238	238

a. For data description and details of estimation, see Rosenzweig and Wolpin (1988, forthcoming).
b. Endogenous variable.
c. Log of variable.
d. Absolute values of t-ratios beneath regression coefficients.
e. Absolute values of asymptotic t-ratios beneath coefficients.

holds appears to be affecting the intra-household and inter-household variations in the inputs and thus the estimated coefficients in this sample of children.

Finally, determination of how the household allocates resources according to the endowments of individuals within the household is not "just" an estimation issue. These household allocative rules have important long-term consequences for inequality associated with particular programme or policy interventions. An increase in schooling opportunities, for example, may benefit the more able and thus could exacerbate earnings inequality. A health programme could reduce disparities in healthiness in the population, depending on the inter- and intra-household distribution of resources and on the nature of the household technology.

CONCLUSION

In this paper, I have briefly reviewed the implications of economic models of the household in order to assess how programme interventions affect the consumption of or investments in individuals who are members of collective decision-making groups or households. While the models discussed ignore many of the problems associated with collective decision-making, richer, more detailed models will likely be characterized by many of the features present in the existing economic models of the household that view the household as maximizing a given welfare function. Such models imply that policy-makers must pay particular attention to the interdependence among household members. Interventions aimed at encouraging particular activities or augmenting the welfare of particular individuals will have cross-effects, will affect other individuals, and may induce other activities, perhaps with less desirable results. These cross-effects come about as long as some resources received by individuals are pooled and reallocated within the collective entity.

A better understanding of how households allocate their resources will no doubt come when the models of household decision-making are imbedded in a broader framework which explains household size and composition and how households form and break up. Work on improving our understanding of the benefits of the family as an organization has already begun (Cain, 1981; Kotlikoff and Spivak, 1981; Rosenzweig and Wolpin, 1985, 1988), but has not yet been integrated with models of intra-household resource allocation.

Despite the limitations of existing models of household behaviour, it would appear that the current binding constraint on knowledge is the state of existing data. The theoretical framework provides a clear indication of the kinds of data needed for improving our knowledge in order to anticipate the consequences of interventions, given intra-household allocative behaviour; few data sets meet these requirements.

First, the models imply that information needs to be elicited on sources of income, by individual, with particular attention to wage rates (cf. Rogers, chapter 1, and Appendix). Most surveys lump all resources together, even though family income is itself an outcome of household decisions and even though different sources of income have significantly different effects on allocations. Second, price variability is critical for understanding how allocations and outcomes vary in response to interventions. Detailed information in one price-income-endowment environment, no matter how accurate, cannot tell us anything about how behaviour changes when there are alterations in the environment in which households exist, yet that is exactly what programmes are designed to do. Third, given price variability, a cost-effective means of obtaining information on the effects of interventions is to obtain information on outcomes of interest. If policy-makers are concerned about health, morbidity, or schooling, then these outcomes should be measured as a priority. Yet many surveys concentrate their efforts on collecting data on *household inputs* rather than on *individual outcomes*. Information on household food consumption or time allocation is useful, but cannot be used to estimate household technology (production functions) or to make welfare judgments without measures of the ultimate consequences of those inputs. Policy-makers as well as researchers must make the decisions about which ultimate consequences are of interest. Poor integration of survey design and modelling so far have been critical impediments to knowledge.

NOTES

1. I do not attempt here to define precisely the decision-making unit. In principle, any collection of individuals who pool resources and/or whose activities are interdependent could qualify as the relevant entity. Thus, co-residence is neither a necessary nor sufficient condition for the existence of a "household." One might operationalize this concept by the following definition: person i and person j are in the same decision-making unit if person i's (j's) resource allocations are not independent of person j's (i's) income or earnings.
2. There may be an additive endowment effect as well. To simplify, I omit a discussion of the distinction between additive and multiplicative endowments.
3. The household decision-makers may also care about whom household members marry or the kind of households of which they become members. These considerations are discussed in Behrman and Wolfe (1983) and Rosenzweig and Boulier (1984).
4. Another difference is that the Philippines data provided information on hours of work for children aged ten and above, while the Indian data only provided information on children's labour-force participation. The Philippines' results indicate the existence of backward-bending supply (hours) "curves" for children. "Own" wage-rate effects on participation probabilities must be positive, of course, as they are in the India data.
5. For example, it is well-known that an infant's intake of breast-milk depends on its ability to suck; immature or ill infants may thus be breast-fed less or not at all, leading to an upward bias in the estimation of the effects of breast-feeding on infant survival or nutritional status.

REFERENCES

Alderman, H., and C.P. Timmer. 1980. Food Policy and Food Demand in Indonesia. *Bull. Indonesian Econ. Stud.*, 16(11): 83–93.

Ashenfelter, O., and J. Heckman. 1974. The Estimation of Income and Substitution Effects in a Model of Family Labor Supply. *Econometrica*, 42(1): 73–85.

Becker, G.S., and N. Tomes. 1979. An Equilibrium Theory of the Distribution of Income and Intergenerational Mobility. *J. Pol. Econ.*, 87(6): 1153–1189.

Behrman, J., R. Pollak, and P. Taubman. 1982. Parental Preferences and Provision for Progeny. *J. Pol. Econ.*, 90(1): 52–73.

Behrman, J., and B. Wolfe. 1983. Who Marries Whom? And How It Affects the Return to Schooling. Mimeo. University of Pennsylvania, Philadelphia, Pa.

Cain, M. 1981. Risk and Insurance: Perspectives on Fertility and Agrarian Change in India and Bangladesh. *Popul. Devel. Rev.*, 7(3): 435–474.

DaVanzo, J., W.P. Butz, and J.-P. Habicht. 1983. How Biological and Behavioral Influences on Mortality in Malaysia Vary during the First Year of Life. *Popul. Stud.*, 37(3): 381–402.

Folbre, N. 1984. Market Opportunities, Genetic Endowments, and Intrafamily Resource Distribution: Comment. *Am. Econ. Rev.*, 74(3): 518–520.

Gronau, R. 1973. The Intrafamily Allocation of Time: The Value of the Housewives' Time. *Am. Econ. Rev.*, 63(4): 634–651.

Heller, P.S., and M.D. Drake. 1979. Malnutrition, Child Morbidity and the Family Decision Process. *J. Devel. Econ.*, 6(2): 203–235.

Kotlikoff, L.J., and A. Spivak. 1981. The Family as An Incomplete Annuities Market. *J. Pol. Econ.*, 89(2): 372–391.

McElroy, M., and M.J. Horney. 1981. Nash-bargained Household Decisions: Toward a Generalization of the Theory of Demand. *Internat. Econ. Rev.*, 22(2): 333–349.

Olsen, R., and K. Wolpin. 1983. The Impact of Exogenous Child Mortality on Fertility: A Waiting Time Regression with Dynamic Regressors. *Econometrica*, 51(3): 731–749.

Pinstrup-Andersen, P., N.R. de Londono, and E. Hoover. 1976. The Impact of Increasing Food Supply on Human Nutrition: Implications for Commodity Priorities in Agricultural Policy Research. *Am. J. Agric. Econ.*, 58(5): 131–142.

Pitt, M.M. 1983. Food Preferences and Nutrition in Rural Bangladesh. *Rev. Econ. Stat.*, 65(1): 105–114.

Pitt, M.M., and M.R. Rosenzweig. 1985. Health and Nutrient Consumption across and within Farm Households. *Rev. Econ. Stat.*, 67(2): 212–222.

Pollack, R.A. 1985. A Transaction Costs Approach to Families and Households. *J. Econ. Lit.*, 23(3): 581–608.

Rosenzweig, M.R. 1976. Female Work Experience, Employment Status, and Birth Expectations: Sequential Decision-making in the Philippines. *Demography*, 13(3): 339–356.

——. 1978. The Value of Children's Time, Family Size and Non-household Child Activities in a Developing Country: Evidence from Household Data. In: J.C. Simon, *Research in Population Economics 1*, pp. 331–347. JAI Press, Connecticut.

——. 1981. Household and Non-household Activities of Youths: Issues of Modelling, Data and Estimation Strategies. In: G. Rodgers and G. Standing, *Child Work, Poverty and Underdevelopment*. International Labour Office, Geneva.

——. 1982. Wage Structure and Sex-based Wage Inequality: The Family as Intermediary. In: Y. Ben-Porath, Income Distribution and the Family. *Popul. Devel. Rev.*, 8 (Suppl.): 192–206.

——. 1988a. Risk, Private Information, and the Family. *Am. Econ. Rev.*, 78(5): 245–250.

——. 1988b. Risk, Implicit Contracts, and the Family in Rural Areas of Low-income Countries. *Econ. J.*, 98(12): 1148–1170.

Rosenzweig, M.R., and B. Boulier. 1984. Schooling, Search and Spouse Selection: Testing Economic Theories of Marriage and Household Behavior. *J. Pol. Econ.*, 92(4): 712–732.

Rosenzweig, M.R., and T.P. Schultz. 1982. Market Opportunities, Genetic Endowments and Intrafamily Resource Distribution: Child Survival in Rural India. *Am. Econ. Rev.*, 72(4): 803–815.

——. 1983. Estimating a Household Production Function: Heterogeneity, the Demand for Health Inputs, and Their Effects on Birth Weight. *J. Pol. Econ.*, 91(5): 723–746.

——. 1984. Market Opportunities and Intrafamily Resource Distribution: Reply. *Am. Econ. Rev.*, 74(3): 521–522.

Rosenzweig, M.R., and K.I. Wolpin. 1985. Specific Experience, Household Structure, and Intergenerational Transfers: Farm Family Land and Labor Arrangements in Developing Countries. *Quart. J. Econ.*, C (402 Suppl): 961–987.

——. 1988. Heterogeneity, Intrafamily Distribution and Child Health. *J. Hum. Resources*, 23: 437–461.

Strauss, J. 1983. Determinants of Food Consumption in Rural Sierra Leone: Application of the Quadratic Expenditure System to the Consumption–Leisure Component of a Household-firm Model. *J. Devel. Econ.*, 11(3): 327–353.

Willis, R.J. 1973. A New Approach to the Economic Theory of Fertility Behavior. *J. Pol. Econ.*, 81/II(2 Suppl): 14–64.

3
Peeking into the Black Box of Economic Models of the Household

JERE R. BEHRMAN

Economics Department, University of Pennsylvania, Philadelphia, Pennsylvania, USA

INTRODUCTION

An organizing framework is essential for asking what empirical dimensions of reality are relevant and for interpreting data about that reality. The economic model of the household, despite its limitations, some of which are noted by Rosenzweig (1984 and this volume), provides a very useful framework for such purposes. It has provided many important insights, particularly regarding the importance of prices in addition to income effects, the difficulty of signing the impact of many exogenous changes, the possibilities of substitution among members of a household within and across generations, the role of overall resource constraints (including those of time), and the influence of often unobserved endowments (or heterogeneities in Rosenzweig's terminology). For empirical work it points to the importance of data on wages for individuals and on prices that the household faces, as well as on endowments of individuals and households. It also suggests that data on individual inputs (e.g. nutrition) that are determined within the household may be difficult to obtain, in part because of intra-household substitution and transfers. Therefore, as Rosenzweig points out, data on the related outcomes (e.g. health measures) may be much more cost-effective to obtain.

But it should be noted, particularly given Rosenzweig's emphasis on the importance of wage data, that if wages depend on consumption of nutrients and other health-related inputs, as Leibenstein (1957) long ago conjectured and as some recent studies report (e.g. Behrman and Deolalikar, 1988; Deolalikar, 1988; Sahn and Alderman, 1989; Strauss, 1985, 1986), then wages are endogenous and do *not* appear in the reduced forms. Thus, the appropriate representation of the opportunity cost of time may be much more complicated and much more difficult to identify empirically than Rosenzweig suggests.

Furthermore, empirical applications of the economic household model as Rosenzweig describes them basically treat the household as a black box,[1] in the sense that observed outcomes respond within a reduced-form framework to exogenous changes

44

in market prices and other variables. In this discussion I shall peak into that black box, first empirically and then theoretically.

AN EMPIRICAL PEEK INTO THE BLACK BOX
OF ECONOMIC HOUSEHOLD MODELS

The reason why most empirical economic applications, including examples given in Rosenzweig's paper, treat the household as a reduced-form black box is that the data requirements make any other option difficult. At times, however, special data in combination with a theoretical framework can permit a glimpse inside the household black box.

To illustrate how this works, I summarize recent work in which I have been involved concerning the nature of household allocations among children.[2] Assume that the parents of the children behave as if they are maximizing (subject to constraints) their preferences defined over the distribution of expected outcomes (e.g. earnings or health) among their children and that the expected outcomes for each child depend on the parental allocation of inputs (e.g. schooling, time, or nutrients) and on child-specific endowments (e.g. genetic characteristics).[3] Two important questions about the parental preferences can then be answered with a specific version of the economic household model and special sibling data on inputs and outputs.

First, to what extent do parents allocate resources so as to compensate for or to reinforce inequalities across children in endowments? Figure 1 illustrates three alternatives for the preference curves of parents between expected outcomes for two children. At one extreme, the preference curve is L-shaped or Rawlsian, showing that parents are concerned only about the worst-off child. They devote all of their resources to that child until the expected outcome for that child is as good as that for

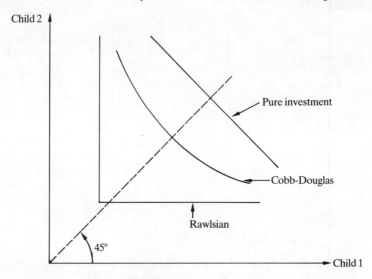

Fig. 1. Alternative parental preferences between expected outcomes for children 1 and 2.

45

the next worst-off child. At the other extreme the preference curve is linear, so that parents follow a pure investment model by allocating resources to their children so that the highest total returns are obtained, with no consideration about the distribution of outcomes. Among all of the intermediate possibilities, there is one of particular interest (which economists call the Cobb-Douglas case), because for this degree of curvature parents are neutral, neither reinforcing nor compensating inequalities in child endowments.

Second, to what extent do parents favour one type of child (i.e. designated by sex or birth order) over others in the sense that an equal outcome is valued more highly for the favoured type child than for others? In terms of figure 1, this question refers to whether or not the parental preference curve is symmetrical around the 45° ray from the origin. If it is symmetrical, as in figure 1, the parents have equal concern, independent of the type of child.[4] If it is not symmetrical, as in figure 2, the parents weigh equal expected outcomes more heavily for one child than for the other (in this case, more for child 1).

With collaborators, I have estimated the curvature and symmetry around the 45° line of parental preferences based on sibling data from samples for the United States and for rural south India. For the United States the expected output data related to adult earnings and the input data to schooling levels for two different recent generations. For India, the expected output data are health outcomes (as indicated by anthropometric measures) and the input data are nutrients for both the lean and surplus seasons (as defined by food availability).

For the United States, the estimates suggest that parental preference curves are shaped approximately like the Cobb-Douglas case for both generations. This implies significant parental inequality aversion and behaviour far different from that of a pure

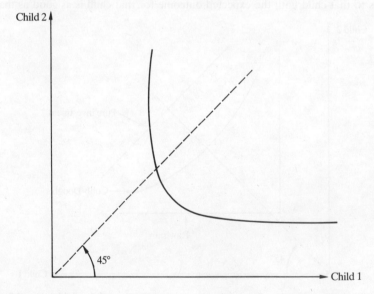

Fig. 2. Parental preferences that weight equal expected outcomes more heavily for child 1 than for child 2.

investment model, but with close to neutrality concerning the compensation or rein-forcement of endowment differentials.[5] Parents also slightly favour older children and girls in the sense that they weigh equal outcomes for such children more heavily than they do for younger children and boys.

For India, the estimates suggest about neutral (Cobb-Douglas) curvature of paren-tal preferences in the surplus season when food is relatively abundant, but much closer to a pure investment strategy in the lean season when food is in short supply.[6] More-over, the allocations suggest preference for boys over girls and for older over younger children in the lean season. The male preference result persists if differential (by gen-der) expected labour-market wages are introduced, thereby suggesting that the greater allocation of nutrients to boys is not due solely to higher expected labour-market returns to investment in boys (than in girls), as is emphasized in Rosenzweig and Schultz (1982). These results do not differ significantly between nuclear and extended households. But the weights on outcomes of children whose mother is not in the household are systematically smaller than for those whose mother is present, consis-tent with the critical role of mothers in the food allocation process that has been emphasized by Engle (this volume) and others. Thus, particularly in the lean season, when food supplies are relatively limited, the results suggest that the most vulnerable – the less well-endowed, the younger, the girls, and the motherless – receive systemati-cally fewer nutrients.

Such studies are valuable in better understanding intra-household allocation, but the data requirements are substantial. For the United States case, information on adult siblings was required; for the Indian study, information on individual nutrients consumed by all siblings. Both types of data are expensive to collect, which precludes widespread replication of these and other studies that empirically look inside the household through large representative social-science samples.

I therefore agree with Rosenzweig that, for many purposes, the most cost-effective empirical approaches may focus on individual outcomes that are determined by intra-household allocation processes as conditioned by changes outside the household, in markets and elsewhere, without explicit representation of the intra-household alloca-tion process. But for some purposes, such as in the studies that I review here, such reduced-forms approaches cannot provide the necessary information.

A THEORETICAL PEEK INTO THE BLACK BOX
OF ECONOMIC HOUSEHOLD MODELS

Several assumptions of the economic household models summarized by Rosenzweig bother many non-economists, and indeed some economists. I will now briefly discuss some of these.

Existence of a Unified Household Preference Function

Rosenzweig explicitly posits that households act as if such a function is being maxi-mized. Others, as Rosenzweig notes and Engle emphasizes in her chapter, question whether such an assumption does not do violence to reality, since they perceive the actual intra-household allocations to be the outcome of bargaining positions based on power.

47

For reduced-form relations tying observed outcomes to exogenous change (but collapsing intra-household allocations into the parameters) estimated from the existing data on which Rosenzweig concentrates, however, it is not clear that substituting other stable household allocation rules would make any difference as long as the allocation procedure did not depend upon additional variables. Reduced forms still would result, indicating that the observed outcomes depend on the exogenous changes. Within such reduced forms, for example, it is not possible to identify to what extent the coefficient on the women's labour-market wage is due to reallocation in response to changes in her opportunity cost of time in a model with a unified preference function or to her altered influence on allocation in a bargaining framework. Only if the alternative frameworks led to different predictions would such identification be possible. To my knowledge, alternative models that permit such identification with data typically available have not yet been developed.

One can conceive, however, of experiments which result in data that can be used to distinguish between a unified household preference function and a bargaining model. For example, transfers could be distributed randomly to different household members and empirical tests could be conducted to see if who received such transfers made a difference. But care would have to be taken to assure that the distribution of such transfers was orthogonal to (i.e. statistically independent of) individual characteristics such as schooling or number of children that may be associated with an individual's human capital and opportunity cost in terms of time. Existing datasets of which I am aware do not have this property. Instead, transfers have been made on the basis of factors such as number of children, income, or family structure that are likely to be associated with the opportunity costs of time.

Of course, all this is not to say that the unified preference approach is correct – it is empirically no more so (nor less so) than the alternatives. Nor is it my intent to discourage the development of alternative models with testable predictions or of alternative datasets with the necessary properties to permit testing between alternatives. To the contrary, such developments would be most welcome, since they could shed useful light on changes in household structures and household formation and dissolution. But at this time, no one has proved that there is a better way of looking at reduced-form relations that result from intra-household allocation.

Existence of Stable Preferences

Economists tend to assume that tastes are fixed, though some economists (e.g. Easterlin et al., 1980) have questioned whether tastes might not be endogenous. Suppose that the latter were true. Would that affect conclusions of the sort that Rosenzweig derives from his empircal explorations?

The answer is: it depends. For example, suppose that tastes depend on schooling and that Rosenzweig includes the woman's schooling in reduced forms for health outcomes because of widespread hypotheses that the woman's schooling positively affects household productivity related to health, but he does not specify an actual dependence of tastes on the woman's schooling. Despite this misspecification, the reduced forms have the correct variables and the interpretation of the magnitude of the impact of a change in the woman's schooling on health is unaffected. The only problem may be in interpretation – for example, if the impact of the woman's schooling is interpreted to be solely a productivity effect.

Suppose, alternatively, that tastes depend on some variable that is not in Rosenzweig's reduced forms. If this variable is correlated with the included variables, then the failure to include it causes omitted variable bias in the variables with which it is associated, since they partially represent the omitted variable in addition to their own effects.[7]

Constrained Maximization as a Representation of Behaviour

Some maintain that maximization is not a good representation of behaviour, because households (or individuals) are constrained by cultural norms or because they do not adjust to every chance for slight gain (due to the costs of adjustment), but instead "satisfice" by following rules of thumb, for instance. Of course, within Rosenzweig's framework, these possibilities could be incorporated as additional constraints – perhaps without changing his reduced forms. If so, these would not alter his basic empirical approach. If not, they could cause biases if the omitted variables were correlated with included ones.

Dynamic Interpretation of Cross-section Estimates

Rosenzweig's estimates of the reduced forms from the economic model of the household generally depend on cross-section associations. Yet the interpretations are dynamic: if one increases this price or expands schooling, then. . . . Such interpretations may be wrong if there are other dynamic changes that are being held constant in the cross-section (e.g. new technology or changed position of a reference group for norms), or misleading (depending on the time horizons) if there are adjustment costs. Of course, these are the problems inherent in any dynamic deduction from cross-section data, and are not peculiar to studies based on economic household models.

CONCLUSIONS

Given the present state of our knowledge, it is pretty dark in the black box of economic models of the household. None the less, Rosenzweig's survey could usefully be extended to show that some peeks inside are possible empirically, as discussed above, although at a data cost which severely restricts replicability. Limited efforts to peek inside theoretically lead to the conclusion that the testing of alternative hypotheses about the functioning of households is indeed difficult, since usually the predictions regarding the reduced forms do not differ for existing data. In such a case, there is nothing to recommend the alternative over the economic household model, or vice versa, except for simplicity. Because of such possibilities, care must be taken in interpretation, because often the identification of the impact of particular variables (e.g. schooling) depends upon assuming away other a priori plausible affects.

NOTES

1. A term that Pinstrup-Andersen and Garcia also use in their paper in this volume.
2. The research presented in this paper was generously supported by a grant from the National Institutes of Health. See in the reference list the citations of which I am author or co-author.
3. Conditional upon the explicit functional forms utilized, the basic features of the model can be estimated, although the endowments are not observed.

4. Except at the Rawlsian extreme, equal concern does not mean that parents maximize by allocating inputs to obtain equal expected outcomes for each child. The parents attain the highest possible preference curve subject to the expected outcome possibility frontier. This in turn depends on total resources allocated to the children, the production relations between parentally allocated inputs and endowments on the one hand and expected outcomes on the other, and on the distribution of endowments across children. Since endowments in general are not distributed equally across children, this production-possibility frontier generally is not symmetrical around the 45° line, and the maximization of parental preferences where the preference curve is tangent to the production-possibility frontier is not on the 45° line (thus *not* implying equal expected outcomes across children).
5. The econometric analysis in Behrman and Taubman (1986) suggests that, due to simultaneity, these estimates probably are biased towards the investment model. If so, actual behaviour may compensate for endowment differentials rather than be neutral.
6. The comment in the previous note about simultaneity bias again applies, but the bias is not likely to be large enough, so that the true lean season value is neutral or compensating instead of reinforcing.
7. There also may be ambiguous private welfare effects since, with endogenous tastes, preferences change with schooling or whatever (see Easterlin et al., 1980).

REFERENCES

Behrman, J.R. 1984. Birth Order, Nutrition and Health: Intrahousehold Allocation in Rural India. Mimeo. University of Pennsylvania, Philadelphia, Pa.

——. 1988a. Nutrition, Health, Birth Order and Seasonality: Intrahousehold Allocation in Rural India. *J. Devel. Econ.*, 28(1): 43–62.

——. 1988b. Intrahousehold Allocation of Nutrients and Gender Effects: A Survey of Structural and Reduced-form Estimates. In: S.R. Osmani, ed., *Nutrition and Poverty*. Oxford University Press, Oxford.

——. 1988c. Intrahousehold Allocation of Nutrients in Rural India: Are Boys Favoured? Do Parents Exhibit Inequality Aversion? *Oxford Economic Papers*, 40 (1): 32–54.

Behrman, J.R., and A.B. Deolalikar. 1988. Wages and Labor Supply in Rural India: The Role of Health, Nutrition and Seasonality. In: D.E. Sahn, ed., *Cause and Implications of Seasonal Variability in Household Food Security*. Johns Hopkins University Press, Baltimore, Md.

Behrman, J.R., R.A. Pollak, and P. Taubman. 1982. Parental Preferences and Provision for Progeny. *J. Pol. Econ.*, 90(1): 52–73.

——. 1986. Do Parents Favor Boys? *Internat. Econ. Rev.*, 27(1): 31–52.

Behrman, J.R., and P. Taubman. 1986. Birth Order, Schooling and Earnings. *J. Pol. Econ.*, 4 (3/part 2): S121–145.

Deolalikar, A.B. 1988. Do Health and Nutrition Influence Labor Productivity in Agriculture? Econometric Estimates for Rural South India. *Rev. Econ. Stat.*, 70(30): 406–413.

Easterlin, R.A., R.A. Pollak, and M.L. Wachter. 1980. Toward a More General Economic Model of Fertility Determination: Endogenous Preferences and Natural Fertility. In: R.A. Easterlin, ed., *Population and Economic Change in Developing Countries*, pp. 81–150. University of Chicago Press for National Bureau of Economic Research, Chicago.

Leibenstein, H.A. 1957. Economic Backwardness and Economic Growth. John Wiley, New York.

Rosenzweig, M.R., and T.P. Schultz. 1982. Market Opportunities, Genetic Endowments and Intrafamily Resource Distribution: Child Survival in Rural India. *Am. Econ. Rev.*, 72(4): 803–815.

Sahn, D.E., and H. Alderman. 1989. The Effects of Human Capital on Wages, and the Determinants of Labour Supply in a Developing Country. *J. Devel. Econ.*, forthcoming.

Strauss, J. 1986. Does Better Nutrition Raise Farm Productivity? *J. Pol. Econ*, 94: 297–320.

——. The Impact of Improved Nutrition on Labor Productivity and Human Resource Development: An Economic Perspective. Paper presented at the International Food Policy Research Institute Workshop on the Political Economy of Nutrition Improvements, West Virginia, 1985.

4

Intra-household Allocation of Resources: Perspectives from Anthropology

ELLEN MESSER

Alan Shawn Feinstein World Hunger Program, Brown University,
Providence, Rhode Island, USA

INTRODUCTION

This paper introduces the various anthropological frameworks used to predict the effects of socio-economic interventions on households and their members. Anthropologists conceptualize household characteristics and processes, and study the changes brought about by development projects from three different perspectives: cultural, social, and biological.

Cultural anthropologists analyse the ecology, economy, technology, symbols, ideas, and values in human environments. Programme planners and project designers are concerned with how knowledge and materials are distributed at the household level, and how distribution of resources affects production, consumption, and health outcomes. Anthropologists generally characterize cultural change by considering structure and content separately. For example, a programme which introduces paid employment for unmarried women, where young women have not worked for pay before, may "increase" female employment and (depending on prevailing rules of distribution) household income. This is a change in content but it may also upset the existing age and gender relationships in that society. This structural change in the culture can lead to longer-term changes which may alter other dimensions of social life, such as increased decision-making power over expenditures of money earned by young women (cf. Fernandez-Kelley, 1983; Nash, 1983). Primary schooling provides book learning for the young and alters their perspectives on society and the economy. In many cases, it also removes children from full-time household chores, causing temporary as well as long-run structural readjustments in the labour force (Minge-Klevana, 1978).

Agricultural and cultural programmes that push native peoples into new relationships with the land may in the short or long run reduce their ability to rely on local subsistence production (e.g. Gross et al., 1979). Cultural anthropology traditionally studies the ways in which culturally determined rules and definitions affect the uses of materials and knowledge in a society. Cultural anthropologists ask whether economic and social changes affect the potential of a household unit to respond to perturbations in the environment, including subsequent socio-economic programmes, and whether new adjustments maintain or eliminate the possibility of falling back on previous emergency strategies. For example, new green revolution agricultural packages may destroy through herbicides the "wild" edible items of an ecosystem (Messer, 1976). New plant forms that must be mechanically processed may eliminate income-earning opportunities for poor people who traditionally processed them by hand (cf. Soekirman, 1978).

Many policy changes and programmes affect not only the material culture and ideas of the society, but its kinship and territorial structure. At the household level, social anthropologists analyse the structure and function of household units, and the effects of social forces beyond the household on its stability and change. Before we can predict the effects projects have on intra-household resource allocation, we must first understand what constitutes "households" and their resources in different cultures, at various times. As I have suggested elsewhere (Messer, 1983, p. 3), for purposes of policy formation and evaluation we are usually interested in "that group of people, their relationships and activities, who acknowledge a common authority in domestic matters, a 'budget unit,' or 'a group who have a common fund of material and human resources and rules and practices for exchange within it.'" To anticipate potential project impacts, "one must examine marriage rules, residence rules, and the social and biological processes leading to cycles of shared residence, work, and consumption of individuals and domestic unit." This includes understanding how labour is recruited, the sex and age division of labour, the rules for transmission of property within and across generations, concepts of ownership of material possessions, skills, information, and time, as well as rules for sharing such resources. Ideally, one should also know who makes decisions at various points in the flow of raw materials from production or purchase, through preparation, distribution, and finally consumption. When measuring changes in allocation of people's time, energy, and material goods, it is of vital importance to know how the structuring of labour changes temporarily or permanently in response to development projects. Do the units themselves change, or do they merely adjust contextually to the demands of the project? Social anthropology provides the tools for studying these questions.

A third subfield, biological anthropology, which includes medical and nutritional anthropology, evaluates the health and nutritional outcomes of local survival strategies, and the impact of socio-economic and policy changes, direct or indirect, on these parameters. Although such outcome measures are usually derived from anthropometry, morbidity and mortality data, social and psychological data should also be used. For a more complete picture, physical development and nutritional and health status should be investigated in relation to indicators of cognitive, emotional, and social functioning, such as work performance in adults or school attendance in children. For example, the net effect of an employment programme for women might include better school attendance by children who no longer have to work to contribute to household income, since their mothers now do. The children might also be better nourished and healthier if mothers' income were directed toward their nutritional and health needs. All of these aspects of biological and socio-cultural function are interrelated (cf. Calloway et al., 1979).

In sum, anthropologists evaluate project impacts in the following terms:
1. The resources available to a social unit – its land, labour time, skills, energy, and potentially productive materials.
2. Its rules for classifying, using, and distributing these resouces – e.g. rules for what

52

work men, women, and children should do, and how they should be compensated for their contributions to the unit's well-being.

3. The nutritional and health consequences of these rules for resource allocation and use. Are people using scarce resources optimally or at least adequately to assure the welfare of all household members? What combinations of resource availability and distribution rules might be changed to improve the well-being of individuals at risk?

Any of these cultural, social, and biological parameters can be viewed from the "scientific" outside analyst's (etic) point of view, or from the native's (emic) perspective. These are respectively termed the "operational environment" (that which can be objectively measured in cross-culturally comparable units such as minutes, dollars, kilocalories, or nutrients), and the culturally specific "cognized environment" described in terms of local ethnic concepts of time (cf. Zeitlin, this volume), costs, energy expenditure, feelings of nutritional well-being or deprivation and perceived cause and effect relationships in the natural and cultural environment (cf. Rappaport, 1968). The "fit" between the scientist's and the native's units of measurement and understanding of the process of change is often a key to the project planner's ability to anticipate outcomes, and therefore shapes the success or failure of a project. A local mother's perception of the opportunity cost of visiting a health clinic, for instance, may be far greater than that anticipated by the project planner, and thus reduce participation rates. In certain cultures, women have daybreak-to-sundown times allocated to specific activities.

The following sections detail some of the data and data-collection processes needed to document household structure and function from these combined anthropological and particularly etic and emic points of view.

ECOLOGICAL AND ECONOMIC RESOURCES

Economists generally evaluate the effects of development projects on "standard of living" in material terms such as income or consumption outcome measures (Mellor and Johnston, 1984). They also use education, health, and nutrition indicators. Yet, attempts to improve these socio-economic indicators may not always work as expected. Consider, for example, programmes to improve economic well-being through (a) cash cropping, (b) livestock production, and (c) cash tree cropping. Substituting cash crops for food crops will limit the absolute amount of food (income in kind) available for distribution among household members, and may result in poorer nutrient intakes unless (1) sufficient income is generated by cash crops to cover the costs of purchasing an adequate diet, and (2) income is allocated to purchasing that diet. On the first point, Dewey (1980), among others, found that when Mexican subsistence farmers were integrated into a cash-crop development scheme, they suffered nutritionally, in part because earned income was insufficient to purchase an adequate diet, and in part because income allocated to food was not necessarily used to purchase the most nutritionally advantageous foods. DeWalt (1983, 1984), in analyses of dietary strategies among another Mexican population, noted that increased income generally improved the variety and nutritional quality of the diet. At levels just above subsistence, however, increased cash and dietary variety did not ensure an improvement in nutritional status: food choices were not necessarily nutritionally optimal.

Cash cropping may also alter the sex division of labour, control over land, and decision-making over crops and their distribution. These changes condition the impact and acceptance of programmes (Kumar, 1979, 1983; Jones, 1983). In Africa, as men assumed responsibility for cash crops, women lost access to land and its products, and lost the power to decide how the land's products would be allocated (Afonja, 1981). These changes reduced women's access to income and their ability to provision their households. Cash cropping, as it changes the nature of the crops grown, may deplete the resources available to marginal members of the population. It may also alter the traditional system of exchange and labour allocation, substituting economic "rationality" for the traditional system of exchanging labour and food within communities. A study in Upper Volta (now Burkina Faso) (Hemmings-Gapihan, 1982) shows how elderly women in particular may find themselves commanding less land and labour for production as the social unit of production changes from the extended to the nuclear family. According to Smith (1980), the development of scrub land into scientifically managed forests may eliminate an important source of free firewood, increasing the time women must spend in foraging for fuel. Similarly, the introduction of improved breeds of swine and poultry which consume commercial feed may result in competition between the food needs of the animals and the human household members. The animals may compete with children for adult time when cash flow is short or if the animals must be managed or fed by adults rather than children. These examples all underscore the importance for programme planners and project designers of understanding the entire ecosystem and rules for its use, before attempting to modify even one aspect of it.

In addition to these ecological and economic consequences, projects can also affect the cultural symbolic-cognitive nature of resources, that is, how resources undergoing change fit into the larger fabric of cultural knowledge and practices. Projects that mechanize food processing, provide fuel (which women no longer have to gather), or provide education or paid employment for women where none existed before, change the meaning of women's lives and their relationships to men, other women, and children. Projects that provide a new agricultural technology which the young master, while the old find their traditional knowledge useless in a changed environment, can radically alter the dominant-subordinate relations between old and young. So do health and nutrition education efforts that indicate to the young that traditional knowledge is obsolete.

New agricultural technologies, such as irrigation, can put the young and old at a sudden disadvantage by altering essential cultural age and sex classifications. Wells and pumps, designed to reduce labour time and provide water which was not previously available, may entirely transform the household labour structure. In one Mexican community with a tradition of pot irrigation by hand, large numbers of sons were traditionally of value to help irrigate more and more land (Messer, 1972). With the introduction of pumps, however, there was suddenly more labour than land to be irrigated. Sons were, consequently, exported to town to learn a trade or commercial activity or to the city for industrial work. The younger generation can no longer count on participating in household production prior to setting up their own households, nor on an assured income thereafter, since the labour of all but a few sons is now superfluous.

The decreased value of child labour in agriculture and food preparation due to new technologies can be viewed as beneficial in that it frees children from farm labour for schooling. For instance, the introduction of labour-saving technology for women, such as grain mills and gas stoves, greatly reduces the household need for female labour. Young girls no longer participating in home production through food preparation might therefore be encouraged to go to school. However, schooling greatly delays the returns to parents' investments in their children's food, clothing, and medicines, so they are more likely to send girls to seek income-generating paid employment as servants in cities. In the short run, it may decrease the allocation of resources to existing children.

Economic interventions may alter the social structure of a community, possibly with some adverse consequences for particular groups. For example, as extended households break up into nuclear units, adults advanced in age may no longer have the labour inputs of younger people available to them (Hemmings-Gapihan, 1983). The elderly as a group seem to have been neglected in the development economists' focus on improving the incomes of adults of productive ages, and in nutritionists' focus on women of childbearing age and pre-school children. It is this elderly group whose knowledge and skills may be devalued by new technologies, and whose control over household resources may be eroded by the breakdown of traditional social relationships.

Migration patterns may also disrupt traditional culturally determined occupational categories. When the youthful labour force is drawn away from the rural home setting to plantations, mines, or cities, personal incomes may seem more assured, but the home base may be left with inadequate labour to carry out agricultural tasks (Richards, 1939). On the positive side, migrants' contributions provide an important share of household income in many parts of the world. Their remittances are used for day-to-day consumption, investment in land and materials, and to offset the loss of the migrants' labour to household production. Aside from cash contributions, migrants also bring home with them new skills and ideas learned in another setting which may have profound consequences for the old, traditional community. For example, time and distance from a home setting may relieve the migrant of many of the cultural rules for favouring some age-groups (e.g. the elderly) or sex-groups (e.g. male) over others. The returning migrant may bring with him/her a modern, and possibly more equitable household form, though, as stressed above, these are not necessarily to everyone's equal benefit.

To predict the full impact of economic policies on intra-household resource distribution, it is crucial to understand the conditions under which migrants at different distances and relationships to the family consider themselves obligated as contributing members of the home household, even though they are no longer co-residents. This is an area in which anthropological approaches can make an important contribution.

PERCEPTIONS OF RESOURCES

Anthropological approaches are particularly suited to identifying the perceptions of individuals about the appropriate uses, rights, and obligations regarding household resources. This brings up the issue of the etic versus emic perspectives on such matters as time and resource availability and costs of participation in work or health programmes (see, for example Minge-Klevana, 1980). In advance of final project design and implementation, it is essential to have some detailed knowledge of the social organization and work schedules and values of the population. Social organization of work, division of labour by age and sex, and time use of the principals and their associates in the household must be identified so that project planners can anticipate what disruptions in scheduling of ordinary tasks or social relationships will occur as a result of their proposed intervention.

It is important to know how people behave, but also how they see themselves allocating time and resources: how much is "adequate" versus "too much" or "too little" time to spend on various tasks, including those to be introduced in a work or health project? Information on these perceptions is needed so that some reasonable assessment of what people are likely to accept in terms of time commitments to a given project can be made in advance of scheduling participation.

The planner's perspective – the etic perspective – on appropriate uses of individuals' time may be quite different from the perspective of the community. The "positive deviants" in the society, who perform tasks efficiently and manage to produce healthy, well-nourished offspring in spite of scarce resources, should be identified from both etic and emic points of view. Their behaviours and practices should be analysed, since they represent positive adaptations which have emerged *within* the cultural context of the community (cf. Zeitlin et al., 1983, for a full discussion of this concept). Both the normal group and the positive deviants might have useful suggestions on how tasks might be rearranged should new tasks be introduced. For instance, they might offer some idea of what constitutes adequate food and child-care provisions for their households and how food and child care will be provided should the principal female be otherwise engaged. These emic assessments can be compared with the operational projections on the same questions. All shed light on what resources a household has, what it perceives it has, and how such resources are structured. Such information will reveal not only how resources might be restructured to produce the least disruption or deficit in household well-being and consumption patterns, but also what types of changes people most likely will not tolerate, or, from the positive perspective, which aspects of their current life-styles they would most like to change.

Beyond the impact on time allocation, development projects may affect women's and children's work and the value of their time and labour in several other ways. Projects which provide industrially processed foods, replacing those which are traditionally home-processed, for example, may remove important sources of cash earnings from local women, while also depriving local society of variety in traditional foods. Basson (1981) describes an example from Jordan, where commercially processed sour milks have replaced traditional home-processed products, thereby removing the possibility of extra income for women, without offering any meaningful alternatives in terms of either income production or status enhancement. While economists generally do not worry about the latter problem, anthropologists recognize that women gain prestige and personal value from producing a good food product and from earning income, and lament the loss of such employment. Projects which jeopardize the status of a particular group may also encounter resistance to participation. In urban areas, traditional food processing by women is one of their main sources of part-time earnings. Where these are replaced by industrially prepared products, the question of providing alternative employment also arises (cf. Simmons, 1975). In either case, where women are the main providers of household food budgets, allocation of resources to all members of the household will be affected.

56

SOCIAL DISTRIBUTION OF RIGHTS AND RESPONSIBILITIES

A key factor determining the impact of policies on household members is the composition of the household unit. In a previous discussion of the household focus in nutritional anthropology, I suggested that:

Prior to initiating a nutrition survey or nutrition intervention, one should begin by defining the group and its members – by co-residence, kinship ties, tasks, food exchange, or some combination of relevant factors. By next investigating how such units conform to structural rules – and, as Arnould and Netting (1982) point out, it may be the "flexibility" rules that are the most significant – one can chart the different patterns in social organization and resource use within cultural groups. From these patterns, one can begin to discuss how they facilitate the interpretation of the dynamics of eating patterns, . . . socialization, and other aspects of household functioning that either favour or interfere with nutrition and health. (Messer, 1983, p. 10)

Clearly, the same considerations would apply to the distribution of all resources (not just food) at the household level.

To analyse how resource production and distribution decisions are made at the household level, I suggested that one consider:

1. Eating units – defined with respect to:
   (a) production units (or common budget units);
   (b) residential groups, further characterized according to:
       (i) all members eat together;
       (ii) some eat together, with others eating outside and foraging outside according to fixed rules;
       (iii) non-co-residents who receive food from this co-resident hearth are included;
   (c) kinship linkages;
   (d) child-care units;
   (e) child-feeding habits or rules for when, what, and how children should eat and who should feed them.
2. Food budget units – defined according to:
   (a) who is responsible for seeing how a particular kinship, co-resident, or activity group or child/set of children are fed;
   (b) from whose earnings the food budget derives;
   (c) who makes the food-related decisions at each step from food production or acquisition to distribution and consumption.
3. Child-rearing units – in relation to:
   (a) where a child eats;
   (b) what a child eats;
   (c) formation of food habits as part of enculturation, socialization, and personality formation.
4. Social networks:
   (a) those which in normal times provide flexibility and options for meeting food needs;
   (b) those to which individuals resort in times of food scarcity. Among the conceptual questions to be investigated in each case are the rules and practices for:
       (i) making demands on kinship relations;

(ii) shuffling of household membership by out-migration of certain members at times of diminishing resources or on a more continual basis in search of improved food resources;

(iii) reorganization of eating and work groups though the residential group may remain the same.

Such eating and budgetary groups are essential units of analysis through which to examine "households" as production, allocation, and consumption units, and the potential labour inputs and welfare of their membership. Although most project design or evaluation teams take the "family" or "household" as units of analysis, these may not be accurate or appropriate units to study. In nutrition studies, for example, it may be that the individual mother, toward whom most nutrition education, food, or health programmes are targeted, is *not* entirely responsible for the food a toddler eats and his/her health environment (Messer, 1981). In Africa the newly weaned child may be fed by a grandmother or other mother surrogate, while in many parts of the world toddlers forage in addition to taking what is offered.

It is also necessary to investigate eating units, child socialization units, and food budget units to determine whether improving the mother's income will make a greater impact, relative to the father's income, on the amount of food available for youngsters. It is generally assumed (cf. Kumar, 1977; Tripp, 1981) that the working mother's income yields resources which directly benefit the child's nutriture and health. This depends, however, on the cultural rules for providing food to blood relatives and others, and the social organization of child-rearing (cf. Engle, this volume). Popkin (1980) has argued that, in fact, added work for mothers means less adequate nutrition for children, but other studies contradict this finding (see Engle, this volume). The anthropological perspective may help to identify the different circumstances under which mothers' work for pay has a beneficial (or detrimental) effect on child nutrition and health.

On the production side, it is generally assumed that a "household head" can allocate the labour of the household's members. Guyer's (1981) review of "household and community" in African studies revealed the fallacy of this view and the consequent shortfalls in labour for certain development projects. Hers is perhaps the most detailed and eloquent plea against taking "the household" as the unit of analysis unless we have additional data on its permanent composition and social relations, and on its seasonal or cyclical variations.

Unfortunately, neither social anthropological descriptions of "social structure" nor the Marxist depictions of "social relations of production" have yet provided adequate models to predict what forms labour organization will take under new conditions of production in a cash-based economy. Nor are we certain to what degree the pre-existing social structure influences transitional or ultimate outcomes of development independently of political, social, and economic environments. One would like to be able to predict how the different household socio-economic units, existing between the societal and individual level, adjust as a result of changing macro-economic conditions. Economic pressures on extended family living environments are often catalysts for the emergence of nuclear family units, in contexts where, in time past, agricultural societies were organized in extended family networks.

The native's emic household constructs and his/her other cultural values, including gender ideologies, that lead to or limit options in residence, work, and resource distribution patterns are as important for predicting project outcomes as are the social scientists' etic definitions. Some circumstances may favour the consolidation of nuclear units, but new tax and economic policies may favour the atomization of these larger units. Studies of single women's extended kinship networks, particularly in urban settings, reveal a variety of arrangements other than the traditional family and household that provide a context in which individuals can find and retain employment, provide food, and be provided for by others (Lomnitz, 1978).

New work arrangements may establish new networks of resort in times of scarcity – the appropriate individuals to whom one turns in times of dearth for sustenance or work. Certain anthropologists and political scientists have postulated that, in the past, there was a rule-governed moral economy which assured people of emergency assistance, but that this breaks down under penetration of the capitalist system (cf. Scott, 1976). Whatever the truth of such a generalization, new social and economic programmes certainly affect such "emergency" networks. For instance, it might be valuable to explore the effects of co-operatives or credit unions on family and extended kinship ties, which were the traditional sources of capital, co-operation, and emergency aid in most societies. It is possible that new institutions like credit unions develop by incorporating such traditional networks for resource distribution. It is also possible that they provide an alternative and thereby destroy the older forms. These questions can best be explored using an approach which incorporates ethnographic analysis.

NUTRITIONAL AND HEALTH CONSEQUENCES

We are by now familiar with the adverse or neutral health and nutritional outcomes of well-intentioned economic development programmes, in both the short and long runs. In building a modern cash economy, development projects may destroy traditional social networks which provided for the poor; they may force the small landholder out of his bare subsistence living, without providing a living in cash (Dewey, 1980); they may support the (male) wage earner nutritionally, at the expense of the health and well-being of women and children (Gross and Underwood, 1971). More generally, the total resources generated by a project may be insufficient to cover the needs it creates.

To evaluate benefits, one must measure what additional products are forthcoming, what income they provide, who controls the income, and how it is spent, before increased income can be predicted to improve the consumption and well-being of all household members. At the community level, questions include whether a locality is more or less self-sufficient and whether resources are renewable as a result of a project. At the local level, does the project make females, for example, more or less equal with men; more or less subordinate in socio-economic relations? Are opportunities more or less open to all? Social and cultural anthropology provide tools which are particularly suited to the investigation of these qualitative questions. These questions should be answered in the process of planning an economic development project.

SUMMARY

This paper has identified the three components which must be considered in anticipating and measuring the effects of projects on intra-household resource distribution: (1) resources, including human time and skills, and the cultural material environment;

(2) cultural rules for classifying time and materials and social patterns of resource distribution; and (3) the health and welfare consequences of available resources and the cultural patterns for allocating them. Knowledge of what these quantities are, the appropriate units for measuring them, and the mechanisms comparing them from the outside observer's/scientist's point of view and from the native's cognitive point of view is a prerequisite for effectively anticipating the kinds of changes a project will bring about, and understanding why, in certain instances, people will reject efforts to "help" them. The anthropological models for analysing project consequences include:

1. Ecological variables, such as measurements of:
   (a) energy flow;
   (b) nutrient cycles from both etic and emic perspectives.
2. Economic variables to evaluate etic and emic values in the production process in terms of:
   (a) materials, technology, and skills in the production process;
   (b) product;
   (c) command over product.

Cross-cutting each of these dimensions are social values in the production, distribution, and consumption process, encompassing the social and cultural values of human relations in production, allocation, and consumption. These go beyond the economic value of what is produced and the scientific notions of what would be most efficient. Time use of men, women, and children in households, what is produced, and who receives and controls the output of the production process are all affected.

3. Social variables, examining the types of production and consumption units involved, with given structuring by age and sex, and flexibility in different contexts.
4. Cognitive-symbolic variables, including the mechanisms and classifications used in the production and consumption of goods. Concepts to be defined are:
   (a) well-being, health, appropriate economic status, and child development;
   (b) good and appropriate foods, health status, ranking of goals, goods, etc.;
   (c) social distribution units, rules of distribution by age, sex, kinship, or proximity;
   (d) perceived "problems" and notions of who should solve them (government, men, women, society?).

Anthropologists are currently improving our ability to examine the kinship and co-residential factors contributing to the formation of production, distribution, and consumption units as they relate to other functional and activity groups within a society and to identify the potential (positive or negative) effects of these patterns on nutritional, health, and socio-economic outcomes. The task remains to incorporate such perspectives on domestic organization into the social and economic models generally used by policy and programme planners. Incorporating anthropological perspectives is equally important whether the objective is to ascertain current nutritional, health, and socio-economic conditions, to identify aetiological factors in the social fabric, or to determine how such conditions contributing to inadequate social welfare might be modified. Moreover, the social historic data on forms and functions of household units can help policy planners anticipate the adjustments that might be made at the household level to particular kinds of economic development initiatives, given structure, function, and flexibility/formation rules of a particular society at a certain point in time. Current socio-economic changes taking place in both rural and urban environments indicate a pressing need to understand how men, women, and children allocate their productive time and arrange social obligations to ensure subsistence and decide on purchases beyond it.

Some of the changes entailed in social distribution of resources brought about by projects are less tangible; for instance, the "value" of being female, a mother, a member of a particular group or the possessor of a particular cultural skill. Anthropologists are sensitive to such concerns. Yet they are aware that, in most cases, people enjoying such "social value" are also amenable to changes that will bring about a less arduous style of life. As anthropologists record the contexts in which changes occur, by choice or default, they also try to understand the shifting trade-offs between exertion and social value, and to anticipate how such changes will affect the acceptance and success of development interventions.

REFERENCES

Afonja, S. 1981. Changing Modes of Production and the Sexual Division of Labor among the Yoruba. *Signs*, 7(2): 299–313.

Arnould, E.J., and R.M. Netting. 1982. Households: Changing Form and Function. *Curr. Anthropol.*, 23(5): 571–575.

Basson, P. 1981. Women and Traditional Food Technologies: Changes in Rural Jordan. *Ecol. Fd. Nutr.*, 11: 17–23.

Calloway, D. 1979. Précis: Collaborative Research Support Program on Intake and Function. Mimeo. University of California, Berkeley, Calif.

DeWalt, K.M. 1983. Income and Dietary Adequacy in an Agricultural Community. *Soc. Sci. Med.*, 17(2): 1877–1886.

——. 1984. Nutritional Strategies and Agricultural Change in a Mexican Community. University of Michigan Research Press, Ann Arbor, Mich.

Dewey, K.G. 1980. The Impact of Agricultural Development on Child Nutrition in Tabasco, Mexico. *Med. Anthropol.*, 4(1); 21–54.

Fernandez-Kelly, M.P. 1983. *For We Are Sold, I and My People. Women and Industry in Mexico's Frontier*. State University of New York Press, Albany, N.Y.

Gross, D., G. Eiten, N. Flowers, F. Leoi, M. Ritter, and D. Werner. 1979. Ecology and Acculturation among Native Peoples of Brazil. *Science*, 206(4422): 1043–1050.

Gross, D.R., and B.A. Underwood. 1971. Technological Change and Caloric Costs: Sisal Agriculture in Northeastern Brazil. *Am. Anthropologist*, 73(3): 725–740.

Guyer, J.I. 1981. The Raw, the Cooked, and the Half-baked: A Note on the Division of Labor by Sex. Working Paper 48. African Studies Center, Boston University, Boston, Mass.

Hemmings-Gapihan, G.S. 1982. International Development and the Evolution of Women's Economic Roles: A Case Study from Northern Gulma, Upper Volta. In: E.G. Bay, ed., *Women and Work in Africa*. Westview Press, Boulder, Colo.

Jones, C. 1983. The Impact of the SEMRY I Irrigated Rice Production Project on the Organization of Production and Consumption at the Intrahousehold Level. Paper presented for the United States Agency for International Development, 20 April 1983.

Kumar, S. 1979. Role of Household Economy in Determining Child Nutrition at Low Income Levels: A Case Study in Kerala. Occasional Paper 95. Department of Agricultural Economics, Cornell University, Ithaca, N.Y.

——. 1983. A Framework for Tracing Policy Effects on Intra-household Food Distribution. *Fd. Nutr. Bull.*, 5(4): 13–15.

Mellor, J., and B. Johnston. 1984. The World Food Equation: Interrelations among Development, Employment, and Food Consumption. *J. Econ. Lit.*, 22(2): 531–574.

Messer, E. 1972. Patterns of "Wild" Plant Consumption in Oaxaca, Mexico. *Ecol. Fd. Nutr.*, 1: 325–332.

——. 1976. The Ecology of Vegetarian Diet in a Modernizing Mexican Community. In: T. Fitzgerald, ed., *Nutrition and Anthropology in Action*, pp. 117–124. V. Gorcum, Assen.

———. 1981. Getting through Three Meals a Day. Diet and Domesticity in a Mexican Town. Presented at the 80th Annual Meeting of the American Anthropological Association, Cincinnati, Ohio, 1981.

———. 1983. The Household Focus in Nutritional Anthropology: An Overview. *Fd Nutr. Bull.*, 5(4): 2–12.

Minge-Klevana, W. 1978. Household Economy during the Peasant to Worker Transition. *Ethnology*, 17: 183–196.

———. 1980. Does Labor Time Decrease with Industrialization? A Survey of Time Allocation Studies. *Curr. Anthropol.*, 21(3): 279–298.

Nash, J. 1983. The Impact of the Changing International Division of Labor on Different Sectors of the Labor Force. In: J. Nash and P. Fernandez-Kelly, eds., *Women, Men and the International Division of Labor*, pp. 3–38. State University of New York Press, Albany, N.Y.

Popkin, B. 1980. Time Allocation of the Mother and Child Nutrition. *Ecol. Fd. Nutr.*, 9(1): 1–14.

Rappaport, R. 1968. *Pigs for the Ancestors*. Yale University Press, New Haven, Conn.

Richards, A.F. 1939. Land, Labour, and Diet in Northern Rhodesia: An Economic Study of the Bemba Tribe. Oxford University Press, London.

Scott, J. 1976. *The Moral Economy of the Peasant: Rebellion and Subsistence in Southeast Asia.* Yale University Press, New Haven, Conn.

Simmons, E. 1975. The Small-scale Rural Food-processing Industry in Northern Nigeria. *Fd. Res. Inst. Studies*, 14(2): 146–161.

Smith, M.G. 1980. Discussion. Conference on Development of Forest Resources. Yale University School of Forestry.

Soekirman. 1978. Indonesia. In: B. Winikoff, ed., *Nutrition and National Policy*, pp. 129–157. MIT Press, Cambridge, Mass.

Tripp, R. 1981. Farmers and Traders: Some Economic Determinants of Nutritional Status in Northern Ghana. *J. Trop. Ped.*, 27(1): 15–22.

Zeitlin, M., M. Mansour, and M. Boghani. 1984. State-of-the-art Paper on Positive Deviance in Nutrition. Mimeo. Prepared for UNICEF (WHO/UNICEF Joint Support Programme), Tufts University School of Nutrition, Medford, Mass.

5

Intra-household Allocation of Resources: Perspectives from Psychology

PATRICE L. ENGLE

Psychology and Human Development Department, California Polytechnic State University, San Luis Obispo, California, USA

SUMMARY

This paper evaluates the contributions of the field of psychology to understanding intra-household resource allocation patterns and their potential alteration. A conceptual framework is then presented which specifies three kinds of resources, and five dimensions of the social context that should be taken into account in analysing the possible changes in intra-household allocation which may result from development interventions. Finally, a longitudinal component for predicting long-term project effects is included.

Several specific implications can be drawn from the psychological constructs:
1. Because cultural patterns assign mothers the primary responsibility for infant care-giving, resources in their hands may tend to be used more directly for the welfare of children than resources in the hands of fathers.
2. Individuals with higher self-esteem or aspirations may be more responsive to interventions.
3. Those with and without power may use different strategies in decision-making, which should be surveyed systematically to determine *all* decision-making. Power relationships within a household may be difficult to change, in that those with and without power may tend to feel that their positions are justified.
4. A number of different allocation strategies may be represented in household allocation patterns. These may not be the same as those of the funding agency. For instance, children most in need may not receive scarce resources in some countries, despite our United States bias to support all children according to need.
5. Changes over a five-year period may be quite different from those immediately following project initiation. Initial responses may be quite different from those which evolve as households adapt to a new situation.
6. Characteristics of the target individual, as well as those of the family, will have a significant effect on project outcomes for the individual.

There are two compelling reasons to pursue analysis of intra-household processes, in spite of the additional effort required. These are: (1) to maximize the effectiveness of the project in the short-term and (2) to avoid the unexpected consequences of long-term changes brought about by development projects. As new resources enter a system, the family will change over time. These adaptations may well determine the success of the intervention.

INTRODUCTION

Designing development programmes to improve the life circumstances of the rural poor is far more difficult than previously believed. Increasing the disposable income of a family or providing food aid has not necessarily resulted in better-fed, healthier children (Kennedy, 1983). Agricultural development projects have not always improved children's nutritional status either (Dewey, 1981). Moreover, development projects have caused unexpected changes in household resource allocation which are at cross-purposes to the anticipated project outcome.

This paper presents contributions from psychology to a multidisciplinary conceptual framework for examining changes that might occur within a household as a result of development interventions. Since the framework focuses on the micro-level exchanges that take place within a household[1] or family, it is particularly useful for identifying household-level issues that are the key to effective planning and to the prediction of long-term consequences of development projects. This framework includes variables that are typically of interest to economists, anthropologists, psychologists, and other social scientists.

What unique role can psychologists play in understanding development policy? Although psychologists have done relatively little work specifically in the area of international development, much of their research has concentrated on issues of cultural differences in behaviour patterns. Their perspective, therefore, differs from those of anthropologists and economists presented by Messer and Rosenzweig in two previous chapters. Traditional cultural anthropologists define culture as a "totality of learned meanings maintained by a human population" (Rohner, 1984). Psychologists are more interested in how individual beliefs, attitudes, and learned meanings vary within a particular culture (Segall, 1984), and their approach is more similar to that of many present-day anthropologists.

Psychological concepts can help refine economic models of household processes as well. For example, Berry (1984) argues that decision-making analysis, which assumes that farmers make rational choices among discrete options, "offers an extremely restricted framework for analysing the complexities of intra- and inter-household processes, and their implications for macro performance" (Berry, 1984, p. 4). Moreover, these models "do not explain how options are determined and how they change over time" (Berry, 1984, p. 6). Psychologists investigate these very complexities as well as the rules for exchange and decision-making in close relationships (cf. Foa and Foa, 1980). Recent work by Kahneman, Slovic, and Tversky (1982) has demonstrated that many decisions made under conditions of uncertainty often are not rationally based. In daily functioning, people ignore statistical probabilities when deciding the likelihood of an outcome. For instance, a teenager's birth-control strategy might be "it could never happen to me."

Who within the family will benefit from a development project is a central question for project planners. A project that increases a family's income may improve the nutritional status of the father but leave that of the children unaffected. A low birth-weight baby may continue to be neglected even after more food is supplied to the household while the nutritional status of an older child improves. A maternal–child health project may be directed toward the youngest child in the family, but the benefit may be felt by the older siblings. Are these failures or successes of the development process? The target group of the project is often defined by the development agency, while cultural and familial patterns may redirect benefits toward a different group. An understanding of intra-household allocation rules will help planners target projects more effectively.

This paper first discusses psychological factors that affect intra-household relationships and thus the outcomes of development projects. It then examines allocation strategies from a psychological perspective. It concludes with the presentation of a framework for examining the longitudinal effects of an intervention on intra-household allocation processes.

CONTRIBUTIONS FROM PSYCHOLOGY

Two issues in the intra-household allocation of resources can be better understood through the application of psychological knowledge: (1) factors influencing power and decision-making within the household, including the ways in which the family role of the income-earner affects how money and other resources are used; and (2) the effects on intra-household allocation patterns of parental beliefs or rules for distributing resources.

Power and Decision-making within the Household

The significance of power and decision-making roles within the household for predicting outcomes of development programmes is based on three hypotheses:
1. Households do not pool income; rather, expenditures are determined by bargaining and by each person's role within the household.
2. Mothers, for a variety of cultural and biological reasons, are more likely to allocate money to the immediate food and health needs of children than are fathers.
3. Women who are income-earners may have more power in decision-making than women who are not income-earners. They may also have more self-confidence and be more assertive, under some working conditions.

Income Pooling

The economic model of household decision-making which suggests that all family members act as a unit to maximize their mutual good (Becker, 1981) is not a particularly accurate model for decision-making in many low-income households. Rather, Dwyer (1983) and Bruce and Dwyer (1988) summarize a number of investigations indicating that male and female household members do not pool their incomes, or pool them only incompletely (cf. Jones, 1983; Baer, 1984; Fapohunda, 1988; Roldan, 1988; Jelín, this volume) Under conditions of greater poverty, pooling is even less common. In fact, a spouse is often kept ignorant of the amount the other earns. In a recent survey of 300 mothers in a Guatemalan town, 41 per cent of the mothers reported that their husbands did not know how much they earned (Engle, in preparation, 1988). Thus, if spending patterns differ between spouses, who earns or loses the income may be crucial to predicting and evaluating the effects of household income changes on children's welfare.

Family Expenditure Patterns and the Attachment Theory

In a village in rural Guatemala, women wove mats in order to earn a very small amount of money each day, which they immediately used to puchase milk for their children (Mejia Piveral, 1972). A number of studies have suggested that mothers' income is positively related to children's mortality (Engle, 1983) and nutritional status (Kumar, 1978; Engle and Pederson, 1989).

The hypothesis that mothers are more likely than are fathers to spend income for the immediate food and health needs of their children has been suggested in recent position papers (cf. USAID, 1982; Rogers and Youssef, 1988). It is sometimes referred to as the "good mother, bad father" theory, which is an unfortunate misunderstanding of the concept. Differential spending patterns could depend on differences in attachment, in mothers' and fathers' prescribed roles in a particular society, or on differences in each parent's ability to perceive the needs of the child. Whatever the basis for these differential spending patterns (cultural, biological, or both), they will influence whether a project should be directed at income generation for women alone, for husbands and wives, or for other family members.

One hypothesis is that mothers are more likely to allocate resources to children than are fathers because they are more attached to their children. Attachments are defined as "specific, enduring relationships characterized by (and growing out of) the infants' use of proximity to adults as a means of assuring protection and care" (Lamb, 1982, p. 202). For most infants, in most cultures, these relationships are fully established by six or eight months of age, and are indicated by the infant's distress at the absence of the attachment figure. Parents also become attached to their infants with a similar bond, usually developed very soon after the birth of their baby (Konner, 1982). The parental attachment is solidified by the biological processes of nursing, the infant's smiling, eye-to-eye contact, and laughter during the second and third months of life.

Infants appear to become attached to both their mothers and fathers during their first year, even though most fathers spend far less time with their children than do mothers (Lamb, 1982). In the second year, however, most infants turn more toward their mothers when distressed. Both mothers and fathers tend to respond similarly to infants' signals (Frodi et al., 1978), but consistent differences in the kinds and frequencies of these responses have been noted, suggesting that mothers tend to respond more often than fathers. In the United States, for example, Power and Parke (1983) reported that mothers' and fathers' behaviours toward their infants were similar in duration, but that mothers showed greater responsiveness to their infants' needs. Green and Gustafson (1983) reported differences in recognition of infants' cries at one month: 80 per cent of mothers but only 45 per cent of fathers could discriminate their infant's cry from those of other infants.

Fathers may assume that mothers bear the primary responsibility for nurturing. In one cross-cultural study in Nigeria, fathers of children hospitalized for severe protein–energy malnutrition were asked to identify its causes. Over 35 per cent of the fathers felt that their children's malnutrition was primarily the mothers' responsibility (Ojofeitimi and Adelekan, 1984), although the episode was more likely to have been

66

caused by poor sanitation and poverty, responsibilities shared by the family, than by lack of maternal attention.

Are these patterns of maternal responsibility for primary care-giving biologically determined or culturally prescribed? The two are difficult to separate. Konner (1982) observes that the mother initiates and sustains the mother–infant bond in the first months of the child's life. Later, the child's responsiveness reinforces the bond. He comments that, "although it is clear that she is aided in this by cultural training and social expectations, it is also possible that the hormonal changes of pregnancy, delivery, and lactation play some role in facilitating the maternal emotions" (Konner, 1982, p. 154). Lamb suggests that in non-traditional Swedish families, "these differences [in maternal and parental behaviour] may reflect the social roles assumed by males and females in traditional families" (Lamb, 1982, p. 199).

Would fathers become as attached to their young children if they spent as much time being primary care-givers as did mothers? Although this question has not yet been tested rigorously, several studies suggest that this occurs. Field (1978) studied small groups of primary care-giving fathers in the United States, and Russell (1982) studied 50 highly involved fathers in Australia. Both found that the fathers resembled primary care-giving mothers in their tendency to smile, vocalize and grimace in imitation of their infants' expressions. Lamb and colleagues (1982a), on the other hand, found that parental styles of interaction continue to differ by gender despite care-giving experience. They followed a group of Swedish families in whom the father planned to assume a primary care-giving role for at least one month during the first nine months of the child's life. At three months postpartum, fathers' and mothers' care-giving behaviours were quite similar. The few differences which did exist were more related to parent gender than to care-giving history. After eight months, when 17 of the fathers had taken paternity leave to be primary care-givers, the same pattern of parental care-giving emerged. "Parental gender appeared to be a more important influence on style of paternal behaviour than family type [traditional or father care-giving]" (Lamb et al., 1982a, p. 134). Despite these persistent gender differences, all studies show that primary care-taking fathers differ from traditional fathers in child care-taking.

Beail (1983), in a survey of research on fathering, noted that fathers are playing a growing role in child care in Westernized cultures, which provides some confirmation for the social origin of these attachment patterns. The changing economic climate worldwide is forcing parents' roles and responsibilities to shift. Employed mothers have already taken on new roles associated with paid work, but working fathers are just beginning to participate more directly in their infants' care and feeding. This growing trend of father participation has been documented as early as the first few months postpartum in a recent study of time use of working mothers in Boston (Schlossman, 1986; Schlossman and Zeitlin, eds., forthcoming). Three-month-old babies of dual-earner couples spent more time being cared for by their fathers when their mothers worked, irrespective of feeding method. Fathers shared in infant care (i.e. changing the baby's diapers and bringing it to the mother for breast-feeding), in infant feeding, or in taking over certain feedings altogether (i.e. night-time feedings when mixed- or bottle-feeding was used).

Mackey (1983) summarized cross-cultural patterns of what he calls the "man–child" bond. After observing adult–child interactions in public places, he concluded that: (1) parenting behaviours are inherent in both men and women, but the threshold for activating and maintaining them is much lower for women than men; (2) there are large differences among cultures, such as the extent of prescribed male roles, that affect men's care-giving behaviours; and (3) men's care-giving behaviours are more sensitive to the child's age than to the child's gender.

In sum, it appears that fathers have the capacity for responsiveness and care-giving equivalent to that of mothers, but that in most cultures the mother is the primary care-giver. This pattern is beginning to change in Westernized societies. As of now, however, the mother is more responsive to the child's needs, and thus may be more likely than the father to spend money to meet those needs. This expenditure will depend on her access to resources, either through decision-making power in the household or through control over her own source of funds. Who makes decisions about expenditures within the family, then, may have a considerable impact on the use of resources for meeting the immediate welfare needs of infants and young children.

Control over Income: Self-esteem, Power, and Decision-making

The third hypothesis is that women's power and status within the household are associated with their income-earning ability. Acharya and Bennett (1981), in their study of decision-making in eight villages in Nepal, found an association between women's statements of the extent of their decision-making in various spheres of influence (e.g. farming or domestic) and their economic activity. Lee and Peterson (1983) studied the relationships of wives' access to resources (defined as the percentage of the total household subsistence base attributable to the labour of women) to their conjugal power (defined as the extent to which wives exercised independent decision-making authority in the home) in 113 patriarchal cultures. The greater the wife's role in subsistence, the stronger was her conjugal power.

These results are significant for policy, particularly if the relationships are causal. If they are causal, one would predict that, as a mother begins to earn money, she will increase her role in decision-making within the family. Given the information on attachment and perception of needs, that money would be preferentially directed toward children's welfare. Making the step from association to causality is not easy. Dwyer suggests causality in her conclusion that for women "control over income – be it earned, inherited, or otherwise transferred – is an immediate gateway to power. By extension, lack of control over income remains a primary basis for women's variable but continuing subordination as well as the heightened vulnerability of many poor households" (Dwyer, 1983, p. 2).

Research on the bases of power, specifically those in close relationships, provides some insights about the psychological characteristics of power. First, power, defined as the capacity to alter the actions of others (Kelman, 1974), can be based on factors other than control over resources (i.e. earning and holding the income, also called coercive power). It may, for instance, rest on expertise (perceived as having special knowledge) or on reference (desire to identify with a certain person, admiration of a person as a role model) (French and Raven, 1959). For example, Guatemalan Indian women were found to have expertise power in their husbands' eyes (Raven, 1974). If so, then there is a variety of ways in which women can increase their power in the household.

A second factor affecting the operation of power within a household structure is the dynamic through which one individual achieves greater power. Evidence from the social psychological literature indicates that those people with more power tend to feel

68

that they deserve that power, and feel that those with less power are perhaps less competent, less valuable, or have less information (Kipnis, 1976). This belief may even be shared by those with less power, who in fact appear to give away their power because of role expectations, greater sensitivity to another's wants, or for other reasons. Bruce and Dwyer (1988) suggest that the income-earner and other household members tend to value men's and women's contributions to a household differently. Women may earn a small income that means the difference between death and survival for her children, but it may be undervalued by both partners. Since the power system rests on a set of beliefs shared by all the family members (both those with and those without power), changing the power relationships within a household may be difficult and even disruptive. The exception is among individuals with higher self-esteem or higher expectations for themselves who appear more amenable to changes in power relationships. In the United States, the associations among self-esteem, assertiveness, and higher status are well known, but little is known about these relationships in developing countries.

The psychological literature suggests that the powerful use different strategies than do the powerless in close relationships. Falbo and Peplau (1980) define power as being held by the person whose preference wins out when there is disagreement. These researchers have identified strategies that couples use to control decisions in the United States. It seems that men, usually the more powerful partners, tended to use direct and interactive means of achieving power, such as stating their goals clearly and trying to persuade their partners. The women in these relationships, usually the partners with less power, more often used indirect means, such as behaving in a non-supportive manner (e.g. "forgetting" to prepare a meal) or acting in a solitary way (e.g. just doing things on their own). Therefore, it is essential to examine indirect as well as direct means of gaining power.

Two key questions remain to be resolved. First, in which kinds of families will changes in power relationships be disruptive? In which will they be positive? Second, what kinds of activities cause increases in power for women within the household? The first question was addressed in Engle (1986b) and will be summarized here only briefly. From studies in the United States and Latin America, increasing women's income appears to be least disruptive of power relationships when the earned income is used towards a shared family goal (e.g. to buy some land).

Several studies pinpoint which income-generation schemes increase status and power in the family and which do not. Jain (1980) reports that among Indian women's organizations, those in which women entered into new relationships with strangers (e.g. bankers or lawyers) resulted in increased respect for the women. Under certain circumstances, financially successful women's projects also result in greater respect for women (Engle, 1986b). All too often, however, as Buvinic (1984) points out, these projects are financially unsuccessful; they take on a welfare function rather than income-generation. It is her perception that those projects that are financially successful tend to get taken over by men (Buvinic, 1984). Her recommendations include focusing on "production-oriented tasks that are innovative, non-stereotypic, and/or allow women to have access to modern productive resources for the first time" (Buvinic, 1984, p. 20). Improved income generation may provide women with the independence they need to escape from a negative relationship, one in which there is alcohol or spouse abuse (Keller, 1983; Engle, 1986b).

Psychologists have been concerned about the long-term effects of the role and status changes associated with changes in income-earning roles between male and female heads of households, and between children and adults. These changes may be so difficult for the household to assimilate that individuals cease to participate in the income-earning project. It is essential to watch these changes *over time*, as introduced changes may alter decision-making and power relationships within the household quite slowly. The kinds of families that should be targeted first for change, and the factors that determine whether they can adapt or whether they are likely instead to experience stress and possible disruption or violence, need to be defined and investigated.

Distribution Rules: Rules of Social Exchange

Rules of exchange governing both the kind of resources allocated and their amount seem to exist in all cultures (Foa and Foa, 1980). When an individual allocates resources to particular family members, the basis for the allocation decisions will affect what kind of family member (e.g. adolescent, mother, or father) receives more resources. These decisions are made within an informal system of rules governing exchange between individuals in social relationships.

Social psychologists have identified a number of allocation rules, and the conditions under which each is applied (Leventhal, 1980). For example, according to equity theorists, "human beings believe that rewards and punishments should be distributed in accordance with recipients' inputs or contributions" (Leventhal, 1980, p. 27). This school of thought suggests that all exchanges are based on a notion of a just reward for contribution; we might say, "equal pay for equal work." Several studies appear to reflect a contributions rule, based on income-earning. In Guatemala, the adult worker received more food than did the children (Flores et al., 1970). Workers ate a slightly higher proportion of the family's calories than non-workers, controlling for age and sex (Engle and Nieves, 1988). In the Philippines, food distribution tended to be greater to girls who were earning an income than to those who were not (Villasenor, 1982). Rosenzweig and Schultz (1982) calculated that girls who worked for income were more likely to survive than those who did not.

Another example of the effects of the contributions rule on food distribution is the frequently observed underfeeding of girls compared to boys. Sex differences in nutritional status, and probably in food distribution within the household, may be due to the perceived utility or the potential contribution of the children:

Differential feeding and care of male and female infants is based on the relative value of males and females in a society and the perceived long range utility of sons and daughters. In some societies, sons are expected to find urban jobs and send money home. In other societies where dowry and bride price are significant, this may influence the perceived value of children. In Nepal, for example, women's families must expend substantial amounts on dowries. (Safilios-Rothschild, 1980, cited in van Esterik, 1984, p. iii)

A parallel finding from African studies is that females apparently are favored in household resource distribution in areas where a high brideprice is paid; where no brideprice is paid or a dowry given, girls did not receive as large a share of the household's food. (Rogers, 1983, pp. 19–20)

Chen and co-workers (1981) found that malnutrition is markedly higher among girls than among boys in rural Bangladesh. Dietary surveys there showed that intra-household allocation of food is biased against girls and women. A review of the literature on the health implications of sex discrimination in childhood, commissioned by UNICEF and WHO (Ravindran, 1986), provides evidence that a strong preference for sons in many parts of the world, but especially in the Middle East and South Asia, leads to discrimination against daughters in the distribution of food inside the household. Some evidence from Latin America also demonstrates sex differences in nutritional status in childhood (Freirichs et al., 1981, in rural Bolivia; Powell and McGregor, 1985, in urban Jamaica; Johnson, 1987, in the Dominican Republic).

A third group of studies also illustrates a contributions rule. Scrimshaw (1982), Schepper-Hughes (1983), and McKee (1984) have described infanticide and under-investment in some children, which they believe indicates that when a child is not expected to be a long-term contributor to the household, fewer resources are directed toward that child. Consciously or unconsciously the family provides fewer of its resources to, or simply neglects the care of, some children while allocating more resources to other children and/or adults. The characteristics associated with the child in whom the family underinvests are: high birth order, female sex, short intergestational period, and, less frequently, sickliness, or other perceived characteristics whose value or desirability are culturally mediated, such as being a twin.

Equity theory (a contributions rule) would suggest that families will not allocate more resources to a needy or malnourished child, which is the assumption underlying targeted feeding programmes and may explain why they so often do not achieve their projected goals. The type of parental feeding promoted by these programmes is closer to a second type of exchange, one based on a "needs rule" (Leventhal, 1980). For example, it would imply that a mother would give her last bit of tortilla to a sickly infant rather than to a hungry older child. In order for a supplementary feeding programme to be effective in increasing the flow of food to an undernourished child, a pregnant woman, or a lactating mother, the needs rule must be applied rather than the contributions rule. How can one influence households to apply this rule if they do not already do so?

A third distribution rule which was spontaneously mentioned by Guatemalan women (Engle and Nieves, 1988) was *equality*: that each person should receive an equal share of the available food. If mothers applied this rule, younger and smaller children would receive relatively *more* than older and larger family members, a consequence that would follow logically from the practice of giving relatively equal-sized proportions to each person.

Which rule is applied depends on many factors, including the type of resource (e.g. education, food, or attention), the resource constraints, and the characteristics or values of the resource distributor. Harbert and Scandizzo (1982), in Chile, found that more educated mothers followed more equitable distribution rules. Although a person's value system (sense of fairness) determines his or her choice of rules, this choice may be influenced by extenuating circumstances (Leventhal, 1980). When resources are severely constrained, one is willing to forgo a sense of fairness. If a family is on the brink of starvation, for instance, normal rules may be replaced by a rule such as "justified self-interest" ("I am starving and must eat").

Preliminary work in a periurban area of Guatemala, investigating the existence of explicit rules, suggests both that mothers *did* have such rules (e.g. equality, contributions), and that food was allocated accordingly. Mothers who reported that boys should receive more than girls actually gave their sons and husbands more food (Engle and Nieves, 1988). Those who said that food should be equally distributed gave children a relatively higher proportion of the food in comparison to the amount they allocated to adults. It was striking that the "needs rule," at least according to the health centre's definition of need (i.e. low weight-for-age), was not applied in the Guatemalan sample. Even though all 45 families were receiving supplementary food because a child aged one to five years was diagnosed as low weight-for-age, only 4 per cent of the mothers reported feeding the target child more for that reason. The calorie and protein intake of these children (per cent adequacy) was *identical* to those of their non-targeted siblings. Similarly, Johnson (1987) in the Dominican Republic found that women reported allocating food equally to boys and girls; yet morbidity and mortality rates were higher for girls. These examples clearly illustrate how crucial it is to understand distribution rules from the household's perspective.

These findings underscore the value of providing policy-makers with a framework within which to identify their own assumptions about distribution rules and to determine whether these are congruent with, or differ from, those of the target group. In designing programmes and projects, it is also vital to understand that not all members of a (homogeneous) cultural group follow the same allocation rules for the same type of resource.

CONCEPTUAL FRAMEWORK

Specific insights from psychology with respect to intra-household and individual factors impinging on allocative behaviour can be incorporated into a broader multidisciplinary framework based on resources and social systems within which allocation patterns for those resources are determined (fig 1). The framework can be used in determining appropriate variables to consider for programme evaluation and impact assessment.

Three kinds of resources are included (listed under "Time 1: Resources" in figure 1), corresponding roughly to economists' categories of resources: (1) land, material, and cash income; (2) time available for labour; and (3) individual skills, abilities, or human capital. These will not be discussed here; the reader is referred to Rosenzweig (this volume) and Behrman (this volume), for a detailed treatment of intra-household resource allocation within the economics framework.

How these economic resources are allocated within the household depends on the social and ecological context of the family and the social system in which it is embedded. Five social-system domains outlined by Triandis (1980) may influence the distribution of resources (listed under "Time 1: Social systems and allocation patterns" in figure 1). These include: (1) the ecological system: physical resources, environment; (2) the subsistence/production system: agriculture, fishing, industrial work; (3) the community (or socio-cultural) system: community-level institutions, norms, roles, beliefs about power, and values as they exist outside the individual; (4) the intra-household system: patterns of social behaviour and child-rearing; and (5) the individual: perception, learning, motivation, and self-esteem.

The model (fig. 1) focuses on how a *change* (such as an economic development programme) affects both the quantity of family resources and the system for distributing these resources *over time*. Time 1 defines the conditions prior to the initiation of the project, Time 2 refers to the period during which the project exists, and Time 3 is the period in which families and households adapt to the changing circumstances

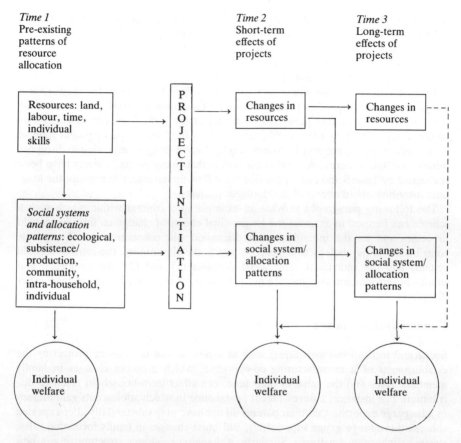

Time 1
Pre-existing
patterns of
resource
allocation

Time 2
Short-term
effects of
projects

Time 3
Long-term
effects of
projects

Fig. 1. Framework for evaluating effects of development projects on intra-household allocation of resources and family welfare.

brought about by the intervention, usually long after its officers have left the project in local hands.

The value of the framework lies in its role for predicting and monitoring the long-term effects of policy change or programmes on individual welfare. The framework's longitudinal orientation makes it equally useful at every stage: in project identification, planning, and evaluation stages.

Prior to the introduction of the project (Time 1), a status quo exists in which resources and allocation systems have resulted in a certain level of nutritional status and well-being in the family members. At Time 2, the short-term impact of the project on both quantity of resources and distribution systems can be observed. These short-term changes will have effects on the children and other family members (arrow down). Most importantly, by including Time 3, perhaps three to five years after the initial project implementation, the model emphasizes the need to monitor long-term project effects on intra-household resource allocation.

During Time 2, when the immediate outcome of the project exerts its effects, changes in resources are expected to have a direct impact on child welfare, though probably not the welfare of other family members. During Time 3, long-term changes in the social system and allocation patterns may have a greater impact on child and family welfare as the family readjusts to new levels of resources, task requirements and allocations, and belief systems.

These long-term changes are often particularly difficult to predict, but they are crucial to the ultimate success of the programme. One must be careful to separate the perspective of the project personnel from that of the individuals concerned. To its officer, the project may seem highly successful on the basis of participation rates at Time 2 (short-term), but may be foundering by Time 3 (long-term) owing to disrupted intra-household patterns. An added concern is that many project officers have been reassigned by Time 3 and cannot provide the follow-up necessary to monitor the long-term intra-household effects of development projects.

The following paragraphs provide an example of a context within which such a scheme can be used to examine the longitudinal effects of change on intra-household processes and on the individual. Our discussion will concentrate on the specific contribution of psychology to areas 3, 4, and 5, the community, the intra-household system, and the individual. The social domains (1) and (2), the ecological and subsistence/production systems, are not presented, as these are borrowed from other disciplines.

Community-level Factors

Social and institutional structures, such as a new school or training project or the establishment of a manufacturing co-operative, which promote changes in family members' roles and the value of their time, can affect intra-household resource distribution. For instance, a development programme in which adolescents gain literacy or a language expertise that their parents do not have may substantially alter expected role relationships (e.g. age superiority), and cause changes in family formation rules, stress, or inheritance patterns. Similarly, a changing economic structure (e.g. a new factory, agricultural project, or training programme) may alter income-earning possibilities and thus change the power relationships in the household as previously discussed.

Intra-household Factors

When new roles emerge for some family members, they are usually accompanied by changes in task, time, and resource allocation patterns within the household. For example, families may encounter severe time constraints and opportunity costs when faced with the time demands of a development project. Projects that do not take into account target individuals' usual activities and time-allocation patterns or constraints represent poor planning, insensitive to intra-household dynamics. Examining how changes in time and task allocation might affect mothers and children is a crucial step in policy and programme implementation. If the project requires time from the mother, or removes a person who had been providing help with household tasks, the mother will have to alter her own time allocation. In the Philippines, King and Evenson (1983) found that as women increased their market time, their leisure time was the first to drop. Not until they were working more than six hours a day did their home production time decline. Similarly, Engle (in preparation, 1988) found that Guatemalan mothers did not report doing less child care until they worked at least six hours per day; they simply added their work time to the amount of time they already spent in home maintenance and child care.

If her work time changes considerably, a mother will be forced to reduce the amount of time she spends in child care, or to replace it with someone else's time. This replacement strategy can be detrimental in the short term to older siblings (particularly to girls) if they are kept home from school to take care of their younger siblings while their mother is occupied. Income-generating schemes that do not make provisions for child care may do more harm than good to women in the long run.

Is this change harmful to the child? Many investigators assume that spending less time with the mother is negative for the child (e.g. Popkin, 1980). Data from the United States, however, do not suggest a simple relationship between time spent with the mother and child welfare (Goldberg, 1981). Furthermore, in many rural agrarian societies, older siblings rather than the mother often perform much of the child care, regardless of the mother's work status (Engle, 1986a; in preparation, 1988).

Individual Factors

The effects of sex and age on resource allocation have been discussed briefly above (pp. 68–70) (for a more in-depth treatment, see Safilios-Rothschild, this volume). Here we focus on other individual characteristics of a child that could affect resource allocation. The psychological literature indicates that parental attention to children depends to some extent on the temperament of the child (cf. Lamb, 1982). Thus, individual differences in children's alertness, healthiness, or perceived brightness can influence the level and the nature of the resources they receive.

Psychologists have only recently begun to examine "invincible children," children from high-risk backgrounds who for some reason manage to flourish in later childhood and adulthood (Werner and Smith, 1982). Rather than concentrate on the problem children, these investigators seek to identify the factors influencing those who manage to overcome severe life stresses to achieve a reasonable life. This approach is similar to the investigation of "positive deviance" (Zeitlin et al., 1984). An investigation of these unusually successful children within the household context might reveal which characteristics make children relatively invulnerable to misallocations within the household.

FUTURE DIRECTIONS

Contributions from psychology to the understanding of intra-household processes are just beginning to be felt. Psychologists are now taking an interest in third-world issues (Wagner, 1986). Some of the areas of investigation that could prove fruitful in the future are the following:
1. Developing culturally appropriate measures of self-esteem and self-confidence. There has been a long history of measurement of these constructs by Western psychologists, and they have proved to be robust predictors of such diverse outcomes as school achievement, teenage pregnancy avoidance, assertiveness, and occupational success.
2. Identifying characteristics of households that are responsive to change, and of those

in which the stresses of change might cause disruption. When a household falls into the latter category, extra care must be taken to use non-disruptive methods.

3. Clarifying the effects of changes in individual income generation on decision-making, power, and status within the household.
4. Determining the circumstances under which particular distribution rules are applied, and what factors might influence changes in these rules.
5. Elucidating the role of individual characteristics, such as temperament, resilience, or intelligence, both actual and perceived, in intra-household allocation processes.
6. Identifying the processes or sequences of change. For example, psychologists have found that changes in behaviour often *precede* changes in attitudes. This information could be applied to projects by recommending small changes in the target population's behaviours prior to a full-scale attitude-change campaign.
7. Identification of factors within a culture that are associated with higher levels of self-esteem and self-confidence.
8. Recognition of the powerful role of positive reinforcement and immediate feedback on programme effectiveness.

NOTE

1. The task of defining a household will not be treated here, as it has been well discussed by Messer (1983) and Heywood (this volume).

REFERENCES

Acharya, M., and L. Bennett. 1981. *The Rural Women of Nepal: An Aggregate Analysis and Summary of 8 Village Studies*. Vol. II, part 9. Tribhuvan University, Centre for Economic Development and Administration, Katmandu, Nepal.

Baer, R.D. 1984. The Interaction of Social and Cultural Factors Affecting Dietary Patterns in Rural and Urban Sonora, Mexico. Unpublished doctoral dissertation. Department of Anthropology, University of Arizona.

Beail, N. 1983. The Psychology of Fatherhood. *Bull. Brit. Psychol. Soc.*, 36: 312–314.

Becker, G.S. 1981. *A Treatise on the Family*. Harvard University Press, Cambridge, Mass.

Berry, S.S. 1984. Households, Decision Making, and Rural Development: Do We Need to Know More? Development Discussion Paper 167. Harvard Institute for International Development, Cambridge, Mass.

Bruce, J. and D. Dwyer. 1988. Introduction. In: D. Dwyer and J. Bruce, eds. *A Home Divided: Women and Income in the Third World*. Stanford University Press, Stanford, Calif.

Buvinic, M. 1984. Projects for Women in the Third World: Explaining Their Misbehavior. *International Report for Office of Women in Development*, pp. 1–29. USAID.

Chen, L.C., E. Huq, and S. D'Souza. 1981. Sex Bias in the Family Allocation of Food and Health Care in Rural Bangladesh. *Pop. Develop. Rev.*, 7(1): 55–70.

Dewey, K.G. 1981. Nutritional Consequences of the Transformation from Subsistence to Commercial Agriculture in Tabasco, Mexico. *Human Ecol.*, 9(2): 151–187.

Dwyer, D.H. 1983. Women and Income in the Third World: Implications for Policy. International Programs Working Paper 18. The Population Council, New York.

Engle, P.L. 1983. The Effect of Maternal Employment on Children's Welfare in Rural Guatemala. In: D.A. Wagner, ed., *Child Development and International Development; Research-policy Interfaces*. Jossey-Bass, San Francisco, Calif.

——. 1986a. Child Care Strategies of Working and Non-working Mothers in Guatemala. Forthcoming in AAAS Selected Symposium and presented at AAAS Meetings, Philadelphia, Pa., May 1986.

——. 1986b. The Intersecting Needs of Working Mothers and Their Young Children: 1980 to 1985. Report prepared for High/Scope and the Carnegie Corporation.

——. 1988. Mothers' Income and Children's Nutritional Status in a Guatemalan Town.

Engle, P.L., and I. Nieves. 1988. Intra-household Food Distribution Patterns and Mothers' Distribution Rules. Mimeo submitted for publication, 1988.

Engle, P.L., and M. Pederson. 1989. Maternal Work for Earnings and Children's Nutritional Status in Urban Guatemala. *Ecol. Fd. Nutr.*, 22: 211–223.

Falbo, T., and L.A. Paplau. 1980. Power Strategies in Intimate Relationships. *J. Personality Soc. Psychol.*, 38(4): 618–628.

Fapohunda, E.R. 1988. The Non-pooling Household: A Challenge to Theory. In: D. Dwyer and J. Bruce, eds., *A Home Divided: Women and Income in the Third World*, pp. 67–85. Stanford University Press, Stanford, Calif.

Field, T. 1978. Interaction Behaviors of Primary versus Secondary Caretaker Fathers. *Dev. Psychol.*, 14(2): 183–184.

Flores, M., M. Menchu, M. Lara, and M. Guzman. 1970. Relación entre la ingesta de calorias y nutrientes en preescolares y la disponibilidad de alimentos en la familia. *Archivos latinos de nutrición*, 20: 41–60.

Foa, E.B., and U.G. Foa. 1980. Resource Theory: Interpersonal Behavior as Exchange. In: K.J. Gergen, M.S. Greenberg, and R.H. Willis, eds., *Social Exchange: Advances in Theory and Research*, pp. 77–94. Plenum, New York.

Freirichs, R.R., J.N. Becht, and B. Foxman. 1981. Screening for Childhood Malnutrition in Rural Bolivia. *J. Trop. Ped.*, 27(6): 285–291.

French, J.R.P. Jr, and B.H. Raven. 1959. The Bases of Social Power. In: D. Cartwright, ed., *Studies in Social Power*, pp. 150–167. University of Michigan Press, Ann Arbor, Mich.

Frodi, A.M., M.E. Lamb, L.A. Leavitt, and W.L. Donovan. 1978. Fathers' and Mothers' Responses to Infant Smiles and Cries. *Inf. Behav. Develop.*, 1(1): 187–198.

Goldberg, R. 1981. Adapting Time Budget Methodology for Child Development Research. Paper presented at Society for Research in Child Development Meetings, Boston, 1981.

Green, J.A., and G.E. Gustafson. 1983. Individual Recognition of Human Infants on the Basis of Cries Alone. *Develop. Psychobiol.*, 16(6): 485–493.

Harbert, L., and P. Scandizzo. 1982. Food Distribution and Nutrition Intervention: The Case of Chile. Staff Working Paper 512. World Bank, Washington, D.C.

Jain, D. 1980. *Women's Quest for Power*. Vikas, Delhi.

Johnson, F.C. 1987. Nutritional Status in the Dominican Republic. Report prepared for USAID/ Santo Domingo Office of Health and Population under Contract 517-000-C-00-6037-00.

——. 1988. The Role of Women's Income in Determining Nutritional Status of Preschoolers in the Dominican Republic. Unpublished doctoral dissertation. Tufts University School of Nutrition, Medford, Mass.

Jones, C. 1983. The Mobilization of Women's Labor for Cash Crop Production: A Game Theoretic Approach. *Am. J. Agric. Econ.*, 65(5): 1049–1054.

Kahneman, D., P. Slovic, and A. Tversky, eds. 1982. *Judgment under Uncertainty: Heuristics and Biases*. Cambridge University Press, Cambridge.

Keller, G. 1983. The Maternal Kin Unit in Bolivian Urban Adaptation. *Internatl. J. Women's Stud.*, 6: 336–351.

Kelman, H.C. 1974. Attitudes are Alive and Well and Gainfully Employed in the Sphere of Action. *Amer. Psychologist*, 29(5): 310–335.

Kennedy, E. 1983. Determinants of Family and Preschooler Food Consumption. *Food Nutr. Bull.*, 5(4): 22–29.

King, E., and R.E. Evenson. 1983. Time Allocation and Home Production in Philippine Rural Households. In: M. Buvinic, M.A. Lycette, and W.P. McGreevey, eds., *Women and Poverty in the Third World*. Johns Hopkins University Press, Baltimore, Md.

Kipnis, D. 1976. *The Powerholder*. University of Chicago Press, Chicago.

Konner, M. 1982. Biological Aspects of the Mother–Infant Bond. In: R.N. Emde and R.J. Harmon, eds., *The Development of Attachment and Affiliative Systems*, pp. 137–159. Plenum, New York.

Kumar, S.K. 1978. Role of the Household Economy in Determining Child Nutrition at Low Income Levels: A Case Study in Kerala. Occasional Paper 95. Department of Agricultural Economics, Cornell University, Ithaca, N.Y.

Lamb, M.E. 1982. Parent–Infant Interaction, Attachment, and Socio-emotional Development in

Infancy. In: R.N. Emde and R.J. Harmon, eds., *The Development of Attachment and Affiliative Systems*, pp. 195–211. Plenum, New York.

Lamb, M.E., A.M. Frodi, C.-P. Hwang, and M. Frodi. 1982a. Varying Degrees of Paternal Involvement in Infant Care: Attitudinal and Behavioral Correlates. In: M.E. Lamb, ed., *Nontraditional Families: Parenting and Child Development*, pp. 117–138. Lawrence Erlbaum, New Jersey/London.

——. 1982b. Effect of Gender and Caretaking Role on Parent–Infant Interaction. In: R.N. Emde and R.J. Harmon, eds., *The Development of Attachment and Affiliative Systems*, pp. 109–118. Plenum, New York.

Lee, G.R., and L.R. Peterson. 1983. Conjugal Power and Spousal Resources in Patriarchal Cultures. *J. Comp. Fam. Stud.*, 14(1): 23–38.

Leventhal, G.S. 1980. What Should Be Done with Equity Theory? New Approaches to the Study of Fairness in Social Relationships. In: K.J. Gergen, M.S. Greenbers, and R.H. Willis, eds., *Social Exchange: Advances in Theory and Research*, pp. 27–53. Plenum, New York.

Mackey, W.C. 1983. A Preliminary Test for the Validation of the Adult Male–Child Bond as a Species-characteristic Trait. *Amer. Anthropol.*, 85(2): 391–402.

McKee, L. 1984. Sex Differences in Survivorship and the Customary Treatment of Infants and Children. *Med. Anthropol.*, 8: 91–108.

Mejia Piveral, V. 1972. Características económicas y socioculturales de cuatro aldeas ladinas de Guatemala. *Guatemala indigena*, 7: 5–300.

Messer, E. 1983. The Household Focus in Nutritional Anthropology: An Overview. *Food Nutr. Bull.*, 5(4): 2–12.

Ojofeitimi, E.O., and M.O. Adelekan. 1984. Partnership with Fathers in Combatting Malnutrition: Their Views as to Causes and Treatment of Protein-energy Malnutrition. *Child Care, Health Devel.*, 10: 61–66.

Popkin, B.M. 1980. Time Allocation of the Mother and Child Nutrition. *Ecol. Food Nutr.*, 9(1): 1–14.

Powell, C.A., and G.S. McGregor. 1985. The Ecology of Nutritional Status and Development in Young Children in Kingston, Jamacia. *Amer. J. Clin. Nutr.*, 41: 1322–1331.

Power, T.G., and R.D. Parke. 1983. Patterns of Mother and Father Play with Their 8-month-old Infants: A Multiple Analyses Approach. *Inf. Behav. Devel.*, 6(4): 453–455.

Raven, B.H. 1974. The Comparative Analysis of Power and Power Preference. In: J. Tedeschi, ed., *Perspectives on Social Power*. Aldine, Chicago.

Ravindran, S. 1986. Health Implications of Sex Discrimination in Childhood: A Review Paper and Annotated Bibliography. World Health Organization/UNICEF/FHE, Geneva.

Rogers, B.L. 1983. Intrahousehold Dynamics: A Critical Factor in Development Policy. Paper prepared for USAID/PPC/Office of Policy Development and Program Review.

Rogers, B.L., and N. Youssef. 1988. The Importance of Women's Involvement in Economic Activities in the Improvement of Child Nutrition and Health. *Fd. Nutr. Bull.*, 10(3): 33–44.

Rohner, R.P. 1984. Toward a Conception of Culture for Cross-Cultural Psychology. *J. Cross-Cult. Psychol.*, 15(2): 111–138.

Roldán, M. 1988. Renegotiating the Marital Contract: Intrahousehold Patterns of Money Allocation and Women's Subordination among Domestic Outworkers in Mexico City. In: D. Dwyer and J. Bruce, eds., *A Home Divided: Women and Income in the Third World*, pp. 119–147. Stanford University Press, Stanford, Calif.

Rosenzweig, M.R., and T.P. Schultz. 1982. Market Opportunities, Genetic Endowments and Intrafamily Resource Distribution: Child Survival in Rural India. *Amer. Econ. Rev.*, 72(4): 803–815.

Russell, G. 1982. Shared Care-giving Families: An Australian Study. In: M.E. Lamb, ed., *Nontraditional Families: Parenting and Child Development*, pp. 139–172. Lawrence Erlbaum, New Jersey/London.

Safilios-Rothschild, C. 1980. The Role of the Family in Development. *Finance Devel.*, 12: 44–47.

Schepper-Hughes, N. 1983. Women, Work, and Infant Mortality: A Case Study from Northeast Brazil. In: N.M. El-Sanatary, ed., *Women and Work in the Third World*. Center for the Study, Education, and Advancement of Women, Berkeley, Calif.

Schlossman, N.P. 1986. Work Resumption, Breast-feeding, and Time Allocation of Mothers in Boston, Massachusetts: The First Half-year Postpartum. Unpublished doctoral dissertation. Tufts University School of Nutrition, Medford, Mass.

Schlossman, N.P., and M.F. Zeitlin, eds. 1989. *Working Mothers and Newborn Babies*. Sage Publications, Beverly Hills, Calif.

Scrimshaw, S.C.M. 1982. Infanticide as Deliberate Fertility Regulation. In: R. Lee and R. Bulatao, eds., *Fertility Determinants in Developing Countries*. National Academy of Sciences Press, Washington, D.C.

Segall, M.H. 1984. More than We Need to Know about Culture, but are Afraid Not to Ask. *J. Cross-Cult. Psychol.*, 15(2): 153–162.

Triandis, H.C. 1980. Introduction. In: J.C. Triandis and W.W. Lambert, eds., *Handbook of Cross-cultural Psychology*. Vol. 1, pp. 1–14. Allyn & Bacon, Boston, Mass.

United States Agency for International Development. 1982. Nutrition. USAID Policy Paper, Bureau for Program and Policy Coordination.

Van Esterik, P. 1984. Intra-family Food Distribution: Its Relevance for Maternal and Child Nutrition. Working Paper 31. Division of Agricultural Sciences Nutrition Surveillance Program. Cornell University, Ithaca, N.Y.

Villasenor, F.R. 1982. A Nash-Mirrlees Model of Intra-family Allocation. In: Economies of Scale in the Household Production Model and Intra-family Allocation of Resources. Unpublished doctoral dissertation. Yale University, New Haven, Conn.

Wagner, D. 1986. Child Development Research and the Third World: A Future of Mutual Interest? *Amer. Psychol.*, 41(3): 298–301.

Werner, E.E., and R.S. Smith. 1982. *Vulnerable but Invincible: A Longitudinal Study of Resilient Children and Youth*. McGraw Hill, New York.

Zeitlin, M., M. Mansour, and M. Boghani. 1984. State-of-the-art Paper on Positive Deviance in Nutrition. Mimeo. Prepared for UNICEF (WHO/UNICEF Joint Nutrition Support Programme), Tufts University School of Nutrition, Medford, Mass.

II.   Methodological Approaches to Measurement

II. Methodological Approaches to Measurement

Methodological Approaches to Measurement

BEATRICE LORGE ROGERS AND NINA P. SCHLOSSMAN

Part I discussed a set of conceptual frameworks for identifying important factors in intra-household resource distribution. Economics, anthropology, and psychology focus on different aspects of the allocation process, tend to identify different sets of variables as central to the process, and so tend to use different approaches to the measurement of these variables. In this section, three papers address methodological issues related to specific techniques used by different social-science disciplines to obtain the most complete understanding of intra-household allocation patterns and their determinants.

Scrimshaw's paper proposes an integration of qualitative methods such as those used in traditional ethnographic studies with more quantitative data-collection methods characteristic of survey research in economics. Each approach, the qualitative and the quantitative, has both advantages and disadvantages; combining the two strengthens both. In fact, the sequence from qualitative description to structured direct observation to survey research is now the method of data collection commonly followed by anthropologists who recognize the importance of statistical reliability and by economists who recognize that they cannot construct adequate models of behaviour without identifying and incorporating culturally specific variables.

Scrimshaw outlines a sequence which might be followed to obtain information for the assessment of programme impacts on the household and its allocative processes. Data collection starts with exploratory ethnographic work, followed by structured observations and guided but open-ended interviews, which lead to the design of structured surveys of statistically representative samples of the population.

Bennett, in her paper, describes an application of these combined methods to one particular problem: the effects of women's work on child welfare. She elaborates the research which would be required to address the various aspects of this question. In so doing, she demonstrates the effective combination of ethnographic investigation, direct, structured observation of behaviour, and quantitative, statistically representative data collection.

To these methods should be added a review of existing literature, which should precede the initiation of any primary data collection, and discussions with professionals – both scholars and development specialists – to obtain information and insights about the location, culture, and environment in advance of field-work. Both published and unpublished literature in the fields of anthropology, sociology, economics, and the specific subject area of the programme or project being assessed (e.g. health, food, nutrition, or agriculture) should be reviewed for pertinent information.

Secondary data is an important and often overlooked source of information for designing and evaluating programmes. Longitudinal, in-depth studies conducted by local research institutes, or by doctoral students from universities in the country or abroad, can be a rich source of information on the local culture and on household processes. Such studies cannot be accepted uncritically, of course, but they can certainly be used to develop questions and hypotheses for later empirical validation.

Jelín's paper in this section describes a study carried on in a small number of households over an extended period of years, using a time-intensive, personal method of gathering information. Her method of data collection is clearly unsuited to the constraints of a donor agency with a limited time horizon. None the less, the insights obtained from the study are of value in understanding how households use resources. Jelín demonstrates that the apparent irrationality of certain household consumption decisions has a logic of its own, based first of all on the expectation of continued high inflation (which makes debt a rational strategy), and secondly on the value of prestige, obtained from specific kinds of publicly observable consumption. She also reveals the importance of the regularity, timing, and reliability of income (at least from the household's perspective) in how the income is used. Once recognized, these factors could be built into more quantitative models of income and its uses. Moreover, the fact that small, regular increments of income are more likely to be used for such expenditures as food should have significant implications for the design of effective income or employment schemes.

Another means of obtaining information is to exploit existing large-scale surveys, such as population censuses, household income and expenditure surveys, health and other special purpose surveys, for what they can reveal about the household. Extracting information about households and their internal dynamics through the analysis of existing large surveys poses its own set of problems. In many countries, large data bases may contain useful data on households. The analysis of Indian census data by Rosenzweig and Schultz (1982) represents one imaginative approach. They compared survival rates of different cohorts of girls and boys, using the known expected ratio of girls to boys at different ages as a baseline, to draw conclusions about differential investment in male and female children.

To be applicable to the analysis of household processes, large data sets must contain disaggregated age/sex characteristics for each household. As Rosenzweig and Behrman indicate in their papers in this volume, individual employment data on each household member can serve as an accurate indicator of the alternative uses of each member's time, and of the total time constraints on the household. Individual education level can reveal both the investment in different categories of individuals and the economic value of their time. Surveys of income will be significantly more useful for household-level analysis if they contain information on individual sources of income (earnings, transfers, wealth income), and even more applicable if earned and wealth income can be associated with the appropriate individual in the household. Special-purpose surveys, covering, for example, health, nutrition, or food consumption, often include valuable information on individual welfare outcomes, which then may be

84

associated with individual characteristics and with household composition and income data.

Of course, interpreting the analysis of such large-scale surveys requires an understanding of the cultural context in which the data were collected. The culturally specific meanings of the variables must be identified before the analysis can be performed. Knowledge of the local culture is essential also for assessing the probable reliability and validity of the data. For example, numerous studies have found that women's market work is underreported in censuses and agricultural surveys because of cultural norms which hold that women are primarily housewives. Not just men, but the women themselves, may report that they (the women) are unemployed, even though they are actively engaged for significant amounts of time in market-oriented production. Another example is the definition of household headship. In many cultures, women are unlikely to be identified as heads of household, even if there is no adult male present. Husbands who are absent long-term, or even pre-school-aged sons, may be reported as household heads in such cases.

It should be noted that computer analysis of such large survey data sets is not cheap, easy, or quick. Typically a great deal of data cleaning is required, and additional modifications may be necessary before the data can be read by a large, main-frame computer. Access to the data itself may be difficult to obtain, especially if it is controlled by a government department or a local research institute. If the problems can be resolved, such secondary analysis is an invaluable tool. Just as data from large-scale surveys must be used with caution and with cultural sensitivity, so must designers of large-scale surveys provide more careful training to their enumerators on culturally appropriate questions of definition, and on how to probe for accurate and meaningful responses.

In the Appendix (table A), we have suggested a sequence of activities to be followed in planning and evaluating the effects of development programmes on the household and its individual members. This series of steps starts with a careful specification of the activities anticipated by the project, and their expected relationships with the desired project outcomes. The likelihood of these relationships occurring can then be assessed using information from existing published and unpublished studies, expert opinions of scholars and development specialists, and field studies employing a combination of qualitative and quantitative methods.

These steps are an integral part of project planning. Moreover, the combination of methods discussed in these papers should be used not only in advance of project implementation, but also in the monitoring and long-term evaluation phases of development programmes. In reality, projects take place in a changing environment, and households may adapt differently to changes in the short and the long run. No substitute therefore exists for ongoing monitoring of intra-household processes as they change over the life of a project and beyond.

6
Combining Quantitative and Qualitative Methods in the Study of Intra-household Resource Allocation

SUSAN C.M. SCRIMSHAW

School of Public Health, University of California, Los Angeles, California, USA

INTRODUCTION

Two fundamental methodological questions plague attempts to measure intra-household resource allocation. The first is how to measure accurately the *actual* behaviours, motivations, feelings, and outcomes related to intra-household resource allocation. The second is how to ensure an accurate understanding of the *meaning* of the behaviours and concepts to be measured. Both of these relate to validity, the accuracy of measurements. Only when validity has been established to a reasonable degree does it make sense to add a concern with reliability (representativeness) and replicability.

Quantitative methods used in isolation tend to jump ahead to a focus on reliability and replicability, but if validity is compromised these efforts are wasted on data which do not reflect reality. Qualitative methods can capture actual behaviour with great accuracy, and can produce detailed information and insights applicable to both the development of testable hypotheses and the interpretation of quantitative data. This is particularly important in cross-cultural research. For example, as Rogers, Messer, and Heywood discuss in other chapters in this volume, "household" and "family" are not synonymous. Family members important to intra-household resource allocation (such as grandmothers) may reside outside the household. Conversely, household members may not all be family members: they may be hired help, friends, or even anthropologists.

The importance of relationships and thus the power of individuals regarding food allocation will vary from culture to culture. To complicate matters further, cultural ideals (e.g. the male head of household makes all decisions regarding how money is spent) may be circumvented in actual behaviour (e.g. the female head is observed making purchases without his authorization). We cannot even make assumptions about the meaning and value of resources. Milk, for instance, is considered children's food in many cultures (and with reason in locations where lactose intolerance is prevalent), so it is not a resource which would interest adults.

This paper will first elaborate on the need to combine quantitative and qualitative research methods. It will then discuss the cross-cultural meaning of concepts such as family, allocation, and resources, and consider why these definitions matter in project design. It will conclude with specific suggestions for measuring the intra-household allocation of resources in different cultures.

WHY COMBINE QUANTITATIVE AND QUALITATIVE RESEARCH METHODS?

In general, quantitative research is assumed to mean large-scale survey methods, including mail surveys, self-administered questionnaires, and telephone or face-to-face interviews (Babbie, 1982; Bailey, 1982; Sanders and Pinhey, 1983), while qualitative research is seen as traditional ethnographic field-work conducted by anthropologists and some sociologists and psychologists. Conventional images of qualitative research methods conjure up an anthropologist sitting in a village taking notes on everything including conversations, observed behaviour, life-histories, and material cultural objects (see table 1). In reality, most present-day ethnographers employ various combinations of participant-observation, observation-only, in-depth unstructured or semi-structured interviews, and structured interviews and surveys (Pelto and Pelto, 1978; Spradley, 1979). Moreover, some observational techniques ethnographers use involve the quantification of many minute observations.

This is illustrated by the work of Johnson and others on time allocation (Johnson, 1975 and this volume), Harris and Dehavenon (Dehavenon, 1978) on video tapes of family hierarchies and food-handling behaviour in East Harlem, New York, and recent research on labour and delivery in women of Mexican origin in Los Angeles (Moore and Scrimshaw, 1983). Thus, the boundaries between quantitative and qualitative work can be nebulous, as ethnographers employ questionnaires and interview schedules or quantify detailed information collected through systematic observation (see table 1).

Researchers trained in disciplines which place a heavy emphasis on quantitative methods (i.e. economics, demography, sociology, and epidemiology) frequently do not understand the methods of qualitative researchers (i.e. anthropologists, some sociologists, and some psychologists) and consequently may view their work as unscientific, unreliable, or biased. Researchers who underrate qualitative methods do not realize that these often include random sampling, standardized questionnaires, and repeated observations which are then quantified. Furthermore, when samples are *not* random and formal interview schedules are *not* used, this is because the kinds of information (such as the meaning of an activity) needed at that point in the research are not readily or accurately available through quantitative means. Qualitative data are not, as some view it, a poor substitute for the "right way to do research." They provide instead an essential method in the array available to students of human behaviour.

The debate on the scientific value of qualitative versus quantitative research is well summarized by Pelto and Pelto (1978). They define science as "the accumulation of systematic and reliable knowledge about an aspect of the universe, carried out by empirical observation and interpreted in terms of the interrelating of concepts referable to empirical observations" (Pelto and Pelto, 1978, p. 22). According to this definition, the fields of anthropology, sociology, social psychology, and economics, which must come to terms with human behaviour, can join experimental fields such as phy-

Table 1. Basic ethnographic methods

1. Formal interview	Written questions on specific topics are asked of individual (respondent) and recorded in detail
2. Informal interview	Open-ended questions are asked on certain topics. The researcher follows a general outline, but additional subjects are incorporated as appropriate. Brief notes are taken on the responses, and the detailed notes are written up later that day or the next
3. Conversations	Important data can also be obtained through very informal conversations with individuals or small groups. Some people are more at ease in these settings and talk freely
4. Observations	Careful observation of events provides valuable non-verbal clues as to what is actually occurring
5. Participant observation	The researcher participates in and observes the socio-cultural context of a household or community and thus gains important insights into everyday life

Source: Adapted from Scrimshaw and Hurtado, 1987, p. 5.

sics in the category of "sciences." The Peltos add that "if the 'personal factor' in anthropology makes it automatically unscientific, then much of medical science, psychology, geography, and significant parts of all disciplines (including chemistry and physics) are unscientific" (Pelto and Pelto, 1978, p. 23).

In fact, scientific research is not truly objective, but is governed by the cultural framework and theoretical orientation of the researcher. This idea will be discussed later in the section on the cultural variations in the meaning of concepts to be measured. As Johnson comments: "It is a vexing ethnocentrism to assume that science is or even can be completely culture-free" (Johnson, 1978, p. 2). The issue then, is to be aware of one's research orientation and potential biases and to collect data as accurately and as objectively as possible.[1] There is hardly a consensus on how to do this, but, increasingly, researchers are arguing that a combination of qualitative and quantitative data-collection techniques is essential (Steward, 1950; Pelto and Pelto, 1978; Johnson, 1978; Van Maanen et al., 1982).

The differences between standard surveys (interview schedules or questionnaires) and the frequently more qualitative anthropological approaches (table 1) and their advantages and disadvantages are summarized in table 2.

The methodological concepts of validity and reliability provide a common foundation for the integration of quantitative and qualitative techniques. *Validity* refers to the accuracy of scientific measurement, "the degree to which scientific observations measure what they purport to measure" (Pelto and Pelto, 1978, p. 33). For example, in my work in Spanish Harlem, New York City (Scrimshaw and Pasquariella, 1970), the phrase "¿sabe como evitar los hijos?" (do you know how to avoid [having] children?) elicited responses on contraceptive methods and was used as the first in a series of questions on family planning. By not using family-planning terminology at the outset, we were able to avoid biasing respondents. The same question in Ecuador, however, produced reactions like "I would never take out (abort) a child!" If the New York questionnaire had been applied in Ecuador without testing it through semi-structured ethnographic interviews, the same words would have produced answers to what was in fact a different question. In another example, Zborowski's classic work on pain perception in different cultures showed that while Jews and Italians (in New York)

Table 2. Plusses and minuses of qualitative and quantitative methods

Qualitative	Quantitative
− Random sampling not possible	+ Random sampling possible
− Little statistical testing of data	+ Statistical analysis
+ Cross-checking (triangulation) used	− Little cross-checking
+ Possible to identify real *v.* ideal behaviour	− Survey questionnaires tend to get reporting of ideal behaviour
+ Sensitive topics can be explored in context: more time, rapport, etc.	− Difficulty in dealing with sensitive topics
+ Attitudes revealed	+ Attitudes may be revealed with careful research design
+ Observation possible	− Little time or rapport for much observation
− Problems in generalizing data to large proportion of the culture due to small samples	+ Large populations can be surveyed
− Takes time	+ Relatively rapid
− Problem of data-collector bias	+ Fewer problems with data-collector bias as more structure, but problem of structural bias
− Replicability difficult	+ More easily replicable
+ Patterning and interrelationships observable	− Must be specifically looked for: difficult if don't know they are there. Must have induction of interrelationships before questionnaire can be devised to survey them
+ Open-ended – i.e. any factors affecting a problem can be observed	− Closed: information usually limited to preselected question, may miss important items

Source: Adapted from Scrimshaw, 1985.

both tended to verbalize feelings of pain to a greater degree than the other culture studied, the underlying *meaning* of pain was different. To the Italians, it was a discomfort which was quickly dismissed when analgesia solved the problem. Jews tended to reject analgesics because of concerns over side-effects and viewed pain as symptomatic of more serious health problems (Zborowski, 1952).

Reliability refers to replicability: the extent to which scientific observations can be repeated and obtain the same results. This means that a study of household-level food-procurement behaviours in a community would yield the identical results with repeated trials. In practice, such replications are complicated by non-controllable factors such as seasonal change and alterations in the economic climate. Even if the first study identified factors leading to particular behaviours, it would be difficult to interpret variations in results from a replication since more than one confounding variable (or circumstance) could come into play. While all research ideally employs meticulous data collection to ensure maximum reliability and validity, in practice investigators must settle for less than perfection. Careful research procedures, including thorough training and monitoring of interviewers, are essential components that should be used in project planning and implementation to minimize error. In general, qualitative methods are acknowledged to be more accurate in terms of validity, while quantitative methods are considered to be better in terms of reliability or replicability.

Surveys are effective tools for collecting data from a large sample, particularly when the distribution of a variable in a population is needed (e.g. the percentage of women who obtain pre-natal care) or when rarely occurring events (e.g. neo-natal deaths) must be assessed. Surveys are also used to record people's answers to questions about their behaviour, their motivations, their perception of an event, and similar topics. While surveys are carefully designed to collect data in the most objective manner possible, they often suffer inaccuracies based on respondents' perceptions of their own behaviour, or their desire to please the interviewer with their answers.

Surveys have difficulty revealing motives (i.e. *why* individuals behave as they do), nor are they likely to uncover behaviours which may be consciously or unconsciously concealed. For example, programmatic attempts to follow up on the consumption of supplementary foods distributed to pregnant and lactating women and young children yield an inaccurate picture if the women alone are interviewed. They may give answers they know the interviewer wants to hear, rather than the facts (i.e. that the male head of household consumes the foods). Alternatively, individuals surveyed may be un-aware of their actual behaviour and thus report it inaccurately. In Barbados, com-parisons of responses to interviews with 48-hour observations of actual behaviour revealed that women nursed their babies twice as often as they thought they did (Scrimshaw, 1969).

A less frequently recognized limitation to survey research is that results can be very different depending on who is interviewed. In Los Angeles, nurses thought Latina women came into the hospital "too early" or in "false" labour in greater proportions than other patients. Observations followed by postpartum interviews with women delivering at that hospital over a two-month period revealed, however, that Anglo women experiencing their first pregnancy were in fact the most likely to come in early. The nurses selectively remembered the Latina women because they were more "dif-ficult patients" owing to language barriers and anxiety about pain and risk of death during childbirth (Scrimshaw and Souza, 1982). In this instance, participant observa-tion helped to establish the most likely source of inaccurate information. More accu-rate data was available from the patients than from the nurses, although interviews and participant observation with both revealed the problem as seen from both sides, staff and patient.

In addition to the aforementioned difficulties in collecting accurate data, surveys may focus so narrowly on specific variables that they may fail to elicit important behaviours underlying a situation. Because anthropologists take a holistic approach which allows them to remain open to new information and to add categories to the data-collection guidelines, they can more readily identify these unanticipated links. For example, Caldwell and Caldwell (1977) point out that demographers examining African birth histories were aware of the limitations of their quantitative approach. They found they were unable to tell whether long birth intervals represented a real social constraint on fertility, defective sampling, or inaccurate reporting. Anthropo-logists, studying the same situation with the methods described in table 1, established that these intervals were in fact due to institutionalized postpartum abstinence, a cultural pattern with important consequences for total fertility rates (Page and Lest-haeghe, 1981).

In another classic instance, physicians and epidemiologists puzzled over the mode of transmission of the uniformly fatal degenerative nervous system disease, kuru, among the Fore people in the New Guinea Highlands. Kuru affected adult women and children and adolescents of both sexes proportionately more than adult men. By the early 1960s, the most accepted of the prevailing hypotheses was that it was genetically transmitted. Yet this did not explain the sex differences in infection rates in adults but not in children, nor how such a lethal gene could persist. Working with Gadjusek of the National Institutes of Health (NIH), cultural anthropologists Glasse and Lindenbaum used in-depth ethnographic interviews to establish that kuru was relatively new to the Fore, as was the practice of cannibalism. Women and children were more likely to engage in the ritual consumption of dead relatives, which was culturally less acceptable for men. Lindenbaum and Glasse suggested the disease was transmitted by cannibalism. In order to confirm their hypothesis, Gadjusek's team inoculated chimpanzees with brain material from women who had died of kuru and the animals developed the disease. Since then, the practice of cannibalism has declined and the disease has now virtually disappeared (Lindenbaum, 1971; Gadjusek et al., 1967).

Research on childbirth among Mexican women in Los Angeles illustrates how a combined quantitative and qualitative approach can work more effectively than either alone. The study was aimed at understanding the relationships between cultural and behavioural factors and the biomedical aspects of labour and delivery. The methods included observation, participant observation and ethnographic interviews, which yielded information and strategies used in the design of pre- and postpartum questionnaires. These were applied to a sample of 518 women delivering in two Los Angeles hospitals. A subsample (not random, but opportunistic) of 45 women was observed throughout their labour and delivery using pre-coded forms for obtaining five-minute time samples of behaviour. Cultural/behavioural factors such as acculturation, social support, anxiety, knowledge of birth, and use of pre-natal services showed logical and predictable relationships when survey data on the entire sample (518 women) were analysed. The medical variables also interrelated in expected ways: the use of pain medications predicted lower baby Apgar scores, labour complications predicted baby complications, and so on. However, the survey data provided few connections between the cultural/behavioural and the biomedical variables, even though we knew some links had to be there. For instance, Mexican women who had arrived most recently in Los Angeles had a higher probability of significantly longer labours, yet there was no evidence for any physiological differences by recency of migration. Three-quarters of the women had arrived in the United States within seven years of the study.

Our behavioural observations of labour and delivery of 45 women helped resolve this problem. In this subsample, the data showed cultural/behavioural influences on factors such as the use of pain medication in labour. We identified relationships between non-verbal behaviour, noise levels, nurse behaviour, and the use of pain medications. Noisier women initially obtained more nurse attention (measured by the amount of time nurses spent in the labour room and by verbal and non-verbal interactions with the patient), and were more likely to be given medication for pain relief. Once the women were medicated, high noise levels no longer were associated with more attention from the nurses (Moore and Scrimshaw, 1983). None of this observed behaviour emerged in the postpartum interview. Women seemed to gloss over the details of their labours. The interview method did not permit time to explore this in depth, nor could already long interviews be extended. A combination of survey and observation techniques greatly enhanced the value of the study results.

It is clear that there are advantages and disadvantages to either methodology alone (Scrimshaw, 1985), and great potential value in combining the two approaches. Johnson suggests that research must balance "the appeal of straightforward techniques to testing hypotheses by using statistics and quantitative analysis against the necessarily complex business of developing cross-culturally valid methods and concepts for the study of human behaviour" (Johnson, 1978, p. vii). The process of developing cross-culturally valid methods and concepts is necessarily dependent on understanding the meaning of the concepts to be measured within each cultural context. Projects which never seek or fail to achieve this understanding run the risk of generating data which reflect superficial findings rather than deeper realities.

THE MEANING OF CULTURAL THINGS

The title of this section is a play on Harris's book title *The Nature of Cultural Things* (1964). In this book, Harris makes the distinction between what he terms the emic (insider) and the etic (outsider) perspectives. He initially intended the terms to apply to data-collection methodologies, where etic referred to observed behaviour and emic referred to subjective statements about the meanings of culture on the part of the informants. The terms retain their original meaning, but can also be applied to research orientations (for example, see Zeitlin, this volume). An etic (outsider) interpretation of behaviours or attitudes is done without reference to the emic (insider) meaning of the observed phenomenon. A great deal of research in developing countries, particularly that using solely quantitative methods, is conducted from the outsider perspective. For example, Rosenzweig in this volume refers to the assumption that all household members *benefit equally* from the production of household "goods" such as cleanliness, sanitation, and meals.

He further suggests that the economic values of each member may in fact condition his or her access to these goods. Economic value is measured as an outsider's etic concept. Household members themselves may have divergent expectations for their differential access to food, such as a belief that some foods are not appropriate for particular age- or sex-groups, or that boys "need" more food than girls. As Engle's contribution to this volume documents, food is *not* equally distributed in all households. A programme which assumes that food supplementation aimed at improving children's nutritional status will benefit all children equally will not, in fact, have those benefits in the situation where boys by right are allocated more food than girls. A different strategy, such as a "snack bar" where children (girls and boys) could go to consume food on the spot might be more successful. Clearly, the challenge is to deal with the *real* process of allocation (the etic) and with the reasons behind it (the emic).

The problem of defining household and family clearly illustrates the need to get at meanings. In a review of the literature on household versus family, Messer (1983) states that while household may refer to the traditional co-residence and food- and fire-sharing, family may reflect kinship ties which extend beyond household. An approach to the related problem of multiple group memberships of individual household members is discussed in Heywood in this volume. To complicate matters, these boundaries and their importance will vary from culture to culture, and they have extremely important implications for resource allocation. For instance, a young couple may be dependent on relatives who do not live with them for as much as 50 per cent of their monthly financial resources.

March (unpublished information) has suggested the terms "soft-bounded" and "hard-bounded" households as an aid to conceptualizing this problem of defining household versus family. He suggests that household boundaries be viewed as a semi-permeable membrance, more permeable in some cultures than in others. This would permit some generalizations about cultures or groups of households, and help avoid the temptation to deal with households only as single, self-contained units. Cultural rules and generalities about what can be exchanged between households could be identified. For example, in United States suburban culture, money is seldom ex-changed between neighbouring (non-kin) households, but food and services (a cup of sugar or babysitting) are frequently exchanged. In the same culture, relatives in a distant city could not provide food or services, but might provide money as needed. All these "items" (food, services, money) could contribute to the nutritional and eco-nomic well-being of the household. Data analysis involving pattern recognition would be particularly effective for quantitative data sets. Patterns of exchange and degrees of household "permeability" could be identified through the analysis of clusters of be-haviours.

A classic example of widely divergent cultural patterns related to food allocation was provided in the actual experience of two young American women and the two Indonesian men they hired to take them by boat on a brief trip to another Indonesian island. The four ended up adrift with very limited supplies of food and water. The men ate food and drank water liberally, even spilling it. Concerned, the women divided the resources (which they had brought) and gave the men half. The Indonesians quickly consumed their rations and conflict erupted when the Americans would not share the remains of their half. The American women could not know that in the men's village culture many foods were freely available and were consumed at will. Potential later shortages rarely were a concern and were never planned for. Hoarding was considered anti-social. Tomorrow would somehow take care of itself. The actions of the Amer-icans and the Indonesians marooned at sea were totally incomprehensible to each other. Fortunately, the four were rescued in time, although the Americans left the Indonesians stranded hundreds of miles from home because they had "behaved irres-ponsibly" (Ciotti, 1986).

Defining a resource also requires a full understanding of meanings. So far, research has tended to focus on resources such as income, which are easy to measure. Time-allocation studies have made an important contribution in revealing less obvious re-sources, such as the extent to which children tending herds free their fathers to work for wages (Nag et al., 1978). Thus children's time becomes an important resource which contributes to the production of income for the household.

An essential aspect of meaning, one particularly well-suited to identification and definition through anthropological techniques, is the distinction between variables and how these variables cluster to form patterns of behaviour. Thus, the fact that some of the children in a household may be from the mother's previous sexual alliance may be an important factor influencing the resources allocated to those children compared to their half-siblings, but this pattern will not be picked up unless it is noted or suspected by the researcher. Individuals are not always conscious of their own patterns of be-haviour (so that their assessment becomes a matter of outsider perspective), yet resource allocation is the product of complex interactions among individuals based on sex, status within the household, health, personality, age, family composition, and so forth. Sometimes these patterns cannot be identified through the analysis of survey data or econometric modelling, because the necessary variables were not included in the data collection or because the researcher did not know what pattern to look for. One of anthropology's strengths is the generation of holistic descriptions (Johnson, 1978; Dehavenon, 1984), which can then be used for generating hypotheses. These in turn can be tested with additional qualitative and quantitative methods. These descriptions can uncover the appropriate factors to be included in a correct, culturally sensitive econometric model, or can be used to design an effective, appropriate intervention. The measurement of outcomes of resource allocation illustrates the complexity of human behaviour. Many outcomes cannot be directly attributed to one resource. For example, nutritional status reflects not only food intake, but freedom from debilitating infections. Susceptibility to infections could be influenced by maternal (or other family member) attention (e.g. keeping a child from playing in the area of the patio used for human wastes), money and time spent on preventive medical care such as vaccinations, time spent on cleanliness, and so on.

Understanding the full range of possible factors affecting a given outcome is essential to more accurate and meaningful research which will result in more effective programme design. Thus, the strengths of the anthropological approach for eliciting and identifying the underlying factors and meaning of behaviours (even on a small scale) are an essential adjunct to the large-scale survey approach for enhancing and refining the understanding of behaviour and its meaning. Generating an appropriate matrix for hypothesis testing is clearly as essential to ensuring more accurate and meaningful research as it is to effective programme planning.

ON COMBINING QUANTITATIVE AND QUALITATIVE RESEARCH METHODS

The basic techniques of anthropology are well known and well described (Wax, 1971; Naroll and Cohen, 1973; Pelto and Pelto, 1978; Spradley, 1980), and volumes exist on quantitative methods from the perspectives of many disciplines, particularly sociology, psychology, economics, demography, and political science. What are optimum combinations of the two approaches for studying intra-household resource allocation? In the following discussion, the assumption is made that time and financial resources are *not* infinite, and that a *realistic* rather than an ideal proposal must be made. For clarity, the suggestions which follow are presented in terms of a village. Studies at the regional or national level can sample accordingly, as can studies conducted in large urban areas.

The discussion on meaning in the previous section makes it clear that at least three phases are necessary, and that a fourth is desirable:
1. Exploratory ethnographic work.
2. Structured observations and interviews in a small sample of households.
3. Survey of a large random sample of households using a brief, focused instrument developed on the basis of results from steps 1 and 2.
4. Additional focused observations and more detailed interviews with a subsample of the survey households, based on the outcomes of the first three steps.

Exploratory Ethnographic Work

The traditional ethnography takes a minimum of a year. This not only ensures deep and accurate knowledge of the culture, but permits the researcher to live each season of the year with people and understand the impacts of seasonal variation on their lives. In a study of something as complex and multifaceted as resource allocation, the importance of seasonality cannot be ignored. Moreover, it takes time to gain a more than superficial understanding of a culture. Development projects, however, do not have the time nor the resources to hire an anthropologist for a year prior to initiating a project. Nor is it a realistic approach for a national or regional project in a country with ethnic, economic, and rural–urban variations in its population. Under these circumstances, a compromise is necessary.

The best strategy is to work with one or more anthropologists, already experienced in the culture(s) to be studied, and to conduct brief, focused ethnographic overviews in a small group of households. These should be sampled to reflect the variation – economics, household size, presence of young children in the household, etc. – present in the community that is important to the research. While specific kinds of behaviour relevant to the project would be the focus, the ethnographer would not be limited by the variables presumed to be of importance, but should be open to all relevant information. The question of seasonality should be handled either by touching base with the households briefly during each season, or by picking the one or two most important seasons for the research and concentrating on them. For example, most agricultural societies have a "lean season," the time just before the crops are ready to harvest and the resources from the previous year are depleted or nearly so. Obviously, it is crucial for projects on resource allocation to study behaviour during the lean season.

If an experienced researcher is involved, this focused ethnographic work can be as little as six weeks to look at 15 households in one community and gather background information on the community. This approach has been successfully utilized in a recent multinational series of studies of health-seeking behaviour at the household level sponsored by the United Nations University (UNU). Researchers in 16 countries focused on the evaluation of primary health-care and nutrition programmes from the household perspective, using guidelines developed by the group (Scrimshaw and Hurtado, 1985). Five hundred and fourteen households in 46 communities yielded rich data on how households were, or were not, affected by these programmes (Scrimshaw, Mitzner, and Scrimshaw, forthcoming, 1989).

One essential aspect of the approach is to focus the data collection fairly narrowly on the project's interests by means of the use of research topic guides. These guides are *not* questionnaires, but "shopping lists" of information required on a series of topics. They are assembled on the basis of project goals and priorities and a knowledge of the culture. The guides developed for UNU's 16-country study on nutrition and primary health care are presented in a field guide entitled *Rapid Assessment Procedures for Nutrition and Primary Health Care: Anthropological Approaches to Improving Program Effectiveness* (RAP) (Scrimshaw and Hurtado, 1987). They are intended to be modified for each programme by adding or deleting topics as appropriate. The information in these guides is collected over a series of visits with each family by means of observation, informal interview, and participant observation. The existence of a guide ensures that the same topics will be covered with each family, although the way in which the topics are discussed and their order will vary as appropriate to each family's situation. The guides are kept in a folder for each family, and supplemented by field notes as indicated. Checking the folder before setting out to visit a family enables the researcher to see what topics still need to be brought up in discussion with that family. Summarizing the information on guide sheets facilitates subsequent comparisons between families and data analysis in general.

The guides are supplemented by the usual ethnographic diary and field notes, and by brief formal interviews on household composition (age, sex, occupation, education, etc., for each household member), ethnicity, religion, and other household conditions (e.g. water supplies) relevant to health. These more formal interviews are usually completed early in the field-work period. They provide a good introduction to the family, and also facilitate data analysis and the comparison of communities through standardized pre-coded questions. The manual developed for the United Nations University projects contains more details on data collection and analysis for this type of brief and rapid interview (Scrimshaw and Hurtado, 1986).

Structured Observations and Interviews

Structured observations and interviews should be developed on the basis of the information gained during the ethnographic overview. For example, if the ethnographer finds that food allocation is carried out by several household members, focused observations of food allocation over a specific period or a sampling of periods should be conducted for each person involved in the allocation. It might be that programme efforts focused only on one type of person (e.g. mothers) when in fact several types (e.g. grandmothers and older siblings of children under five) should be involved in the programme as well.

Observation instruments should be developed on the basis of behaviours observed by the ethnographer, and might include a behaviour checklist of the type psychologists often use. For instance, Dehavenon (1978) used video cameras in people's homes to observe the family hierarchies reflected in food-allocation and request/compliance behaviours. Because it is so labour-intensive, she suggests this technique primarily be used in the design of observational and interview instruments. In recent research on labour and delivery in Mexican women, Engle and I started with field notes taken during labour, then structured those notes within specific time periods, and finally developed precise instruments collecting 78 columns' worth of data over five minutes, which could then be coded and entered into a computer for analysis (Scrimshaw, in press, 1989). As indicated by Johnson in this volume, observations on time allocation should be supplemented by interviews and informant recording of information.

Surveys

The range of survey methodologies is well documented (Babbie, 1982; Bailey, 1982; Sanders and Pinhey, 1983). The integration of quantitative and qualitative research can be difficult if the specialists in each method do not *really* respect or appreciate the contributions of the "other" method. It is essential either to have researchers who are familiar with and value both methods, as many now do, or to have quantitative and qualitative researchers work as a team throughout the project.

Just as the anthropologist or other qualitative research specialist has to compromise on the ideal project in phase 1, the quantitative specialist must be willing to carry out a parsimonious survey in phase 3, incorporating questions derived from and designed on the basis of the previous two phases. Dehavenon (1983, 1988) boiled down her voluminous data on East Harlem families to a four-page interview instrument used annually to measure hunger and food emergencies in a sample of 500 families from that same community.

Integration of qualitative information in the survey design phase must be followed by integration in data analysis and the presentation of results. A good report weaves the two together, illustrating survey findings with concrete examples, pointing out discrepancies between what people say they do and what they actually do, exploring interrelationships according to qualitatively derived hypotheses, and validating qualitative findings with survey data.

SUMMARY

Obtaining data on a topic as cross-culturally and individually varied and as elusive to people's memories and awareness as intra-household resource allocation calls for a multifaceted methodological approach. A combination of quantitative and qualitative research techniques is needed in order to understand the process being studied in culturally appropriate terms, to obtain accurate information on behaviour, and to interpret the meanings behind the behaviours. A three-phase approach is suggested involving initial ethnographic work, focused observations and interviews, and large-scale surveys. The inclusion of ethnographic phases does not need to be lengthy or costly, but can be scaled up or down according to time and resource availability. The essential ingredient is the co-ordinated *combination* of methodological approaches.

ACKNOWLEDGEMENTS

This paper has been guided by discussions with Mary Scrimshaw, Daniel March, Patricia Engle, and Anna Lou Dehavenon. Their comments and suggestions are greatly appreciated.

NOTE

1. The question of observer bias in ethnographic research has been discussed at length in the literature. Pelto and Pelto recapitulate the Robert Redfield/Oscar Lewis debate, the discussion of Ruth Benedict's *Patterns of Culture*, and other anthropological controversies (Pelto and Pelto, 1978, pp. 23–33). More recently, Derek Freeman's (1983) attack on Margaret Mead's work has been well analysed by several anthropologists (Brady, 1983; Shepper-Hughes, 1984).

REFERENCES

Babbie, E.R. 1982. *Social Research for Consumers*. Wadsworth, Belmont, Calif.
Bailey, K. 1982. *Methods of Social Research*. The Free Press, New York.
Brady, I. 1983. Speaking in the Name of the Real: Freeman and Mead on Samoa. *Am. Anthropologist*, 4: 908–944.

Caldwell, J.C., and P. Caldwell. 1977. The Role of Marital Sexual Abstinence in Determining Fertility: A Case Study of the Yoruba in Nigeria. *Popul. Stud.*, 31: 193–217.

Ciotti, P. 1986. In Unfamiliar Waters. *Los Angeles Times Magazine*, 16 February.

Dehavenon, A.L. 1978. Superordinate Behavior in Urban Homes: A Video Analysis of Request-compliance and Food Control Behavior in Two Black and Two White Families Living in New York City. Unpublished doctoral dissertation. Columbia University, New York.

——. 1983. The Tyranny of Indifference and the Myth of a Caring Society: A Study of 669 Households with Children in Food Emergencies in East Harlem in 1982. East Harlem Interfaith Welfare Committee, New York.

——. 1988. Homeless Families in New York City: A Study Using Emic Life History and Etic Survey Data. Paper presented at the 12th International Congress of Anthropological and Ethnological Sciences, Zagreb, Yugoslavia, 1988.

Freeman, D. 1983. *Margaret Mead and Samoa: The Making and Unmaking of an Anthropological Myth.* Harvard University Press, Cambridge, Mass.

Gadjusek, D.C., C.J. Gibbs, and M. Alpers. 1967. Transmission and Passage of Experimental "Kuru" to Chimpanzees. *Science*, 155; 212–214.

Harris, M. 1964. *The Nature of Cultural Things.* Random House, New York.

Johnson, A. 1975. Time Allocation in a Machiguenga Community. *Ethnology*, 14: 301–310.

Johnson, A.W. 1978. *Quantification in Cultural Anthropology: An Introduction to Research Design.* Stanford University Press, Stanford, Calif.

Lindenbaum, S. 1971. Sorcery and Structure in Fore Society. *Oceania*, 41: 277–287.

Messer, E. 1983. The Household Focus in Nutritional Anthropology: An Overview. *Fd. Nutr. Bull.*, 5(4): 2–12.

Moore, D.S., and S.C.M. Scrimshaw. 1983. Latina Women in Labor: The Relationship between Nursing Contact and Patient Behavior. Presented at the American Public Health Association Annual Meeting, November 1983.

Nag, M., B.N.F. White, and R.C. Peet. 1978. An Anthropological Approach to the Study of the Economic Value of Children in Java and Nepal. *Curr. Anthropol.*, 19(2): 293–306.

Naroll, R., and R. Cohen, eds. 1973. *A Handbook of Method in Cultural Anthropology.* Columbia University Press, New York.

Page, H.T., and R. Lesthaege, eds. 1981. *Childspacing in Tropical Africa: Tradition and Change.* Academic Press, New York.

Pelto, P.J., and G.H. Pelto. 1978. *Anthropological Research: The Structure of Inquiry.* Cambridge University Press, New York.

Sanders, W.B., and T.K. Pinhey. 1983. *The Conduct of Social Research.* Holt, Rinehart & Winston, New York.

Scrimshaw, S.C.M. 1969. A Critique of the Anthropological Method as an Instrument for Research on Human Reproduction: A Case Study in Barbados. Unpublished master's thesis. Columbia University, New York.

——. 1985. Bringing the Period Down: Government and Squatter Settlement Confront Induced Abortion in Ecuador. In: P.J. Pelto and B. deWalt, eds., *Micro and Macro Levels of Analysis in Anthropology: Issues in Theory and Research.* Westview Press, Boulder, Colo.

Scrimshaw, S.C.M., and E. Hurtado. 1987. *Rapid Assessment Procedures for Nutrition and Primary Health Care: Anthropological Approaches to Improving Program Effectiveness (RAP).* United Nations University, Tokyo.

Scrimshaw, S.C.M., and R. Souza. 1982. Recognizing Active Labor: A Test of a Decision-making Guide for Pregnant Women. *Soc. Sci. Med.*, 16(4): 1473–1482.

Spradley, J.P. 1979. *The Ethnographic Interview.* Holt, Rinehart, & Winston, New York.

——. 1980. *Participant Observation.* Holt, Rinehart & Winston, New York.

Steward, J. 1950. *Area Research: Theory and Practice.* Social Science Research Council, New York.

Van Maanen, J., J.M. Dabbs, and R.R. Faulkner. 1982. *Varieties of Qualitative Research.* Sage, Beverly Hills, Calif.

Wax, R.H. 1971. *Doing Fieldwork.* University of Chicago Press, Chicago.

Zborowski, M. 1952. Cultural Components in Responses to Pain. *J. Soc. Issues*, 8: 16–30.

98

7

An Approach to the Study of Women's Productive Roles as a Determinant of Intra-household Allocation Patterns

LYNN BENNETT

Women in Development Division, World Bank, Washington, D.C., USA

INTRODUCTION

Development projects often focus on improving the welfare of vulnerable individuals by providing resources to their households. The distribution of benefits derived from these resources, however, cannot always be assumed to conform to the priorities of the project designers. Households allocate resources according to their own priorities; it is therefore important for project planners to understand what these priorities are.

This paper suggests an approach to studying the factors which determine how household priorities are established. In particular, it focuses on women's productive roles as a determinant of their bargaining power within the household. Research on this and related questions would improve programme design by improving the understanding of how programme resources are likely to be used.

Women fill a dual role in most households, being both mother/caretaker and economic provider. These two roles, which complement each other in many circumstances, can also cause conflicts in time use and in the allocation of responsibilities. This dual role has led to what can be described as schizophrenic programming on the part of development agencies in their effort to work with third-world women. The question is whether women's income-producing work – which is increasingly recognized as crucial to the survival of poor families – results in an improvement or a deterioration in the health and nutritional status of their children, given the potential conflict with their caretaking role. Most women, however, have no choice about whether or not to work. For these women the issue is instead how to balance paid work (from wages or in-kind payments) with child-care responsibilities.

Welfare agencies generally focus on one or the other of the two roles. At the policy level, copious recognition is given to the importance of both roles, but, at the operational level, activities carried out by specialized agencies or divisions tend to focus on one role and ignore the other. A policy is often implemented through several separate divisions of an agency. One division may be charged with health and nutrition or family planning, and therefore would tend to focus on women as mothers, while

99

another, charged perhaps with agricultural development, employment, or, more frequently, "women in development," may focus on women as producers.

Many of the issues raised by the trade-offs between women's mothering and productive roles remain unresolved. This not only hampers the wholehearted adoption of a more integrated programme approach by governments and donors, but also constrains the design of effective intervention strategies.

In recent years, a number of authors have reviewed the available literature seeking to clarify the issues and highlight what is known about the relationships between women's work and their child-care responsibilities (cf. Safilios-Rothschild, 1980; Engle, 1980, 1981; Clark, 1981, 1982; Nieves, 1981, 1982; Carloni, 1983; Dwyer, 1983; and, in this volume, Engle and Safilios-Rothschild). What is clear from all the reviews is that there is a great deal of partial and conflicting evidence. In numerous studies, the children of working mothers have lower nutritional status than those of mothers who do not work outside the home (Hart, 1975; Popkin and Solon, 1976; Popkin, 1980; Blau, 1981). However, these studies have neither controlled for the family's income level nor for other important variables, such as the presence of an employed male or the family's land tenure status (Carloni, 1983). Hence, the poor nutritional status among the children of working mothers in many of the studies may well be due to the conditions of poverty which drove the mothers to work in the first place and to the low wages which such women earn, rather than the fact of their working per se.

RESTATEMENT OF THE PROBLEM: FOCUS ON WOMEN AS MAXIMIZING INDIVIDUALS WITHIN THE HOUSEHOLD

A framework which incorporates more than the roles of the mother is needed to identify the determinants of child health and nutrition (Carloni, 1983; Dwyer, 1983). A mere examination of the trade-off between the time women spend in income production time and in child care will not suffice. What is required is an investigation of how this trade-off is itself conditioned by the economic and socio-cultural environment. It would be equally important to concentrate on the household[1] as the locus of the trade-off; to know what other members of the family and kin group are also contributing in terms of domestic service and income, and whether or not these contributions influence household decision-making patterns in ways that would affect child well-being and nutritional status.

A growing number of detailed household studies include data on the time allocation and income contributions of individual family members (cf. Johnson, this volume), but most lack either the complementary data on child health and nutrition (Acharya and Bennett, 1981) or pertinent data on decision-making or income control (King-Quizon, 1978; Kumar, 1978; Nag et al., 1978; Cain et al., 1979; Mueller, 1979; DaVanzo and Lee, 1983). One of the key steps in understanding women's roles in the determination of child health and nutritional status may be a careful investigation of the process of resource allocation within the household. It is essential to understand gender-specific priorities for expenditure and the degree to which men and women control or influence various areas of decision-making. It is a difficult task, amenable only to limited quantitative measurement and statistical analysis. But the attempt must be made if we are to move beyond the accepted premise of the New Household Economics (Becker, 1965, 1981) that a single joint utility function can adequately represent the dynamics of household decision-making.

The joint utility concept is based upon a number of inaccurate and ethnocentric assumptions about the nature of the family. These assumptions are consistent with what both Yanagisako (1979) and Rosaldo (1980) have noted as a tendency in Western thought to idealize or sentimentalize the family as an "unchanging, nurturant, and altruistic core" which is somehow above the more instrumental and political modes of the public sphere. One of these assumptions is that all household members share the same priorities for the use of household time and resources. In the words of its own proponents, the assumption of a joint utility function "means simply that all household members agree to certain management rules regarding the distribution of income within the household and the allocation of household members' time" (Evenson et al., cited in Binswanger et al., 1980). Scholars from various disciplines (Fapohunda, 1978; Clark, 1982; Guyer, 1982; Roldan, 1982; Kumar, 1983) have called this concept into question. They cite data from Africa and elsewhere which illustrate that (1) household income is not always pooled, and (2) men and women often have separate, culturally designated obligations to meet different sets of needs within and beyond the conjugal family. In particular, it has been noted (Fapohunda, 1978, and Guyer, 1982, for Africa; Roldan, 1982, for Mexico; and Peluso, 1980, for Indonesia) that women are often responsible for providing all or part of the resources needed to support their children. These studies and my own work in Nepal (Bennett, 1981, 1983) all indicate that what the "household" decides to do with its resources is not the outcome of spontaneous utopian "agreement," but instead grows out of serious *bargaining* (covert or overt) among its individual members (cf. Safilios-Rothschild, this volume).

This brings us to the two other assumptions commonly associated with the concept of the joint household utility function: (1) that all household members have equal bargaining power to enforce their own definition of utility; and (2) that all members benefit equally from the way resources are actually allocated. Any observed inequality in the distribution of household resources, therefore, is interpreted as the most efficient reaction to the prevailing wage-price conditions (i.e. as part of the household unit's maximizing behaviour). Folbre's (1984) reanalysis of time allocation and nutrition data from Laguna, Philippines, presents an alternative and more compelling explanation for reported inequalities in household distribution patterns. Among the more obvious disparities between men and women revealed by these data are the observations that men had significantly more leisure time than women, and that they consumed 101 per cent and 116 per cent, respectively, of their required daily allowance (RDA) of calories and protein, while women's diets were markedly deficient, providing only 87 per cent of their caloric RDA and 79 per cent of their protein RDA (see Appendix of Pinstrup-Andersen and Garcia, in part III of this volume, for exact values of caloric RDAs in the Philippines).

Folbre (1984) sees this phenomenon, and all inequitable household distribution rules, as arising from structural asymmetries in the economic, social, and legal position of men and women which give the two sexes unequal bargaining power. Rather than viewing the household as a single maximizing unit, she posits that the household is a group of maximizing individuals, "in which individual family members co-operate with one another primarily to further their own personal interest" (Folbre, 1984). Of course, there will often be a high degree of overlap in the allocation priorities of household members. The overlap, however, will rarely be 100 per cent. This ability to realize personal allocation priorities, which Folbre calls "bargaining power," appears to be affected by "the individual's contribution to the household income," by his or her potential earnings outside the household, "and even support from extra-household coalitions struck by members of the same class, race or gender" (Folbre, 1984, p. 3). From my own work among Hindus living in the hills of Nepal (Bennett, 1981), I would suggest that a number of additional social factors, such as support from family of origin, freedom to divorce and remarry, polygamy, and individual personality, also affect women's bargaining power. Moreover, I would add that the concept of "maximization," which is appropriate for trying to understand individual decision-making inside the household, cannot be understood within a purely economic framework.

Instead of assuming an exogenously given joint utility function or household distribution rule, it would be more useful to investigate how the rule itself varies in different cultural and economic settings and to uncover the process through which household members establish the rule.[2]

PROPOSED FRAMEWORK FOR ANALYSIS

This paper proposes a conceptual framework which could be used as the basis for empirical research into some of these questions. In it I have tried to set out relationships in quantifiable terms; what follows may seem very abstract and overly neat. The arrows and boxes may obscure the fact that some of the most important aspects of the household decision-making process cannot be quantified. Instead, they need to be captured through in-depth anthropological observation, what Geertz (1973) has called "thick description," of the social bargaining process within the family. Statistical correlations mean little without a thorough knowledge of the context in which they occur. In spite of the quantitative nature of the model presented here, the approach envisioned is similar to those used by Acharya and Bennett (1981, 1983), van Esterik (1983), and Nag and colleagues (1978, 1982). All these projects combine survey methods with an ethnographic approach involving extended residence in the community under study. Data from both sources then must be integrated at the analysis stage.

Focus on the Internal Dynamics of the Family

In the proposed framework depicted in figure 1, biological and environmental factors are bracketed and child health and nutritional status are analysed as outcomes of the social economy of the household.[3] This procedure would document the income and services which flow into the household from each family member, and would examine the process through which these resources are allocated to produce welfare for each member.

The final welfare outputs in which we are particularly interested are the health and nutritional status of children in the household (particularly of infants and children under five). We recognized that there are many other welfare outputs which are crucial to the development of the child such as shelter, clothing, the child's own leisure and play time, education, support for special life-cycle rituals, and even the leisure time of the mother and father, which may enable them to be more creative and involved as parents. If data on these sorts of outputs are gathered along with the data on

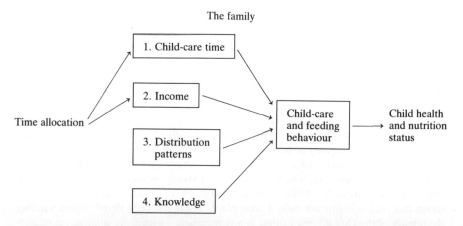

The family

1. Child-care time

2. Income

3. Distribution patterns

4. Knowledge

Time allocation

Child-care and feeding behaviour

Child health and nutrition status

Fig. 1. Tentative framework for analysis: the major family determinants

the child's food consumption and care time, etc., they can also be examined within the same framework. By expanding the data collected to include the dietary intake and health and nutrition status[4] of the mother as well as her children, it would be possible to look at the factors affecting both these interrelated dependent variables within the same framework. This would be especially useful in identifying situations in which the child's welfare was being purchased at the expense of the mother's.

Figure 1 shows the four main determinants within the family of the child's health and nutritional status: (1) child-care time; and (2) income to purchase material goods such as food, clothes, medicine, and shelter, or home-produced equivalents. Two other factors impinge on how the first two inputs are used: (3) the priorities and bargaining power of different family members, which determine the pattern of distribution of household resources; and (4) the *knowledge* and skills of various family members, which determine how efficiently the time and income inputs are transformed into child welfare.

One of the main resources the family has is the time of its members. Time can either be used to produce services for the family (i.e. domestic work like cooking, cleaning, laundry, and child care) or it can be used in production. This includes wage/salary work in the market, which generates income, and unpaid subsistence production of food and other goods on the family farm, which spares income.

While it has always been relatively easy to measure the contribution to family welfare made by the wage-earner contributing cash income, this has not been the case with subsistence production. Often this crucial contribution has been overlooked in macro-economic analyses because it has been so difficult to assess individual input into what, in many cultures, is viewed as pooled or communal family production,[5] and also because much of the food produced is consumed by the family and never reaches the market, and therefore is not counted as part of a country's GNP. It can be done, though. Acharya and Bennett (1983) developed a technique using time-allocation data and detailed household production data to estimate the relative value of each household member's contribution to household subsistence production without relying on imputed wage rates.[6]

It then becomes possible to look at the income inputs of not only wage-earners working in the market economy (who generally are men), but also of those who work without pay for the family (generally women), saving income in income-sparing activities.

Disaggregation

This opens the way for disaggregation of inputs, which is illustrated in figure 2. Disaggregation permits us to begin to analyse the trade-offs between different members of the family for certain types of inputs. For example, it allows us to determine, in cases where the mother works outside the home and cannot spend as much time on child care and food preparation, whether or not other family members make up the difference. Evidence from the Philippines (Evenson, et al., cited in Binswanger, 1980) shows that such substitution indeed takes place. There has been debate about whether the quality of the care given by other family members – especially siblings – is equivalent to that provided by the mother. This issue could be addressed through separate assessment of the knowledge and skills that various care-givers had in child care and food preparation.

Disaggregation of inputs is also vital to the examination of relationships between income-earning and "bargaining power," i.e. the ability to influence how household resources are used. Among the hypotheses that could be tested are:
1. That increases in maternal income are positively associated with increased maternal influence over income allocation.
2. That increases in maternal influence over income allocation lead to increased allocation, better dietary intake, and higher health and nutritional status for the child.

In figure 2, the welfare outputs are also disaggregated, first according to what is received by each individual family member, and second by the stages of the consumption or utilization process. Data should be collected on the allocation of both cash and in-kind resources to each family member. This first stage of output is the result of the total amount of income the family has (determinant 2 in figure 2) and the influence of the various members on the way that income is distributed (determinant 3).

As mentioned above (p. 103), time for child care, food preparation, and other domestic work (determinant 1), and the knowledge and skills (determinant 4) needed to transform income into a nutritious meal or adequate health care, are required for this income and raw material to be consumed. Data to measure this second stage of welfare output would be (a) the protein/calorie intake of each member; (b) feeding patterns (i.e. initiation, frequency, and duration of breast-feeding, age of introduction of supplementary foods, or frequency of meals); (c) health-care behaviour (i.e. treatment of diarrhoea, expenditure on medical care, or utilization of health services); and (d) total child-care time.[7]

Thus, the second-stage welfare output is conceptualized as the result of the per person income/raw material available plus the knowledge and time inputs of each family member. Factors outside the family such as the availability of foods and health care also must be included here, although they are not shown in the model.[8]

These types of biological and environmental factors outside our model would be expected to have a proportionally greater effect on the final-stage welfare output: the health and nutrition status of each family member. Although this output would be

104

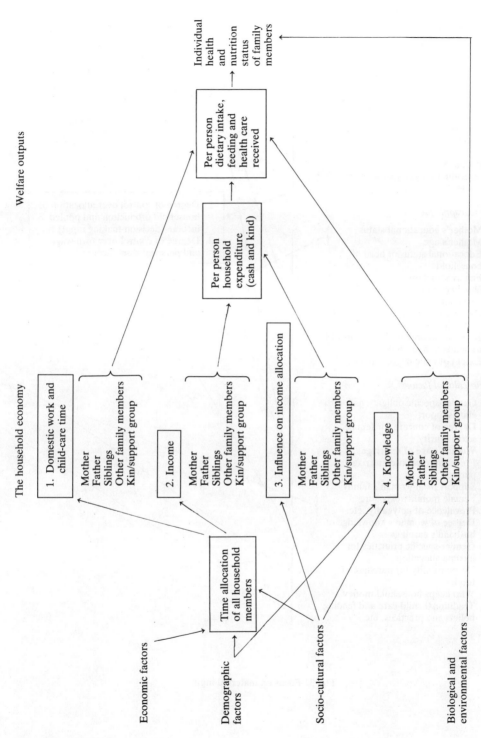

Welfare outputs

The household economy

Fig. 2. Tentative framework for analysis: disaggregation

105

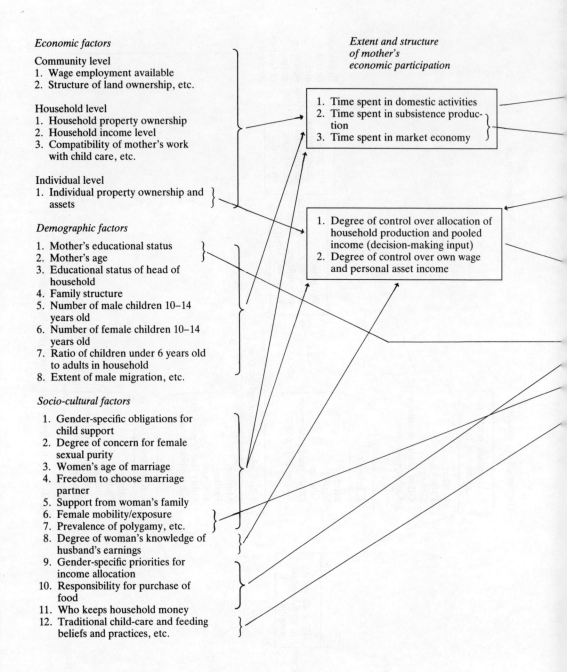

Economic factors

Community level
1. Wage employment available
2. Structure of land ownership, etc.

Household level
1. Household property ownership
2. Household income level
3. Compatibility of mother's work
   with child care, etc.

Individual level
1. Individual property ownership and
   assets

Demographic factors

1. Mother's educational status
2. Mother's age
3. Educational status of head of
   household
4. Family structure
5. Number of male children 10–14
   years old
6. Number of female children 10–14
   years old
7. Ratio of children under 6 years old
   to adults in household
8. Extent of male migration, etc.

Socio-cultural factors

1. Gender-specific obligations for
   child support
2. Degree of concern for female
   sexual purity
3. Women's age of marriage
4. Freedom to choose marriage
   partner
5. Support from woman's family
6. Female mobility/exposure
7. Prevalence of polygamy, etc.
8. Degree of woman's knowledge of
   husband's earnings
9. Gender-specific priorities for
   income allocation
10. Responsibility for purchase of
    food
11. Who keeps household money
12. Traditional child-care and feeding
    beliefs and practices, etc.

*Extent and structure
of mother's
economic participation*

1. Time spent in domestic activities
2. Time spent in subsistence production
3. Time spent in market economy

1. Degree of control over allocation of
   household production and pooled
   income (decision-making input)
2. Degree of control over own wage
   and personal asset income

Fig. 3. Focus on maternal inputs

106

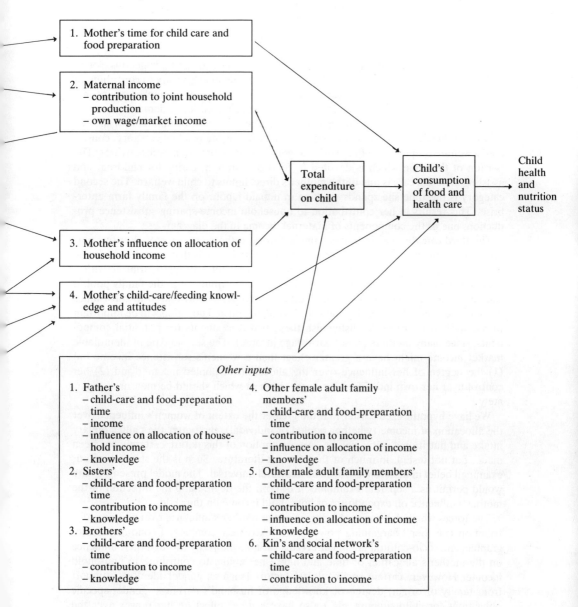

Mother's inputs

1. Mother's time for child care and food preparation

2. Maternal income
   – contribution to joint household production
   – own wage/market income

3. Mother's influence on allocation of household income

4. Mother's child-care/feeding knowledge and attitudes

Total expenditure on child

Child's consumption of food and health care

Child health and nutrition status

Other inputs

1. Father's
   – child-care and food-preparation time
   – income
   – influence on allocation of household income
   – knowledge
2. Sisters'
   – child-care and food-preparation time
   – contribution to income
   – knowledge
3. Brothers'
   – child-care and food-preparation time
   – contribution to income
   – knowledge
4. Other female adult family members'
   – child-care and food-preparation time
   – contribution to income
   – influence on allocation of income
   – knowledge
5. Other male adult family members'
   – child-care and food-preparation time
   – contribution to income
   – influence on allocation of income
   – knowledge
6. Kin's and social network's
   – child-care and food-preparation time
   – contribution to income

107

measured, it would be a less sensitive indicator of what we are examining: the internal dynamics of the household economy as it affects the child.

Focus on the Mother

Our model includes intra-household demographic factors and exogenous socio-cultural and economic factors, since they affect each member's ability to contribute to child welfare along the four major dimensions (time, income, influences on income allocation, and knowledge). Figure 3 details some of the cultural, demographic, and economic data that will need to be examined. The allocation of time is now broken down into three major work categories[9] (with leisure as the residual category, considered a welfare output). The first work category is time spent in domestic activities. The portion of this time which is devoted to food preparation, caring for children, and assisting in health care is one of the mother's direct inputs to child welfare. The second category is the time she spends working in unpaid labour on the family farm enterprise. This results in her contribution to household income-sparing subsistence production, one of the components of maternal income in the diagram.

The third category encompasses women's work in the market sector. For our purposes one of the most important aspects of this kind of work is that it produces income – either from wages or as the profit from own-account entrepreneurial activities. Whether she keeps this income to spend herself or contributes it to the family pool, it can be identified as her own earnings. Like the mother's contribution to subsistence income, the effect of her market income on child health and nutrition will be important to measure. It is crucial to distinguish these two components (or potential components, since many mothers do not earn wage income). The second type of identifiable market income might have a greater effect than a women's subsistence income on: (1) the degree of her influence over the allocation of pooled income; and (2) her control over her own individual earnings – both of which should be measured separately.

We have hypothesized earlier that the greater the extent of women's influence over the allocation of income (whether pooled or individal), the better the child's dietary intake and nutritional status will be. An assumption of this nature certainly has been made, but not tested, in much of the relevant literature. Such is the strength of our examined belief in maternal altruism as a cultural universal. The model presented here would permit us a separate examination of both the degree and the direction of the mother's influence on expenditure of household income on the child.

The forces which determine the degree of the mother's influence over resource distribution (i.e. her "bargaining power") are extremely complex. Economic, demographic, and socio-cultural factors affect this variable *indirectly* through their influence on the mother's allocation of time and hence her ability to contribute to household income. However, certain socio-cultural factors (such as gender ideology, support from family of origin, degree of knowledge of husband's earnings, gender-specific obligations for child support, etc.) also have a *direct* effect on her power over the disposal of household resources.

The direction of the mother's influence is based on her own priorities, which will be, at least in part, socially conditioned and can be observed and measured separately. Dwyer (1983) has pointed out that women's allocational priorities are often geared toward survival strategies, while men's priorities may focus on mobility. Women's priorities may be conditioned by the need to protect against or prepare for divorce or desertion – especially in cultures where land ownership is in male hands. They may have to compete with a co-wife to secure family resources for their own children. The need to keep natal kin and neighbourhood support networks active by fulfilling certain social obligations may be more important to women. Societies also differ as to whether women can express their individual priorities openly or must pursue them covertly.[10]

The "knowledge" input would be measured with reference to certain specific practices regarding breast-feeding, weaning, supplementary feeding, response to diarrhoea, etc., determined by nutritionists and physicians to be central to child survival.[11] This variable is seen as conditioned primarily by socio-cultural factors, particularly by the traditional child-care and feeding practices which prevail in the community. However, demographic variables such as the age and educational status of the mother (and, in some situations, economic variables such as labour-force participation, which affects exposure to new ideas) will obviously influence the degree to which the individual has absorbed these traditional beliefs and practices and the degree to which he or she has access to and adopts alternative ways of doing things.

Potential Programme and Policy Relevance

This framework should do much to clarify the relationship between women's roles as mothers and producers. In particular, it should help identify the social and economic conditions under which women's income-producing work results in healthier, better-nourished children and those conditions in which it fails to do so. This will be important to programme-planners attempting to build up the traditional support networks of working mothers and, in some countries and some sectors of the economy, to assist in creating such facilities where they do not exist. Moreover, because this model does not define women's productive work narrowly in terms of "labour-force participation," it will permit a much more accurate assessment of the actual extent of women's contribution to the income variable. It also permits an examination of the differential effects of various kinds of income-producing work on the child's welfare.[12]

But perhaps the most important potential contribution this kind of study could make in terms of support to the design of programme interventions would be to provide a clearer grasp of the factors determining decision-making patterns at the household level as they relate to child health and nutrition. A number of specific questions can be addressed within the proposed framework:

1. What are the respective male and female obligations within the family (particularly with regard to support for child feeding, health care, etc.) in different cultural settings?
2. To what extent is income pooled in the family? What is pooled income spent on and who spends it? On what is the non-pooled income of different family members spent? Which type of income support goes to the child?
3. How does income earning or market participation affect the extent of women's input in various areas of household decision-making? Can it actually outweigh or change the effect of traditional gender ideology? What other factors affect women's "bargaining power?"
4. What are the women's allocation priorities? Is it true that income earned by women is more likely to be spent on food and basic needs than income earned by men? Is there a positive relationship between the extent of women's control over the alloca-

109

tion of household resources (pooled and individual) and child health and nutrition-al status?

5. Of the four determinants of inputs (i.e. time, income, influence on income distribution and knowledge), which contributes most to child health and nutrition status? Even more importantly, for each input, does it make a difference which family member contributed it?

Statistical analysis of some of these issues may have important global policy implications in addition to intrinsic theoretical interest. However, the most useful information in terms of concrete project design and formulation of country-level policy by governments in the developing world is likely to be the insight gained from in-depth observation of how men, women, and children in poor families work out their individual and collective strategies for survival.

NOTES

1. Although the terms "family" and "household" have been used interchangeably in this discussion, they are of course not synonymous. The term "family" implies that members are related by some conjugal or consanguineal tie, though the form which the family takes, the number of generations it encompasses, etc., vary greatly between cultures. One family may have several "households," as in the case of polygamous marriages or the husband's long-term migration for employment. A consistent definition of "household," and yet one that is not culturally bound, would have to be evolved as appropriate to the research or project.

2. This alternative to the joint household utility function can be conceptualized as a series of individual utility functions, each accompanied by a coefficient representing that individual's power in the household and hence his/her ability to achieve or enforce his particular priorities for his own and others' welfare as these differ from those of the household head. This alternative household utility function or distribution rule might look something like this:

$$x(U_f) + y(U_m) + z(U_c) = U_h$$

where U_f = utility as perceived by the father, and x = the father's power to enforce his perception, with $x + y + z = 1$. Similarly, U_m = utility as perceived by the mother, and y = her power to enforce her perception. U_c = utility as perceived by the child, and y = his/her power to enforce his perception.

The relative power of each member to enforce his/her preferences is indicated by the coefficient. For example, in a culture where the household head has close to absolute power, x would be close to 1, and y and z would approach 0. Folbre (1982, p. 9), points out that the adult child who has left the family but is earning income has a great deal of power over what (s)he chooses to send his/her parents for their support. Likewise, grown sons in the patrilineal extended family may have equal or even greater bargaining power than their parents. These coefficients then would change over the life-cycle of the individual and with variations in the developmental cycle of the family itself.

Other factors determining the strength of each individual's bargaining power would be the structure of the economy, the socio-cultural definition of a particular role in the family, and the personality of the individual filling the role. In extended family structures other members of the household – and perhaps even the extended kin group – would need to be added.

3. Many parts of the model – especially those dealing with health and nutrition – are not yet clearly formulated. The question of how to measure the set of household "outputs" which I have grouped together as "Child Food Consumption and Health Care" will need the attention of nutritionists and health experts. It is clear, moreover, that for a "feeding practice" such as breast-feeding there are many biological factors not encompassed in this model which influence the mother's decision whether or not to breast-feed and for how long. This framework may therefore be more suitable for investigating the determinants of certain child-care and feeding "outputs" than for others.

4. It is suggested that as far as possible data on welfare outputs, including (1) per person expenditure, (2) dietary intake, and (3) anthropometric measurements of health and nutritional status, be gathered for the following age/sex groups: (a) 0–1 infants (male/female); (b) 1–5 young children (male/female); (c) 6–15 children (male/female); (d) adult women (unmarried, no children; children under five; childbearing age; past childbearing age); (e) adult men (heads of household; dependent adults). In addition, data on leisure time of all household members, which is also an important welfare output, should be available from the time-allocation data. A meaningful composite category of leisure activities can be constructed if separate activities are carefully coded.

5. In many parts of Africa where women sometimes have rights to their own plots in addition to family lands, or where certain crops are identified as belonging to women, this problem has been less severe. The value of the produce (or income from selling it) in such cases probably should be included under the second category of "own income" shown in figure 1.

6. In the Nepal study (Acharya and Bennett, 1983), monetary value was only calculated for household work which resulted in a *product* which could be valued on the basis of the market purchase price of an equivalent product. The study was conservative in its approach and did not attempt to value unpaid domestic *service* since it is particularly difficult to establish wage rates for services (such as cooking and child care) which are not purchased in a traditional subsistence economy like that of Nepal. The recent work of Goldschmidt-Clermont (1983), however, suggests that it may be possible to develop a similar output-related approach to valuing domestic service as well.

7. The proposed method of collecting data on time allocation is based on that used in an earlier study in Nepal (cf. Acharya and Bennett, 1983). This method allows child care to be recorded as the simultaneous activity it often is in developing countries. There are some conceptual problems since child-care time is being treated as both an input and an output. Perhaps child-care time should not be included as part of this variable.

8. In considering the issue of breast-feeding as part of the health-care and feeding behaviour "output," it perhaps would be necessary to consider the mother's dietary intake and biological factors such as her health, age, etc., which are not considered in this model, in addition to the mother's time and her knowledge (and that of other senior females in the household).

9. It may be useful to follow the procedure used in Nepal and separate the third category, market work, into work which takes place in the local area and allows the worker to sleep at home, and migrant employment for which the worker resides outside the home community. This distinction is necessary if the random spot-check observational method is used as it was in Nepal to gather time-allocation data (cf. Acharya and Bennett, 1983, for discussion).

10. Such cross-cultural differences would have to be kept in mind when seeking to measure this variable – as would the difference between normative female priorities and actual observed priorities.

11. Conceptualization of how this factor operates and the linkages between what the mother knows, how she learns it, and what she actually does need further work.

12. Several authors (e.g. Nieves, 1982; Carloni, 1983) have pointed out the fallacy of assuming that women's traditional agricultural work is more compatible with child care than are other more modern types of employment. This may be so for women who simply tend a small kitchen-garden and look after a few animals. But, for women who must work as wage labourers – who, according to studies in Bangladesh (Saleka and Greeley, 1980), are often among the poorest section of the population – or whose family lands are far from the homestead, agricultural work and even "domestic chores" such as fuel- and water-gathering take the mother out of the house for long periods in difficult physical conditions which are not suitable for a child.

REFERENCES

Acharya, M., and L. Bennett. 1981. *The Rural Women of Nepal. The Status of Women in Nepal.* Vol. II: *Field Studies*, part 9. Tribhuvan University, Centre for Economic Development and Administration, Kathmandu, Nepal.

——. 1983. Women and the Subsistence Sector: Economic Participation and Household Decision Making in Nepal. Staff Working Paper 526. World Bank, Washington, D.C.

Becker, G.S. 1965. A Theory of the Allocation of Time. *Econ. J.*, 75(2); 493–518.

———. 1981. *A Treatise on the Family*. Harvard University Press, Cambridge, Mass.

Bennett, L. 1981. *The Parbatiya Women of Bakundol. The Status of Women in Nepal.* Vol. II: *Field Studies*, part 7. Tribhuvan University, Centre for Economic Development and Administration, Kathmandu, Nepal.

———. 1983. *Dangerous Wives and Sacred Sisters: Social and Symbolic Roles of High Caste Women in Nepal.* Columbia University Press, New York.

Blau, D.M. 1981. Investment in Child Nutrition and Women's Allocation of Time in Developing Countries. Center Discussion Paper 371. Yale University Growth Center, New Haven, Conn.

Cain, M., S.R. Khanam, and S. Nahar. 1979. Class, Patriarchy and Women's Work in Bangladesh. *Popul. Devel. Rev.*, 5(3): 405–438.

Carloni, A.S. 1983. The Impact of Maternal Employment and Income on the Nutritional Status of Children in Rural Areas of Developing Countries. United Nations Administrative Committee on Coordination, Subcommittee on Nutrition, New York.

Clark, C. 1981. Women's Work and Child Nutrition. The Rand Paper Series, Rand Corporation, Santa Monica, Calif.

———. 1982. The Microeconomic Approach to the Relation of Women's Market Work and Child Welfare. Presented at the Roundtable for International Center for Research on Women, Washington, D.C., 1982.

DaVanzo, J., and D.L.P. Lee. 1983. The Compatibility of Child Care with Market and Nonmarket Activities: Preliminary Evidence from Malaysia. In: M. Buvinic, M.A. Lycette, and W.P. McGreevey, eds., *Women and Poverty in the Third World*. Johns Hopkins University Press, Baltimore, Md.

Dwyer, D.H. 1983. Women and Income in the Third World: Implications for Policy. Working Paper 18. Population Council, New York.

Engle, P.L. 1980. The Intersecting Needs of Working Women and Their Young Children. Report to the Ford Foundation, New York, 28 August.

———. 1981. Maternal Care, Maternal Substitutes, and Children's Welfare in the Developed and Developing Countries. Presented at the International Center for Research on Women Conference on the Interface between Poor Women's Nurturing Roles and Productive Responsibilities, Washington, D.C.

Evenson, R.E., B.M. Popkin, and E. King-Quizon. 1980. Nutrition, Work, and Demographic Behavior in Rural Philippine Households: A Synopsis of Several Laguna Household Studies. In: H.-P. Binswanger, R.E. Evenson, C.A. Florencio, and B.N.F. White, eds., *Rural Household Studies in Asia*. Singapore University Press, Singapore.

Fapohunda, E.R. 1978. Characteristics of Women Workers in Lagos: Data for Reconsideration by Labour Market Theorists. *Labour and Society*, 3(2): 158–171.

Folbre, N. 1982. Exploitation Comes Home: A Critique of the Marxian Theory of Family Labor. *Camb. J. Econ.*, 6: 317–329.

———. 1984. Household Production in the Philippines: A Non-neoclassical Approach. *Econ. Devel. Cult. Change*, 32(2): 303–330.

Geertz, C. 1973. *The Interpretation of Culture*. Basic Books, New York.

Goldschmidt-Clermont, L. 1983. Output-related Evaluation of Unpaid Household Work. A Challenge for Time Use Studies. *Home Econ. Res. J.*, 12(2): 127–132.

Guyer, J.I. 1982. Dynamic Approaches to Domestic Budgeting. Cases and Methods from Africa. Presented at Seminar on Women and Income Control in the Third World Conference, New York, October 1982.

Hart, G. 1975. Women's Participation in the Labour Force: Implications for Employment and Health/Nutrition Programs. Mimeo. Department of Agricultural Economics, Cornell University, Ithaca, New York.

King-Quizon, E. 1978. Time Allocation and Home Production in Philippine Rural Households. *Phil. Econ. J.*, 17(1–2): 185–202.

Kumar, S.K. 1978. The Role of Household Economy in Child Nutrition at Low Incomes: A Case Study in Kerala. Occasional Paper 95. Department of Agricultural Economics, Cornell University, Ithaca, N.Y.

———. 1983. A Framework for Tracing Policy Effects on Intra-household Food Distribution. *Fd. Nutr. Bull.*, 5(4): 13–15.

Mueller, E. 1979. *Time Use in Rural Botswana*. Population Studies Center, University of Michigan, Ann Arbor, Mich.

112

Nag, M., R. Anker, and M.E. Khan. 1982. A Guide to Anthropological Study of Women's Roles and Demographic Change in India. Work Paper 115. Population and Labour Policies Programme. International Labour Organization.

Nag, M., B. White, and C. Peet. 1978. An Anthropological Approach to the Study of the Economic Value of Children in Java and Nepal. *Curr. Anthropol.*, 19(2): 293–306.

Nieves, I. 1981. A Balancing Act: Strategies to Cope with Work and Motherhood in Developing Countries. Prepared for the International Center for Research on Women Policy Roundtable on the Interface between Poor Women's Nurturing Roles and Productive Responsibilities, Washington, D.C., December 1981.

———. 1982. The Interface between Poor Women's Nurturing Roles and Productive Responsibilities. Paper prepared for Second Annual Women, Work and Public Policy Workshop, Harvard Institute for International Development, Harvard University, Cambridge, Mass., April 1982.

Peluso, N.L. 1980. Survival Strategies of Rural Women Traders, or Women's Place Is in the Market: Four Case Studies from Northwestern Sleman in the Special Region of Yogjakarta. Rural Employment Policy Research Programme. International Labour Organization, Geneva.

Popkin, B.M. 1980. Time Allocation of the Mother and Child Nutriture. *Ecol. Fd. Nutr.*, 9(1): 1–14.

Popkin, B.M., and F. Solon. 1976. Income, Time, the Working Mother and Child Nutriture. *J. Trop. Ped. and Environ. Child. Health.*, 22(4): 156–166.

Roldán, M. 1982. Intrahousehold Patterns of Money Allocation and Women's Subordination: A Case Study of Domestic Outworkers in Mexico City. Presented at the Population Council Seminar on Women, Income and Policy, March 1982.

Rosaldo, M.Z. 1980. The Use and Abuse of Anthropology: Reflections on Feminism and Cross-cultural Understanding. *Signs*, 5(3): 389–417.

Safilios-Rothschild, C. 1980. The Role of the Family: A Neglected Aspect of Rural Poverty. In: Implementing Programs of Human Development. Staff Paper 403. World Bank, Washington, D.C.

Saleka, B., and M. Greeley. 1980. *Women, Employment and Agriculture: Notes from a Bangladesh Case Study*. Institute of Development Studies, University of Sussex, Brighton.

Van Esterik, P. 1983. Integrating Ethnographic and Survey Research: A Review of the Ethnographic Component of a Study of Infant Feeding Practices in Developing Countries. Working Paper 17. The Population Council, International Program, New York.

Yanagesako, S.J. 1979. Family and Household: The Analysis of Domestic Groups. *Ann. Rev. Anthropol.*, 8: 161–205.

113

8
Household Organization and Expenditure in a Time Perspective: Social Processes of Change

ELIZABETH JELÍN

Centro de Estudios de Estado y Sociedad (CEDES), Buenos Aires, Argentina

INTRODUCTION

Household dynamics involve processes of change that are best studied in a time perspective. Changes in household organization over time are catalysed by two sets of distinct but interacting influences. First, there are the inevitable changes in household organization as members age and their status changes in culturally prescribed ways during their life-cycle. Superimposed on these are external forces including cultural, political, historical, and social factors that propel households to reorganize.

This paper addresses methodologic and conceptual issues pertaining to the measurement and analysis of processes of social and political change, and their effects on household dynamics. It illustrates the contributions of qualitative studies in the investigation of intra-household dynamics. Qualitative methods are particularly effective for uncovering patterns of social organization and mechanisms of change, and play an important role in identifying dimensions and measures to be included in subsequent, more representative, quantitative studies (cf. Scrimshaw, this volume). The paper is based on insights from an in-depth, longitudinal study of fifteen working-class households in Greater Buenos Aires, Argentina, from 1976 to 1983, a period of economic recession, political repression, and profound social transformations.

SOCIAL CHANGE AT THE HOUSEHOLD LEVEL: METHODOLOGICAL ISSUES

The household is a dynamic institution, its organization constantly adapting to internal and external influences. But how exactly does one assess these changes? Household organization itself is difficult to measure (cf. Heywood, Messer, this volume). Moreover, households do not exist in a vacuum. They function day-to-day in a larger context – including cultural, social, historical and political components – that changes over time. Their organization must be examined in a time perspective in order to understand how households reorganize as they adapt to these influences.

Measuring the time dimension, however, poses a critical methodological problem. Most surveys and cross-sectional studies take a static view of family and household: reality is what is being chronicled at the moment. Time-use studies that record the allocation of time by each member to various tasks, such as outside work, housework, or leisure, focus on everyday life (cf. Johnson, this volume). But everyday life is only one point in the progression of individual life-courses and family cycles (Balan and Jelín, 1979). Shifts and transitions in the life-cycle are revealed in daily life, at times as very small, gradual, and almost imperceptible cumulative changes, at other times as dramas and crises. In this sense, the effects of time are not linear but occur in stages. Significant transitions qualitatively alter the life condition of the individual and the distribution of power and tasks in the household.

Furthermore, household members age simultaneously but along different personal and social paths. The transitions the various household members make may require mutual adaptations and shifts in the organization of the entire household: as children reach adulthood and start working, younger siblings may need to contribute to household tasks; a grandmother becomes ill and can no longer help with household maintenance, so her daughter takes care of her in addition to her own children; the birth of a baby, marital separation, or widowhood all are junctions accompanied by significant task redistributions.

Analytically, a dynamic perspective requires separating the various time dimensions that result in the cross-sectional picture. One of these time dimensions is the biographical life-cycle development of each person. "Normal" life consists of continuous change linked to the biological and social aspects of the aging process. The life-cycle is a socially structured pattern of shifts over time (Elder, 1975, 1978; Balan and Jelín, 1979). A second dimension is what Hareven (1977) calls "family time." This consists of the interaction between each individual's life-course and those of other family and household members. Although there are strong cultural norms regarding an ideal family cycle (Glick, 1947), the increasing variability and choice in family life-styles and household structures today call for the development of more flexible models. In family time, for instance, co-residence (household composition) may not always be the crucial factor determining mutual obligations and rights, as exemplified by the duties and responsibilities of divorced parents toward their children, or the financial and time obligations to care for aging parents living outside the home.

Just as in project identification and programme planning (cf. Rogers, this volume), the perspective from which a given problem is approached determines the ideal type of data to be gathered. The dynamic life-cycle perspective implies a longitudinal approach, with data collected via retrospective life-histories or follow-up studies. In so far as there are interrelationships among the life-cycles of various persons in the family and household, information must be gathered from all household members. Finally, since it is essential to understand the meaning of actions for the subjects involved in order to construct accurate analytical models, links should be established between the interviews of the household members.

Even in cases where the available sources of information are not longitudinal nor based on personal testimonies, cross-sectional data can be interpreted with a life-course perspective, taking time into account as a basic dimension of social reality. This is a particularly useful approach for programme planners and project designers who do not have the time to do long-term studies.

That the life-cycle unfolds in a social environment undergoing change makes the analysis even more complex. The historical circumstances, the specific conditions in which processes of family and individual change take place, are variables that must be included explicitly. Historical time has to be part of studies of household dynamics.[1] Only then can one untangle changes due to the "normal" life-course from the transformations that life-courses undergo in the process of macro-social change.

CONCEPTUAL ISSUES IN THE ANALYSIS OF HOUSEHOLD PROCESSES

Households are the social units in charge of the organization of reproductive tasks, both those geared towards long-term reproduction of the population (i.e. childbearing and child-rearing) and those which maintain daily household function. Even in highly monetized and market-oriented societies, the production of goods and services for household consumption is a key household economic activity. In fact, the participation of household members in the labour force (i.e. in the social process of production) rests on the provision of a considerable amount of domestic work, very often socially invisible, carried out in the "private" realm of the household (Glazer-Malbin, 1976; Michel, 1978; Himmelweit and Mohun, 1977; Jelín, 1984a).

A household is not an undifferentiated set of individuals who equally share all activities linked to its maintenance. It is a social organization, a microcosm of relations of production, reproduction, and distribution. Structured power relations and shared ideology cement the organization and assure its reproduction (cf. Safilios-Rothschild, this volume). Internal differentiation and stratification of households are revealed in the diversity of activities and tasks individual members perform, and in the ways in which goods and services are distributed. Although the household is a unit with a common goal, it is also the locus of divergent interests and capabilities. Both solidarity and conflict are rooted in the social relations governing the intra-household division of labour and distribution of goods and services (Hartmann, 1981). In so far as recruitment criteria are based on kinship and family ties, household organization and its internal division of labour follow the lines of age/sex/kinship distinctions embodied in the Western patriarchal tradition.

Household organization and dynamics can be analysed at two levels: (1) in relation to external political and social institutions; and (2) in relation to the intra-household division of labour and allocation of resources. Regarding the first perspective, societies differ as to how productive and reproductive responsibilities are allocated among social institutions. The question of where the responsibilities of the state, of private enterprises functioning within the free market, and of other non-profit organizations leave off, and those of individual households begin, is an issue of political and ideological importance. At the core of the issue is the social distribution of costs and benefits. In modern times, this question is especially controversial when it comes to deciding who bears the costs of maintaining and reproducing the population: how many state services, and for what sector of the population? What tax structure? How will taxes be spent? Since they are practically powerless to influence the inter-institutional division of responsibility in matters related to these areas, households *adapt* to, rather than struggle against, given conditions. A few neighbourhood or community organizations may be formed to defend local interests, to demand certain public services, or to provide collectively for certain basic needs, but they are not household-based orga-

116

Table 1. Source and type of resources in urban working-class households

Source	Type of resource	
	Monetary	Non-monetary
Work of household members	Labour-force participation	Household production
Formal transfers	Retirement, pensions	Access to public services, indirect subsidies
Informal transfers	Mutual help based on reciprocity in exchange networks	

nizations. The determinants of these institutional changes, although extremely important, will not be treated in this paper. These changes, however, have relevance beyond their impact on the specific economic conditions in a country, in that they usually imply the adoption of significant social policies affecting household tasks.

The second analytical perspective probes the internal dynamics of households. The pertinent issues here are: (1) the intra-household allocation of tasks (division of labour); and (2) the intra-household distribution of goods and services (consumption and expenditure patterns). From the point of view of family well-being, the first is revealed in the way households obtain resources to carry out maintenance and reproductive activities. The second issue is the question of how patterns of consumption are established. Households elaborate mechanisms for the creation, defence, reproduction, and administration of resources. Urban working-class households procure resources in several ways (table 1).

How households combine their various resources and establish strategies for their own defence and improvement can be studied from long-term and short-term perspectives. In the life-cycle framework, when a new household is established (usually at the time of marriage in Western culture), the members provide the new household unit with material goods, ranging from clothes and household equipment to property or dwellings. They also bring "personal capital," their time and working capacities, to be sold on the labour market or utilized in domestic production. Third, they bring "social capital," a network of social relations based on kinship, friendship, and other criteria. Finally, they bring their social and citizenship rights, which give them access to a set of public goods, and their "cultural capital," in the form of information about goods, public services, the market, and how to gain access to them.

Social expectations exist about the progression of household goods over time: better household equipment, more social relations, and more cultural capital. The individual members' working capacities also change with time. The assignment of household members to market or household production is a key element of domestic organization. It can be observed in the division of labour at a given moment, and identified by studying the transitions in the life-cycle of members as they move from one phase of activity (such as studying) to another (gainful employment, for instance).

The assignment of tasks to various members involves a strong ideological "operation" geared to convince the members of their responsibilities to the group and to each other (Safilios-Rothschild, this volume). At stake are decisions affecting the extent of contribution to the common budget of personal income, the performance of domestic chores for the benefit of others, and so on. Moral rewards and punishments, based on traditions and social definitions that ideologically sanction the division of labour be-

117

tween genders and generations, blur the visibility of the authority system, especially in the modern nuclear family where democratic and egalitarian values are acknowledged explicitly, if not observed in practice. Culturally prescribed sex-typing of family roles (i.e. the father being the breadwinner and the mother being responsible for the domestic and reproductive activities), and the social norms governing rights and duties of parents and children, constitute the traditional ideological pillars on which the perpetuation of this internal authority system rests.

The effects of these hidden dimensions of social organization on intra-household processes can only be uncovered through in-depth research on the various domestic activities and practices, on the assignment of household responsibilities, and on control and discipline within the household. Such research must be comprehensive, including: investigation of actual behaviour; verbal descriptions of activities; expressions of norms and values; and ideological contents and meanings (Jelín, Llovet, and Ramos, 1986).

The dynamics of budget and consumption patterns are usually more difficult to grasp than the logic of the division of labour. There is no clear-cut set of cultural norms governing resource distribution as there is for task allocation. In daily life, decisions about consumption are part of a wider pattern of intra-household social relations. And this takes place in a setting where love, affection, duties, and obligations are also present but not easily measured (cf. Engle, Safilios-Rothschild, this volume).

Given the chronic scarcity of monetary resources, bargaining about distribution among household members is an arena of intra-household conflict. Consumption involves constant and recurrent decision-making; it is a function of the flow of earnings, changes in relative prices, and individually felt needs. The division of labour and other arenas of domestic discussion and decision-making are relatively more stable, not requiring daily negotiations. They become subjects of discussion and decision-making during crisis situations (i.e. illness or unemployment) or at times of transition in the life-cycle (i.e. beginning school, childbirth, or leaving home). This is not to say that decisions about the division of labour are conflict-free. On the contrary, conflict over these issues may be particularly intense because it is rooted in deeply felt values and cultural norms. The most obvious example is the conflict over whether a woman "can" or "should" go out to work.

Outside the household, the socio-economic and political context, and its change over time, influences household dynamics. The impact of processes of social change on households can be assessed in two ways: first, the short-term quantitative effects (deterioration or enhancement of the standard of living, and increased or decreased labour-force participation); second, the long-term effects on household dynamics, both on the division of labour and on patterns of consumption.

MICRO-SOCIAL RESEARCH ON HOUSEHOLD ORGANIZATION AND EXPENDITURES IN BUENOS AIRES, ARGENTINA

We used the life-cycle approach to study certain aspects of household dynamics. In our longitudinal empirical study,[2] we first examined activities and tasks in relation to the set of institutional constraints in which households have to adapt. Times of recession, repression, and crisis (such as the study period) often are accompanied by a reduction in social services, increasing the burden on households. We then looked inside the household specifically at consumption and expenditure patterns, disaggregating data according to sex, age, and kinship.

The Setting

During the last decades, political instability in Argentina has been chronic; the economy has gone through drastic ups and downs within a generally recessive framework; and the society has experienced periods of intensive public mobilization followed by harsh repression.[3] The period of military rule, from 1976 to 1983, witnessed profound structural adjustments in the polity, economy, and society. High inflation, limited employment opportunities, and low wages were characteristic. The results for the working classes have been longer working hours, fewer available social services, and more household members in the workforce. At the same time, the government became committed to an ideological shift, the "change of mentalities," intended to destroy collective identities and to replace them with the market-place – the impersonal arena where individuals, never collectivities, exchange their goods and services – as the basic mechanism of social life.

On the political and ideological level, the exclusion of all channels of expression of dissent and the prevalence of fear led to increased levels of uncertainty in personal and family life. Longer-term personal and family plans were postponed while more immediate issues of day-to-day survival came to the forefront. The dimensions of public policy and economic performance most directly affecting the organization and daily life of urban working-class families were: (1) conditions of the labour market; (2) inflation and shifts in relative prices of consumer goods; and (3) provision of public services. Budgeting and planning expenditures became impossible, and consumption patterns changed to follow a different logic. Money was spent as soon as it was earned or became available, often before it reached the pocket of the earner. In low-income families, this contributed to a chronic state of debt, current income being used to pay off previous debts. In sum, under such conditions, the dynamics of consumption seemed to follow both the logic of indebtedness and a strategy of substituting goods and services in response to changes in relative prices.

Little is known about how these conditions affect the behaviour of families and individuals. Although our study offers some hints as to how working-class families live and organize under such constraints, there are limitations to the study. The method can identify issues to explore, but is not suitable for a problem-oriented, focused project evaluation or planning study. First, although the study was longitudinal, it covered a period in which there was comparatively little macro-social change. Because we do not have long-term time-series information about these factors under changing socio-political and economic conditions, it is not possible to separate the effects of the Argentine recession and repression from more stable patterns inherent in working-class life. Second, because we do not have inter-class comparisons, it is impossible to discern whether the findings are peculiar to the working class or would be similar in other social strata. The exploratory nature of the study does allow us to suggest ideas and hypotheses about the range of variation in behavioural patterns, and to present selected methodological considerations. Programme planners and evaluators are encouraged to make use of such studies as a context in which to plan or evaluate projects.

The Research Process

Longitudinal micro-social research can be carried out only on a small number of cases at the same time, given the personalized and committed relationships which must be developed with the subjects. Case selection involves a purposeful search for "meaningful" or conceptually "relevant" cases. Statistical representativeness is thus not part of the research design.[4] The project is in itself a process taking place in time. Three separate stages are carried out simultaneously or with much overlap: information gathering, data formation, and analytical model construction.

First, information gathering is anchored in the inter-personal relationship between researcher and subject. This relationship is an integral part of the overall organization and interpretation of the social reality under study. Initial encounters with the families are geared to gain the researcher access to their everyday life. Enough information is obtained in these encounters to construct a preliminary, albeit naive, picture of the family situation. At this stage in our study, we collected information on personal and social dimensions: household composition, job conditions of the members, access to services, dwelling conditions, kin and networks of social relations, income and expenditures, and so on. Some of the more dramatic and traumatic experiences in family life were shared with the researcher, promoting greater intimacy and trust. As time passed, it became possible to penetrate more deeply into the subjects' reality, not so much by gathering information about new dimensions, as by dealing repeatedly with the same issues, but in more depth. The foundation was thus laid for collecting information about processes of household change: hidden themes and issues emerged that were not disclosed during the initial encounters. The task then proceeded along two lines: we continued gathering new information towards a deeper understanding of the data already obtained, thereby enriching the picture of the subjects' social reality; and we remained open to disclosure of previously hidden aspects of reality. We began to understand the meaning of activities, tasks, and events in the subjects' lives, for the individual, and how this subjective interpretation affected his/her actions. The process of information-gathering is not cumulative and unidirectional; the descriptive picture of everyday life is continuously revised. New pieces of information may produce a reinterpretation of the situation as previously understood, bringing new meanings to the information already gathered. This feedback may even alter the viewpoint from which information is subsequently gathered.

Second, data construction involves the transition from a superficial or "thin" description to a deeper and more complex one (Geertz, 1973). This is done by synthesizing the growing body of information and by incorporating meanings of actions into the description of the subjects' realities. This process of selection, ordering, and re-elaboration of empirical material requires stepping back from that material.

Finally, the construction of analytical models is anchored in the empirical evidence of the range in social patterns. Verbatim quotations from interviews are used in constructing analytical concepts. The quote or description of a given case expresses the typical patterns of behaviour, partially embodied in concrete human beings. The researcher chooses the cases that most clearly express the variability under study, and illustrate the complexity of types encountered in reality.

Results: Priorities in the Satisfaction of Needs and the Micro-social Dynamic of Family Expenditures

Selected results are presented in the next sections to illustrate the dynamics of expenditures during a period of uncertainty in Argentina, as they were revealed in this life-history approach.

The Categories of Expenditure

In periods of high inflation and deteriorating real wages, consumers face chronic instability in the prices of basic articles of consumption. This compounds their difficulties in organizing the budget. Under such conditions, expenses are broken into: daily or "out-of-pocket" expenses, and "fixed" expenses. Pocket expenditures include transportation to and from the workplace or school, food purchased away from home, and cigarettes; they require having cash available each day. Fixed expenditures include those billed monthly: rent, credit payments, electricity, taxes, etc., in addition to goods and services purchased on formal or informal credit. Wage workers usually keep for themselves a certain amount of income for their out-of-pocket expenses before contributing to the family budget. Normally, the wife manages the household budget, but neither she nor members of the household with no personal income (e.g. children, elderly relatives) have access to cash to cover these personal daily costs. Moreover, out-of-pocket expenses seldom are budgeted.

One way in which people handle this apparently chaotic situation is by establishing a direct relationship between the type of earning and the type of expenditure. Obviously, this can occur only in those households where there is more than one source and type of income: the most stable and predictable earnings pay for fixed expenses, and the variable income covers more elastic expenditures.

Two examples:

Family 1

The father is a boot-black with a variable daily income; the daughter is a clerk with a monthly wage. The daughter pays for the rent and electricity; the father gives money daily to the mother for the purchase of food.

Family 2

Several members work and contribute wages to a "common fund" for various expenditures. The mother earns a monthly wage cleaning a school, augmented by her overtime hours which are paid by the week. She uses her overtime income to purchase meat. Her monthly income is put into the "common fund" for fixed expenditures.

In the short run, food is a very elastic consumer need: non-perishable foodstuffs can be accumulated when more money is available or the price is lower; meat consumption is curtailed when less money is available. The purchase of food can also be converted into a fixed expenditure through a system of local credit, the *libreta*.[5] Households receiving their principal income in stable monthly earnings use this type of credit more often. Access to credit in the neighbourhood grocery, however, is limited to cases of occupational and income stability. When family earnings are very scarce, unstable, or unpredictable, the risk run by the store-owner is too great, and access to any form of credit is unavailable.

Two examples:

Family 3
Basic family income is earned by the father, a public servant. He receives a monthly salary, and the second week of every month he gets additional payments for travel expenses. His wife organizes the budget and relies almost exclusively on *libretas* and other forms of monthly payments.

Family 2 (described above)
Given the variety of sources of earnings, they managed without the *libreta*, taking money from the "common fund," and assigned overtime earnings to meat purchases. When the husband's earnings became monthly and he no longer worked overtime, they found it more difficult to plan and manage the monthly budget, so they adopted the use of local credit at the greengrocer's.

Under conditions of recession and scarcity, two alternatives exist: to postpone consumption, or to postpone payment. People might delay home improvements; they might not purchase medicines when needed, but they always pay their electrical bills on time. The purchase of non-durable consumer goods may decline: one buys fewer clothes, less food, or food of lesser quality. Consumption theory suggests that households follow orderly patterns when adapting to declining income. From our study, however, it appears that during periods when money is very scarce, daily consumption is the result of unrelated, on-the-spot decisions, more than of a premeditated consumption plan.

Families seem to follow one line of logic for paying fixed expenditures, related to their links with the creditor, and another for "cash" consumption. The first takes into account the formality of the ties and the potential penalties for default, more than the nature of the goods or services or their urgency. Informal credits are loose; there is some slack in payment deadlines. These credit lines are established through close personal relationships or more distant kinship relationships. Affective-emotional ties may also come into play. Formal debts, on the contrary, are paid more punctually.

The second line depends in some cases on how indispensable the expenditure is, or how long the purchase can be delayed; in others, there appears to be no apparent logic except to spend on "some" thing when "some" money is available. Each individual with access to cash may decide for him/herself, suggesting an alternative to the unified preference function (cf. Becker, 1981; Rosenzweig, this volume). Moreover, there are no clear personal criteria for setting priorities between one and the other type of expenditure. Instalments usually are paid, often before knowing whether there will be any money left over to buy food.

A hierarchy of control over income and expenditures of the different household members is inherent in this dynamic. The power derived from bringing in money tends to be transmitted to decision-making. The members with the most stable work decide on renting a house, purchasing land or consumer durables, and securing the corresponding loans, generally formalized in contracts. Women, through their control of daily expenditures, manage the less formal debts and maintain the networks of infor-

122

mal relations of mutual aid, while men tend to operate in the transactions of the formal market.

The Consumption Patterns

Consumption patterns reveal how households and individual family members exert their power and influence. Moreover, investigating apparently illogical purchases or "overconsumption" of certain types of goods provides a key to understanding the coping strategies families and individuals develop to mitigate the constraints and uncertainty of a recessive economy.

Electrical Appliances

The purchase of electrical appliances is "overloaded" with meanings linked to hiding social subordination and the deterioration of living standards. For low-income households, these purchases constitute evidence that they still have a margin of choice. They can show that their living conditions are not "so" deplorable and unhealthy. For the adult who decides on the purchase, usually the father, to do so indicates his power as a consumer in the market-place and as a provider for the satisfaction needs of his family. For the adolescent who enjoys them and talks about them, the goods are a means of publicly presenting him- or herself and his social condition as relatively privileged. The most pragmatic side of this type of object-purchase is expressed by the mother who views these electrical appliances as an investment. Usually mothers argue that when there is some money, it disappears with no trace if it is not invested in consumer durables. Indeed, they consider that even when the objects are not used, they function as securities because they can always be sold or pawned for cash.

While living spaces tend to be small and crowded, and furniture tends to be old – second-hand purchases or hand-me-downs from relatives – electrical appliances are numerous and constantly accumulated. They are acquired solely through their purchase in the market-place, but in cases of emergency (a broken iron or sewing machine) they can be obtained by loan or transfer through informal networks. They are not part of those public goods and services that can be received by "right" or through charity; these are privately acquired goods for family use. Each appliance has a certain use-value which contributes to family well-being: saving domestic labour (refrigerators, washing machines), improving access to information or contributing to recreation (television, record-player, tape-recorder).

Although the use-value influences the decision to purchase, additional factors explain the abundance of appliances in the homes of the popular sectors.[6] For several decades, the Argentine working-class family has been able to acquire the basic home appliances such as refrigerators, gas stoves, radios, and sewing machines. In the last few years, goods of a distinctive nature have been added, namely objects which are tied to the leisure time of the young: cassette-players, colour televisions, and record-players. Access to these new consumer goods, which until recently were seen as luxuries for the rich, function as a mechanism to compensate for, and/or hide, the deterioration in public services such as health and education.

In macro-social terms, the meaning of these appliances cannot be derived from a theory that sets out "basic human needs" and studies the historically and culturally specific "satisfiers" of these needs. As Leiss (1976) pointed out, the character of human needs cannot be comprehended without explicit reference to the actual means and ways in which they are satisfied in particular social systems. These objects are therefore tangible evidence of the logic of a consumer society, in which individuals orient their needs toward the type of satisfactions embodied in a growing number and variety of goods.

Clothing

The contrast observed in clothing between different family members is enormous. Pre-school children dress practically in rags. The mother wears very worn and old clothes in the house, while maintaining a "presentable" outfit if she works outside. The father is usually somewhat better dressed, in view of his greater presence outside the house. But, without a doubt, adolescents are the best dressed. Their clothing is not only in good condition and clean, but it always follows the latest fashion.

Teenagers' clothing is a subject of permanent discussion and decision-making in the family circle. The adolescents plead, demand, order, and appear to have power in decisions regarding their own clothing. They do not directly control the money, but they demand it in such a way that their parents finally give in to pressure. The desires and needs of the young adults also dominate in decisions to purchase electrical appliances, records, and cassettes. How is it possible for adolescents to have so much influence over decisions on expenditures? It should be noted that we are not speaking of the young who work and spend their own earnings, but of dependents who have no earnings of their own. Why do parents give in to such an extent?

Undoubtedly there are altruistic feelings on the part of parents, who feel satisfaction when they see their children happy with the things they like to have. But the family interaction around this subject seems to reflect the acceptance of adolescent clothing as a "need." Why? It is our contention that a mechanism of "public presentation" of the family operates through the adolescents. They are the ones who participate most in commercial leisure activities, who go out most, who have the most contacts outside kinship circles. That a son or daughter would "have nothing to wear" or not be able to go dancing for lack of money would be a very obvious manifestation of failure. This is not considered a failure of the young but rather it is parents who view it as their own by not giving their children what they need.[7]

CONCLUSIONS

Our experience with the life-history method and the in-depth longitudinal study of households leaves many more questions than answers, especially answers applicable to the general population. None the less, we consider this methodology essential to raise for consideration issues that are taken for granted or seldom questioned in the most common household studies.

While census reports and large-scale surveys simply describe household composition and organization, our study shows very clearly how much can be gained in analytical depth if the two dimensions of household organization, namely the patterns of intra-household division of labour and of internal allocation of resources, are studied in and of themselves, rather than having assumptions made about them that are based simply on household composition.[8]

Second, the introduction of a time perspective into household studies has very often been limited to time-budgets, i.e. the allocation of time to different activities on a daily basis. We disaggregated the various dimensions of time: daily time, biographical time, family time, and historical time. The detailed focus on time-budgets tends to mask longer-term processes. It is important to realize that these longer-term dimensions and their effects are present in all instances of activity, and do not constitute a separate object of analysis from that of everyday life. This systematic analysis and combination of the various time dimensions allows for a constant consideration of development and change, bringing to light processes that otherwise remain hidden and invisible.

Finally, this type of study demonstrates the importance of the interrelationship between households and their environment. Households are open social structures, moulded and transformed both by their internal dynamics and by external factors. Although for analytical purposes it may be convenient to draw boundaries to households and talk about "household composition" as given, a dynamic perspective has to focus on the way external forces – changes in social policies, the general macroeconomic and political conditions, specific development programmes and projects – interact with intra-household dynamics in shaping a household response. Any study concentrating its analytical efforts inside the household must also study the specific ways in which households as units and their individual members enter into significant relationships with other institutions.

NOTES

1. The processes examined and exemplified in the present paper are more fully analysed in Jelín, 1984c.
2. Research methods: Data were collected through in-depth interviews and participant observation. During the three-year study period (1979–1982) a four-person research team frequently visited 15 low-income households in Greater Buenos Aires. All adults and adolescent members of the household were interviewed repeatedly, and these interviews were complemented by observations of household activities under a variety of circumstances. Most interviews were tape-recorded, and although there were thematic guidelines in most cases, the interviews were open-ended and often did not follow the format that the researcher had in mind.

   Guidelines were developed for the collection of life-histories, for dwelling histories, for weekly changes in household activities and patterns, for monetary and time budgets. The exact use of the guidelines in actual data gathering was not a priority of the study. Rather, the respondent's own views, criteria, and discourse took precedence over the systematic recording of data based on analytical categories and questions.

   Given the focus of the study on daily activities and household organization, the primary respondents, with whom the rapport was established and maintained during the period of field-work, were the women in charge of the domestic tasks.

   The larger study on which this report is based has led to a series of papers and publications devoted to specific theoretical, methodological, and empirical issues. These include: Jelín and Feijoo (1980); Ramos (1981, 1982); Feijoo (1983); Llovet (1984); Jelín (1984a, 1984b, 1984c); and Jelín, Llovet, and Ramos (1986). The study was funded by PISPAL, Ford Foundation, ILO, Inter-American Foundation, IDRC, and CLACSO.
3. Political and economic characteristics of Argentina after the Second World War can be found in O'Donnell (1976) and Canitrot (1975). On the more recent period, see Canitrot (1980, 1981), Landi (1982), and Rouquie (1982).
4. The issues discussed in this section are discussed at length in Jelín, Llovet, and Ramos, 1986.
5. The *libreta* is a form of credit in a specific establishment (neighbourhood grocery, vegetable stand, meat market, etc.) or with a household delivery service (soda, milk, wine, etc.). Acquired goods are listed in the booklet each day. Payment is made according to the periodicity in which family income is received. The *libreta* system converts the purchase of basic food-

stuffs into a "fixed" expenditure to be paid monthly along with the rent, taxes, electricity, and commercial credit payments.
6. It is necessary to distinguish phases in the period covered by this study. During 1979–1980, with the free-trade policy, the market was "flooded" with imported electrical appliances, including products new to Argentine consumption (sound equipment and colour television). Families from the popular sectors were active buyers in this market. The deep recession of the later period led to a severe decline in the sale of these products. What we are describing was the case during 1979–1980 and does not apply to the later period.
7. Parents' emphasis on wanting their adolescent children to start working and earning their own income is not based on their direct contribution to the family budget, but on their ability to buy more or better clothing without stressing the family budget. In family 2, the adolescent daughter did not work outside the home. The mother said that, if she got a job, "she could buy what she want[ed], because we buy her what we can but not all she wants." The father did not want his daughter to work and to support his negative view he compensated her with money to buy clothes whenever he was paid. In family 4, the mother complained constantly that her son made demands but did not take seriously his search for work. Not that he should contribute to the family budget, but should have an income to pay for whatever "pleasures he wants to give himself," which range from shampoo and deodorant to tickets for a Queen concert and the latest style in bluejeans.
8. This is especially clear in the way the category "household head" has been constructed and utilized. Usually, the existence of an adult male in the household is taken as an indication of his role as household head, without any further questioning as to the division of labour and the allocation of resources (Jelín, 1982).

REFERENCES

Balán, J., and E. Jelín. 1979. *La estructura social en la biografía personal*. Estudios CEDES. CEDES, Buenos Aires.

Becker, G.S. 1981. *A Treatise on the Family*. Harvard University Press, Cambridge, Mass.

Canitrot, A. 1975. La experiencia populista de redistribución de ingresos. *Desarrollo económico*, 15(59).

———. 1980. *La disciplina como objetivo de la política económica. Un esayo sobre el programa de gobierno argentino desde 1976*. Estudios CEDES. CEDES, Buenos Aires.

———. 1981. *Teoría y practica del liberalismo. Política antiinflacionaria y apertura económica en la Argentina, 1976–1981*. Estudios CEDES. CEDES, Buenos Aires.

Elder, G.H. 1975. Age Differentiation and the Life Course. *Ann. Rev. Soc.*, 1(1): 165–90.

———. 1978. Approaches to Social Change and the Family. *Am. J. Soc.*, 84 (Suppl.): S1.

Feijoo, M. del C. 1983. *Buscando un techo. Familia y vivienda popular*. Estudios CEDES, CEDES, Buenos Aires.

Geertz, C. 1973. *The Interpretation of Cultures*. Basic Books, New York.

Glazer-Malbin, N. 1976. Housework. *Signs*, 1(4): 905–922.

Glick, P.C. 1947. The Family Cycle. *Am. Soc. Rev.*, 12(2): 164–174.

Hareven, T. 1977. Family Time and Historical Time. *Daedalus*, 106: 57–70.

Hartmann, H.I. 1981. The Family as the Locus of Gender, Class, and Political Struggle: The Example of Housework. *Signs*, 6(3): 366–394.

Himmelwelt, S., and S. Mohun. Domestic Labour and Capital. *Camb. J. Econ.*, 1(1): 15–31.

Jelín, E. 1982. *Coping with Uncertainty: The Role of Women in Households*. Estudios CEDES. CEDES, Buenos Aires.

Jelín, E. 1984a. *Familia y unidad domestica. Mundo publico y vida privada*. Estudios CEDES. CEDES, Buenos Aires.

———. 1984b. Daily Lives of Urban Women. In: Unesco, *Women on the Move*. Unesco, Paris.

———. 1984c. Las relaciones sociales del consumo: El caso de las unidades domesticas de sectores populares. In: CEPAL, *La mujer en el sector popular urbano: America Latina y el Caribe*. CEPAL, Santiago.

Jelín, E., and M. del C. Feijoo. 1980. *Trabajo y familia en el ciclo de vida femenino: El caso de los sectores populares de Buenos Aires*. Estudios CEDES. CEDES, Buenos Aires.

Jelín, E., J.J. Llovet, and S. Ramos. 1986. Un estilo de trabajo: La investigación microsocial. In: *Problemas metodologicos en la investigación sociodemografica*. PISPAL/El Colegio de México, Mexico City.

Landi, O. 1982. Conjeturas políticas sobre la Argentina post Malvinas. Mimeo. CEDES, Buenos Aires.

Leiss, W. 1976. *The Limits of Satisfaction: An Essay on the Problem of Needs and Commodities*. University of Toronto Press, Toronto.

Llovet, J.J. 1984. *Servicios de salud y sectores populares. Los anos del proceso*. Estudios CEDES. CEDES, Buenos Aires.

Michel, A. 1978. *Les femmes dans la société marchande*. PUF, Paris.

O'Donnell, G. 1976. Estado y alianzas en la Argentina, 1956–1976. Documento de trabajo 5. CEDES, Buenos Aires.

Ramos, S. 1981. *Las relaciones de parentesco o de ayuda mutua en los sectores populares urbanos. Un estudio de caso*. Estudios CEDES. CEDES, Buenos Aires.

——. 1982. *Maternidad en Buenos Aires: La experiencia popular*. Estudios CEDES. CEDES, Buenos Aires.

Rouquie, A., ed. 1982. *Argentina, hoy*. Siglo XXI, Mexico City.

III. Measurement of Key Variables

Measurement of Key Variables

BEATRICE LORGE ROGERS AND NINA P. SCHLOSSMAN

The conceptual frameworks presented in part I identified a series of issues related to the question of how a proposed policy change or new programme might alter intra-household processes, and whether these alterations might affect the success of the project and the welfare of individuals involved, directly or indirectly, in the change. The following set of questions was derived from these frameworks as a way of organizing data collection for the analysis of project effects on households and individuals:

1. Who will participate in the project's activities?
2. Will the project require or cause a change in household structure, composition, or function?
3. Will the project change any person's access to productive resources or any person's control over what is produced (including control over income from his/her labour)?
4. Will the project affect any person's wage rate (returns to labour) or the rate of return to assets under any person's control?
5. Will the project require changes in the inventory of tasks performed by household members, or in the organization of tasks?
6. Will the project change the allocation of tasks among members or the time use of members?
7. Will the project change any person's access to consumption goods (food, health care, education, etc.) which affect individual welfare?

The relevance of these questions to programme planning is discussed in part I. The need to answer the first question should be self-evident: participants must first be identified before their behaviour can be predicted. The question of household structure is important because of the potential for resistance to or rejection of the project (see Safilios-Rothschild's paper in this section), and because it may indicate how project benefits may be dispersed. Fundamental changes in the household may also cause emotional stress, as discussed by Messer in part I and by Safilios-Rothschild in this section. Moreover, a change in household composition, such as male outmigration or the physical separation of nuclear from extended family units, may increase the work burden on remaining members (by reducing the possibilities for sharing tasks), the

131

income on which they can draw, the resources available to them, and the possibilities for support during an emergency.

The question of individual access to income and capital is key because of the potential harm that projects may do to certain categories of idividuals if this issue is not resolved equitably. Since different individuals have distinct priorities for the uses of income, and since the person who earns the income generally has a greater degree of control over its uses, altering access to income may also have significant consequences for the ways in which income is used (see the papers by Messer, Engle, Behrman, Bennett, and Safilios-Rothschild for further discussion).

The task allocation and time-use questions are related. Time burdens may reduce or prevent participation in the project, or may interfere with the performance of other tasks equally important to the welfare of household members. For example, a project which imposes increased demands on a mother's time may reduce the amount of time she can spend in child care, including food preparation and feeding. This reasoning applies to all household members. An employment or schooling project, for instance, takes children's labour time away from the household, increasing the work burden of remaining members, and possibly reducing the total amount of time devoted to particular tasks.

Answering these questions requires information on a variety of specific key variables:

1. Household structure and composition.
2. Individual incomes (cash, in-kind).
3. Individual and household asset ownership.
4. Tasks performed and their allocation among members.
5. Uses of individuals' time.
6. Allocation of consumption goods among household members.

Some of these variables are best measured using a qualitative approach, while others are more suited to quantitative methods. The papers in part II addressed these methodological approaches, along with their advantages and limitations for identifying aspects of intra-household processes.

The papers in this section confront the problems of measuring the key variables and propose some solutions. In the first paper, Heywood discusses the difficulty of applying any single definition of the household, especially if it is not specific to the culture being studied. He suggests that, rather than attempt a fixed definition of the household, one should record information on individual members in such a way that the individual can be assigned to any of several differently defined and possibly overlapping household units, depending on the requirements of the specific analysis or project.

The other papers deal with the measurement of specific variables which are particularly critical to intra-household-level analysis. Time and income are the two major categories of resources available to a household. Measurement of income and of time use are therefore central to any study of resource allocation within households. Johnson reviews and discusses the pros and cons of time-use and task-allocation methods, and emphasizes the importance of standardizing measurement techniques. Reflecting the concerns expressed by Scrimshaw, he underlines the importance of validating recall or descriptive data with structured direct observation of time use. Zeitlin, in her paper, suggests that, when direct observation is not possible, there are ways of making recall data more reliable by incorporating local perceptions of time and its

132

measurement. These papers together confirm the importance of defining variables for measurement using both the outsider's (etic) and the local culture's (emic) perspectives, as discussed earlier by Messer.

The measurement of income and asset-ownership is not specifically addressed in these papers. Measurement of household income is treated in a variety of publications, but there are certain principles which are of particular importance to analysis at the intra-household level. First, Rosenzweig argues persuasively that income must be measured for the individual earner, and that wage rates as well as total earnings are important for assessing the relative value of household members' time. Because wage rates are a major determinant of resource allocation patterns, it is important to know what proportion of income is earned (and thus affects the value of time in all its uses), and what proportion is obtained from other sources, such as transfers or returns to wealth.

Jelín's paper stresses the importance of the timing and reliability of income as determinants of its use. It is important to know whether income is received weekly, daily, or seasonally, and whether it comes from steady employment or from irregular, occasional work. Messer and Engle in their conceptual frameworks, and Bennett and Safilios-Rothschild in their papers, contend that both the size of an individual's economic contribution to the household and the degree of his/her economic independence are significant determinants of that person's access to household resources and his/her control over the consumption and allocation decisions of the household. This perception is based on the conflict-resolution model of household decision-making. It is not only earned income which affects an individual's degree of economic independence. Unearned income may also be attributable to a single individual in the household, as when a son sends remittances to one parent, or when one member of a couple receives transfers or access to productive resources from his/her natal family.

For intra-household analysis, income and assets should be associated with the individual responsible for them, if possible. Measurement of income is notoriously difficult, both because it is a sensitive subject about which respondents may be unwilling to talk, and because in many cases they may simply not know how much income they earn. For purposes of assessing the relative contributions of individuals within the household, approximate amounts are enough; absolute accuracy is not necessary.

Allocation of consumption goods is another category of information needed to assess the effects of development projects on individual household members. In this section, Pinstrup-Andersen and Garcia evaluate several measures of food consumption, and conclude that household-level food consumption information is a very poor proxy for individual consumption levels. Their results underscore the importance of individual-level data for the assessment of intra-household patterns. Food is in some ways the best indicator of allocation of consumption goods: consumption of health-care and educational services is conditional on a variety of factors, including service availability and perceived need. But all households at every economic level consume food, and food represents a critical element in human capital formation in addition to being a consumption item.

The final paper in this section deals with the measurement of a variable which is much harder to define, but no less important. We know that development interventions introduce changes in the economic and social environment that cause households to adapt in a variety of ways, reallocating tasks, responsibilities, roles, and access to consumption. In order to assess the probable effects of an intervention, planners would like to predict just how the reallocation will occur, who will gain and lose, and in what ways. Safilios-Rothschild addresses the question of how to predict the degree and direction of adaptation in households to a given project-induced change. She focuses on one particular aspect of household adaptation, the relative power of men and women, and suggests that households will accept the changes induced by development programmes more readily if the changes do not visibly alter the distribution of power.

In this argument Safilios-Rothschild disagrees with Bennett and with Engle, who suggest that the visibility of a woman's economic contribution is precisely what enhances her decision-making power. However, she agrees with Rosenzweig that individual time-use may adapt more readily than a person's sense of power. This may be an indication of the phenomenon discussed by Engle, that behaviour changes more readily than attitudes, and that the traditional knowledge-attitudes-practices model should really start with behaviour change.

The papers in this section demonstrate that a focus on intra-household allocation, in both implementation and research, poses unique measurement questions, many of which have yet to be resolved. Some problems, such as defining the household, are simply intractable; the solution lies in redefining the objective. In the case of measuring food consumption and income, short-cut methods are not available; there is no way around the need to expend additional effort to get the information required for intra-household analysis. A meassage inherent in all these papers is that responsible planning involves addressing the measurement questions directly; the need for intra-household analysis, and its pay-off in terms of programme success, merit the extra effort.

9
Multiple Group Membership and Intra-household Resource Allocation

PETER HEYWOOD

Papua New Guinea Institute of Medical Research, Madang, Papua New Guinea

INTRODUCTION TO THE PROBLEM OF MULTIPLE GROUP MEMBERSHIP

The field of anthropology is responsible for much of what we know about how families and households function in different cultural settings (see Messer's discussion of intra-household dynamics in the context of anthropology in part I). However, defining the household is far from straightforward (Messer, 1983). Is a household a reference group defined by those who live together? Under one roof? Who sleep there? Who eat at the same table? Who contribute money (income) to the common coffer? Or is the household defined in terms of members' kinship ties? Often a member of a household is also a member of several other reference groups, depending on the task at hand. Can these multiple group memberships be taken into account in studying the household unit?

Household composition, structure, and function vary among and within cultures and within individual households over time. In many cultures, the functions we associate with "the household" in a Western context are divided among several reference groups. This means that defining the household, no easy task in any setting because of the fluidity of boundaries over time, also depends on the particular household function of interest. Thus, recognizing that there is no single definition of "household" which will serve all purposes, this paper addresses the particular problem of assigning, to a given individual, membership in a variety of reference groups, each of which may be considered a household for some purposes. Examples are taken from our work and experience in the subsistence cultures of Papua New Guinea (PNG).

In many cultures, there is an interplay between the members of a household and the resources they bring in. The resources are generated through group as well as individual processes, and each individual may be a member of several different groups. Food production, food consumption, health-care behaviour, and cash income generation are group processes that may be performed within very different reference groups, even within a given cultural and economic setting. The groups, whose memberships cut across the boundaries of the primary household unit, may make demands on the individual's time for joint processes. In return, the individual gets his or her share of the resources (food, income, etc.) generated by the group effort. These resources are then brought into the household, that is, the primary group to which the individual belongs.[1] Resources can be time, cash, or consumable goods.

Development policies seeking to affect these resources cannot ignore multiple group membership. Policy-makers and programme planners as well as survey researchers must take this into account in order to identify correctly target individuals for programmes, or respondents for research. The most effective programme designs incorporate an understanding of intra-household dynamics and the individual members' relationships. Since (1) the household is not a static unit, (2) different groups may be formed according to specific tasks being performed, and (3) an individual member can be part of several different (perhaps overlapping) units depending on the task at hand, the household may be defined differently depending on the aims of the project or investigation.

For instance, nutritionists and programme planners focusing on food and nutrient consumption often define the household in terms of "eating units" or "food budget units" (Messer, 1983). We used this approach in our study of changes in food intake patterns over 25 years in a village in the Simbu Province of PNG (Harvey and Heywood, 1983). We defined a household as the group of people who ate together in the same house, since the aim of the study was a comparison of *individual* food intakes with earlier data on individual food consumption patterns.

MULTIPLE GROUP MEMBERSHIP IN SUBSISTENCE CULTURES IN PNG

In societies which are at least partly dependent on subsistence production, household members who eat together are not always part of the same unit(s) that produced the food for the household. Projects seeking to effect changes in consumption and production, then, cannot assume that the same unit (identical members) is always responsible for both food production and consumption. Although in many parts of the highlands of PNG the consumption group would also be a production unit, there are variations. For instance, in Southern Highlands Province, Huli men grow and cook their own food while women and children eat food produced by the women (Brown, 1978).

Elsewhere in PNG, the pattern differs. The Garia in Southern Madang Province (Lawrence, 1984) engage in shifting cultivation, clearing and cultivating new sites each year. Plots are prepared by groups working with a garden leader, generally a middle-aged man, experienced in co-ordinating the activities of his fellow workers, and recognized as a performer of successful agricultural rituals. At the beginning of the agricultural year, he may seek out associates to work with him, or he may announce publicly that he intends to clear bush in a particular area. Those who desire to work with this leader then approach him in the next few days to form a team.

Members of the Garia food production unit are not grouped by kinship ties. Agnates (i.e. members of the paternal family line) rarely work together in the same garden. A nuclear family also rarely works together: husband, wife, and adolescent children may even plant on separate sites. Moreover, an individual may work with more than one garden leader. The result is that a single nuclear family, through its individual members, may be associated for the period of the agricultural cycle, approximately 18 months, with distant kin and non-kin in up to six food-producing gardens. Among the Garia, then, a household as defined by kinship, resource-sharing, or common dwelling, might be represented by its individual members in a number of food-production units. The total amount of food produced by the household is therefore derived from several gardens through the participation of its members.

There is yet a different pattern of food production in Western Madang Province (Rappaport, 1984). Here, the Tsembaga men and women co-operate in making gardens, and usually work in pairs: a woman may make more than one garden with different men, including her husband, her own or her husband's unmarried brothers, or her widowed father. Likewise, a man may cultivate several plots with his wife, his or her unmarried sisters, or his widowed mother. As among the Garia, the total food consumed by a Tsembaga household is produced through the participation of individual household members in several, though smaller, food-producing units. It is clear that defining the household in such a subsistence setting is not straightforward: the food-producing and consuming units are not identical. A project seeking to affect food consumption must address the various roles which an individual has as a member of multiple groups.

Decision-making which ultimately affects the level of household resources is also determined in part by household and multiple group membership. Clearing and initial preparation of the land are generally group activities in which the adult members of a number of households participate. Heavy work like felling trees is usually carried out by the male members. The type and amount of ground that can be cleared is determined by the size of the group and the characteristics of its members, particularly of the men. Thus, many of the decisions affecting household food production, and consequently the amount of food within the household, will be made by the production group, a different group from the primary dwelling or consumption unit. If the male household head is absent, there may be a very marked reduction of the total resources available at the household level. In contrast, food consumption decisions, given the available quantities of food, tend to be made within the household of an individual wife and her children.

CODING SYSTEM FOR RECORDING INDIVIDUAL AND GROUP MEMBERSHIP

In PNG, we have attempted to incorporate multiple group membership into a general system of recording information on household members. This coding system is currently in use in the larger population studies being carried out by the Papua New Guinea Institute for Medical Research (PNGIMR). It is informed by anthropologic data which indicates that the larger populations are organized into clans, subclans, and families.[2] This pattern of settlement varies among geographic areas. In the Tari Basin (Riley, 1979), the settlement is dispersed; in Eastern Highlands Province, it is in villages that correspond to subclans. A seven-digit census number incorporating the anthropologically derived relevant subgroup memberships is assigned to each individual for use in large-scale surveys. The first two digits of the code indicate the clan, the third the subclan, and the fourth and fifth identify the heads of household within the subclan. The sixth and seventh digits represent the individual, as follows:

−01: male head of household;

−10: first wife of head of household;
−11: first child of first wife of head of household;
−12: second child of first wife of head of household;
−20: second wife of head of household;
−21: first child of second wife of head of household;
−22: second child of second wife of head of household;

and so on. Thus, census number 5120910 identifies an individual who is a member of clan 51, of its second subclan, and of the ninth household within subclan 2. She is the first wife of the head of household 9.

The system allows easy identification of the major groups to whom individuals belong through the census number, which is unique to each individual. As an individual's status changes (e.g. through marriage), his or her census number changes, but previous numbers are also recorded, allowing cross-checking and identification of changes of status over time. This system has been used in the Tari Basin for approximately 15 years, and, over time, it has become clear that too much information was being stored in the census number. This number has been retained, but now it indicates only the current status of the individual. Old numbers are kept on file and can be used for cross-referencing and tracing changes in status over time. A separate, unique ID number is now used for each individual.

This coding method has been successfully modified for use in other geographic areas with different settlement patterns, although the basic principle remains the same. Such a system could also easily be modified for other purposes by adding digits to represent membership in other production or consumption units. For example, the first wife of the head of household 9 might also be identified as a member of a particular group of market women, or as a participant in her brother's gardening unit. An ethnographic study would be needed to identify the reference groups of interest; this would be used to define relevant groups. The resulting coding system could be applied in a larger-scale survey.

This system is one approach that has been successfully used in large-scale, longitudinal, epidemiologic, and demographic studies in several populations in PNG. Other approaches may be more useful in other populations. This does, however, in conjunction with other information, allow membership of some groups within the community to be recorded efficiently. Other communities with other bases of group membership will require different ethnographically derived systems for recording membership. The principles, none the less, remain the same.

It is obviously impossible to try to devise one system for recording household members which will fit every need. In large-scale studies with multiple objectives (even when they appear closely related, such as household food consumption, production and expenditure studies), it is particularly important to be able to derive multiple definitions of group membership from the information recorded in the individual's record so that macro- and micro-studies can be co-ordinated. This will facilitate the most efficient two-way flow of information between large- and small-scale studies on the same overlapping populations and samples.

CONCLUSIONS

The examples of work done in PNG illustrate the importance of identifying multiple group membership for studying the intra-household allocation of resources and other intra-household dynamics. Such studies can clearly benefit from combining the methods of anthropology with those of other relevant disciplines (cf. Messer; Engle; Scrimshaw; Safilios-Rothschild, in this volume). Ethnographic investigations are necessary to determine the extent and nature of multiple group membership, and to generate initial and specific hypotheses about its nature and effects on intra-household processes. Testing the hypotheses in a broader context and in a wider population will often depend on operationalizing definitions of group membership in such a way that information can be collected on large numbers of individuals by people who have little or no training in ethnography. The specific group memberships to be recorded will depend on the household process being investigated. It will not usually be possible to collect and code information on all memberships related to all intra-household allocative processes; it will be necessary to select the specific processes for study, and to identify the effects of specific memberships on them. So long as the studies are set up to look at specific effects and to test specific hypotheses, the data coding and analysis should be relatively straightforward. The important point is that the design of macro-studies should be influenced by the results of micro-studies, and vice versa. This is essential if the effects of very diverse social, economic, and biological phenomena on intra-household resource allocation are to be understood.

A similar co-ordination between the two types of studies is important in understanding the allocation of resources within households. Anthropologic insights about the nature of groups to which an individual belongs, and the demands he or she makes on the group and vice versa, should help identify the information to be collected on the larger population in order to make realistic determinations of multiple group membership. Large-scale studies of their effect on intra-household processes should then be possible. A system of recording members, which allows precise multiple definitions of the many groups to which the various members of the household belong, may permit a single study to be used for an even wider and more diverse set of aims and objectives.

NOTES

1. For some activities, individuals keep control of the (monetary) resources they bring into the household; in others, the resources are pooled within the primary group.
2. Clans and subclans are localized, territorial patrilineal groups and, depending on size and area, they may form all or part of a village. Alternatively, the settlement pattern may be dispersed.

REFERENCES

Brown, P. 1978. *Highland Peoples of New Guinea.* Cambridge University Press, Cambridge.
Harvey, P., and P. Heywood. 1983. Twenty-five Years of Dietary Change in Simbu Province, Papua New Guinea. *Ecol. Fd. Nutr.*, 13: 27–35.
Lawrence, P. 1984. *The Garia: An Ethnography of a Traditional Cosmic System in Papua New Guinea.* Melbourne University Press, Melbourne.
Messer, E. 1983. The Household Focus in Nutritional Anthropology: An Overview. *Fd. Nutr. Bull.*, 5(4): 2–12.
Rappaport, R. 1984. *Pigs for the Ancestors: Ritual in the Ecology of a New Guinea People.* New, enlarged edition. Yale University Press, New Haven, Conn.
Riley, I.D. 1979. Pneumonia in Papua New Guinea. M.D. thesis. University of Sydney.

10
Time-allocation Research:
The Costs and Benefits of Alternative Methods

ALLEN JOHNSON

Department of Anthropology, University of California, Los Angeles, California, USA

INTRODUCTION

Many social scientists are converging in their focus on detailed accurate descriptions of everyday behaviour. In the past, theory has tended to concentrate on activities outside the home (i.e. in the workplace, school, hospital, or church), and has paid correspondingly little attention to behaviour within the home. Although such focused theoretical social-science research is valuable, it may miss important areas of study. First, human activities that are not currently at the centre of theoretical or policy debates may be overlooked. For example, until recently, activities taking place within the household (including housework, food preparation and distribution, and child care), as well as the division of labour by age and sex, suffered such neglect. Second, activities that may provide a context in which to understand the focal variables of the research are overlooked. For example, when a married woman with children takes on gainful employment, every aspect of home life and all members of the household are bound to be significantly affected by changes in the allocation of her time and resources. Knowing the amount of time a woman spends at work, or at any other single task, is therefore not sufficient to understand the effect of her working on the household. We need to understand how gainful employment affects her total *allocation* of time, how she partitions her time, how she organizes and sequences tasks, and how other family members reallocate and reorganize their time (or fail to do so).

Social-science research has increasingly turned to research methods which can describe broadly defined human activity patterns, in particular time allocation. A relatively new focus of social research, time allocation is currently measured with a wide range of specific methods, each having its own strengths and limitations. In this paper, I will first discuss the basic goals of research on time use, and then briefly indicate the "trade-offs" of the several quite distinct research techniques that have been used to measure time allocation. Finally, I will suggest certain rules of thumb for ensuring that findings from research on time allocation can be used most effectively by project planners and policy-makers.

140

TIME-ALLOCATION RESEARCH: AN OVERVIEW

Time-allocation data are important for comparing patterns of human behaviour across diverse settings. Time is a "currency" we know how to measure accurately by the clock, irrespective of our research subjects or the settings in which we study them. Given that time is such a natural, universal, and objective scale of measurement (if one is using a clock), it is perhaps surprising that time allocation is not universally studied in comparative behavioural research. But social scientists do not carelessly neglect promising research methods. The reasons for the limited use of time-allocation research include shortcomings of existing data and current data-collection methods. The specifics of those shortcomings indicate the directions such research must take in the future.

The Unfulfilled Promise of Time-allocation Research

Time-allocation research, the effort to gather reliable and valid data on how people spend their time in the ordinary course of their lives, has grown with astonishing rapidity over the past decade (As, 1978; Andorka et al., 1983; Gross, 1984). Social scientists in several disciplines have made systematic, detailed behavioural descriptions of time use. The recent dramatic increase in computing power has made it practical to organize and process large datasets with thousands of individual observations, and has no doubt contributed to the growing interest in collecting time-allocation data. Yet little attention has been paid to standardizing techniques. Researchers devise their own individualized methods of measuring time allocation, making it difficult for other researchers and policy-makers to understand what they have done or to use the data for comparisons across cultures, economic systems, social categories, or political boundaries.

Within limits, a proliferation of research strategies is a sign of healthy growth and creativity in this relatively new field. Successful research requires techniques to be creatively fine-tuned to different settings. Furthermore, experience with a variety of methods is necessary to assess their relative costs and benefits. This methodological variety, however, has hindered our ability to compare results between studies and thus strengthen existing theories and make appropriate policy decisions. Findings from numerous individual studies of time allocation have been published, but it is difficult to draw comparisons between them, owing to differences in how the data were collected, and how the results were reported. Resolving the following specific problems in time-allocation research would significantly enhance the comparability, and thus the usefulness, of these studies.

First, primary time-allocation data, from which behavioural patterns of given populations are compiled, and the specific definitions used to code the primary data into activities are almost never available for examination. Hence, it is impossible to know how actual behaviour was transformed into primary data, and how the primary data were grouped to form the categories in the published tables. For example, two unrelated studies might report that fathers in each case spent 5 per cent of their time in "child care." But one might code "father plays ball with son" as "child care," while another might code the same activity as "recreation." Thus we would not know the specific behaviours each researcher counted as "child care" and we could not conclude that fathers in each of the two cases spent comparable times in child care.

Second, methods of sampling the subjects of time-allocation research are seldom reported, leading to difficulties in assessing the representativeness of the sample. Most time-allocation researchers are well aware of the principles of sampling, but have not reached a consensus on what sampling techniques are most appropriate to this kind of research.

Third, most studies report the general technique by which the data were gathered (e.g. 24-hour recall, diaries filled out by the research subjects themselves, random "spot checks" of directly observed behaviour), but provide little information about how their techniques bias the data or to what degree any given method is capable of replicating the results of the others.

Fourth, for interpreting results it is crucial to know how each technique is related to its ethnographic setting, and how varying methods of data collection influence possibilities for data analysis. For example, in some research settings it is easy and natural to drop in casually in both public and private settings to make momentary observations ("spot checks") of individual activities; in others it is inappropriate or simply impossible. If informant reports must be used instead of direct observations, a substantially different kind of data is collected, and this must be analysed and interpreted accordingly.

For these reasons, although scores of time-allocation datasets are now available from virtually every kind of cultural and economic system around the world, very few comparative studies have been published. Indeed, the few that have been usually involve comparisons between communities that were studied in a single research project, using the same methods (e.g. Gross et al., 1979; Szalai et al., 1972). When comparisons among studies are made (e.g. Minge-Klevana, 1980), they require questionable assumptions (for example, that "work" has been defined comparably in each study), and the lack of standardization leaves their conclusions open to challenge.

To begin to unify the field, at the University of California at Los Angeles we are creating a standardized cross-cultural time-allocation database.[1] Time-allocation studies from all areas of the world and levels of societal complexity are compiled into monographs that provide the original data (on computer diskette), as collected by the field researchers, as well as the same data translated into a standardized coding format to facilitate comparison between studies. The monographs also describe sampling and coding methods, a census of the research population, and an extensive summary of background information on environment, economy, social organization, culture, and the encompassing political system (cf. Johnson and Johnson, 1987).

The monographs and the database should prove to be excellent tools for use in project identification and design. An initial understanding of time-use patterns and constraints could be obtained from time-allocation studies previously done at the proposed project site, or in another similar type of society, helping to define the problem and to assess the feasibility of alternative interventions.

Time-allocation Research: A Theoretical Framework

Time-allocation research has the potential to generate objective measures of human activities that apply without prejudice to all people in all circumstances, regardless of personal differences, geographical location, the nature of the economic system, or of the broader cultural context. Activities of all kinds, whether economic, social, psychological, or political, can be described quantitatively in terms of the time allocated to

142

them, if they may be observed at all. Even though time is a one-dimensional measure that does not take the qualitative diversity of human activities into account, time allocation is extremely useful for comparing human activities in varying contexts, just as in other contexts monetary costs, or the earnings derived from an activity, are useful measures for comparison. Time-allocation studies give an indication of when during the day the activity takes place (e.g. day or evening), the way tasks are organized (e.g. certain activities are always done together), who does the task or activity, and with whom the task is done. This information is essential to effective project planning and implementation.

Time-allocation theory has been based on the assumption that people in general experience their time as scarce and allocate it among alternative activities in order to maximize individual utility (i.e. personal satisfaction). Micro-economic reasoning is thus applied to the analysis of time use, assuming that people are maximizing the value of their time (Becker, 1965, 1981). The application of this reasoning is more complicated in the household context, where members cannot be assumed to have the same priorities or interests (cf. Rosenzweig; Behrman; Safilios-Rothschild, in this volume).

The goal of the earliest time-allocation in the social sciences was to describe human activity patterns in quantitative terms (Sorokin and Berger, 1939). Sorokin collected over 5,000 records of daily activities of 100 Americans, which were analysed for time of day, age, sex, occupation, motivation, and social interaction. Curiously, sociologists appear to have made little use of these early studies:

The groundwork for the quantitative study of time in this country. . . [was] primarily laid by sociologists, such as Bevans (1913), Lundberg et al. (1934), Sorokin and Berger (1939), and Reiss (1959). Despite the attention given it by prominent sociologists, however, the empirical potential of time to function as a "currency" for sociology – representing a "hard" measure of human preferences and values – is mostly an unfulfilled aspiration. Linder (1970: 6) claims that this inability of sociologists to use their own results is due to their failure to recognize the time-scarcity problem. (Robinson, 1977, pp. 4–5)

Time-allocation methods have also been used to some extent by researchers in psychology (Zelkind and Sprug, 1974), agricultural economics (Clark and Haswell, 1970; Pimentel and Pimentel, 1979; Ruthenberg, 1980), and comparative sociology (Szalai et al., 1972; McSweeney, 1979).

PRACTICAL APPLICATIONS OF TIME ALLOCATION RESEARCH

In anthropology, patterns of time use were traditionally reported in the description of the daily round that usually formed part of the ethnographic monograph in which anthropologists reported their field research, but these were non-quantitative descriptions of the typical day and seasonal round. Since early quantitative research in anthropology was primarily in the realm of economics, quantitative time-allocation data were reported mainly as a measurement of labour inputs in production, rather than as a general description of activity patterns. Foster (1948), Lewis (1951), and Erasmus (1955) in their studies of Latin American communities, for example, provide detailed estimates of the amount of time spent in food production and manufacture, but only the broadest outlines of time spent in social and leisure activities.

The use of time-allocation data in the description of economic systems has continued in the study of New Guinea horticulturalists and foragers (Salisbury, 1962; Pospisil, 1963; Waddell, 1972; van Arsdale, 1978; Grossman, 1981, 1984), African foragers (Lee, 1969; Tanaka, 1980) and farmers (Tripp, 1982), Nepalese and Javanese villagers (Nag et al., 1978), and South American forager-horticulturalists (Johnson, 1975, 1978a; Lizot, 1977; Gross et al., 1979). Data from these Amazonian studies have contributed to the continuing debate on the role of limiting factors in lowland South American Indian adaptations, and have inspired researchers to expand this database to include other lowland societies (Baksh, 1984, 1985; Johnson and Baksh, 1987; Paolisso and Sackett, 1985). Theoretical explorations of the anthropological usefulness of formal models from evolutionary ecology, such as optimal foraging theory, and from micro-economics, such as linear programming solutions of the "diet problem," have been made using these data (Behrens, 1981, 1984; Hames and Vickers, 1982; Hawkes et al., 1982; Johnson and Behrens, 1982; several studies in Hames and Vickers, 1983).

Time-allocation data have also been instrumental in the study of technological change. Labour-saving associated with the adoption of the steel axe was studied by Salisbury (1962), Townsend (1969), and Sillitoe (1979) in New Guinea, and Carneiro (1979a, 1979b) in Amazonia. Hames (1979) and Yost and Kelley (1983) have similarly assessed the impact of the shotgun on Amazonian hunting efficiency. Gross and co-workers (1979) have used time-allocation studies to uncover changes in labour investments accompanying greater market involvement among tropical horticulturalists.

Information on time allocation is also essential to determining daily energy expenditure in studies of nutrition (Richards, 1939; Fox, 1953; McCarthy and McArthur, 1960; Hipsley and Kirk, 1965; Norgan et al., 1974; Montgomery and Johnson, 1977; Edmundson, 1977; Dufour, 1983) and energy flow in human ecosystems (Rappaport, 1971; Thomas, 1976).

A number of hypotheses in cultural evolution have been tested in time-allocation studies. Sahlins (1972) used time data on several foraging groups to support his argument that hunters and gatherers meet their food needs with relatively little effort. Boserup (1965) found time studies supported her hypothesis that per capita labour requirements increase with the shift from extensive to intensive cultivation. Reviews by Minge-Klevana (1980) and Ember (1983) have demonstrated how total labour requirements and types of labour change with the shift from an agrarian to an industrialized economy.

Apart from the main emphasis on problems in ecology, economics, and economic change (see Carlstein, 1982, for an overview), time-allocation research in anthropology has concentrated on socialization. Here researchers have found time allocation to be a valuable measure in charting the amounts of time caretakers of various kinds (e.g. mother, father, sibling, babysitter, etc.) spend with children, and in describing the varying ways in which children of different ages actually spend their time (Munroe and Munroe, 1971; Munroe et al., 1983; Rogoff, 1978). Whiting and Edwards (1974) used such data to show that differences in the tasks assigned to different children affected their social behaviour, for example that boys assigned child-care responsibilities will become less aggressive in play than other boys.

It will be apparent from even this brief overview that time-allocation research has a place in many kinds of policy-related research. Indeed, whenever patterns of time use are relevant, as in estimating how hard people work (say, for nutrition studies) or how their activity patterns change following an intervention, time-allocation research should be built into project design. Neumann and Bwibo (1987) provide an excellent recent example of how such research fits into a complex, multifaceted project design.

COSTS AND BENEFITS OF TIME-ALLOCATION RESEARCH METHODS

The ideal approach to the collection of time-allocation data would be to get a sort of "god's-eye view" of what each subject in the research population was doing all the time. This ideal is both technically impossible and ethically untenable. A research subject's right to privacy implies that whenever the research is felt to be inordinately intrusive the subject should exercise the power to stop it. Thus, any realistic method of measuring time allocation will, from the outset, be a compromise between the ideal of complete unimpeded observation of research subjects and the practical limits set by available resources for research and the subjects' willingness to be observed. Since there are a number of different ways to compromise the ideal in favour of practical reality, several distinct research strategies have evolved in time-allocation research, each with its own rationale and constituency.

A Basic Dimension of Contrast: Direct Observation v. Subject Self-report

Many researchers prefer to use the informant as an observer of his or her own behaviour. Several techniques depend on the subject recording his own behaviour throughout the day, or recalling behaviour over a given time period. This resolves most ethical issues, because the informant decides which behaviours to report and which to hide. It also saves a great proportion of the researcher's time, since the research subjects themselves do the work of observation and recording.

The major drawback to informant self-reports is that, in general, there is a surprisingly low correspondence between informants' reports of their own behaviour and that behaviour as measured by outside observers. Bernard and colleagues (1984) have found that, in virtually all cases where both kinds of data were collected simultaneously, informant self-reports have been weakly correlated, if at all, with direct observations made by scientific researchers. For example, in a study of rural women's time use, McSweeney (1979) found that when the informant-recall technique was used, women failed to report 44 per cent of their work as recorded by direct observations. The main reason for such discrepancies is probably not deliberate deception by informants but rather that people tend to remember their own behaviour selectively, in terms of cultural models of "appropriate" or "significant" behaviour (cf. D'Andrade, 1974; Johnson, 1978b). It follows that the closer in time the informant is to the actual behaviour being described, the more accurate will be the description.

Methods of Direct Observation

Two primary methods of direct observation are commonly used. The first comes closest to giving a "god's-eye view," whereas the second saves much labour and cost by introducing sampling methods.

Following the Subject

The most straightforward approach to studying how people spend time is to follow them around all the time. When this is done (e.g. Lewis, 1951; Lee, 1979) it is necessary to focus on a specific individual or on a close-knit group such as a household or a migratory camp. Depending on the level of accuracy desired, a researcher can find it difficult to describe even the behaviour of a solitary individual, so the major shortcoming of this method is that the results are limited to very small numbers of individuals and short periods of time (e.g. one or two weeks). The representativeness of such data, as a sample of a community and of the varying seasons of the year, is highly doubtful. Such studies are normally done by a single researcher. Many details of behaviour are lost, since no observer can focus on details of behaviour for more than a few minutes at a time without requiring rest and diversion. If a group is the subject of observation, as soon as individuals undertake separate tasks (the normal situation), the observer must select which one to follow.

In order to obtain a representative sample of individuals in a community, as well as representative samples of times of day and seasons of the year, sampling procedures must be used. Note that in a modification of the "following the subject technique," Peet has introduced a degree of representativeness in his research in Nepal by following each of his research subjects for a 24-hour period once a month (Nag et al., 1978). However, true random sampling requires larger numbers of observations than are practical using this method.

Spot Checks

A solution to the problem of representativeness is to sample behaviour over time, making periodic spot checks of the behaviour of many individuals (Erasmus, 1955; Johnson, 1975). The spot-check technique uses a random pattern of visits or "checks" to determine what the members of the study population are doing at a given moment. By randomizing the observations by person and time, a representative sample, based on hundreds or thousands of brief observations, allows a statistically accurate picture of patterns of time use in the community to emerge.

In recent years this has become the technique of choice in cross-cultural behavioural studies (e.g. Gross et al., 1979; Hames, 1979; Tripp, 1982; Grossman, 1984; Baksh and Paolisso, 1986). This technique has seldom been attempted in complex urban societies, perhaps because the method of randomly dropping in on research subjects for brief visits is not as feasible in privacy-oriented modern groups as it is in the small communities anthropologists study. On the other hand, the willingness of modern individuals to accept random visits from an anthropological researcher – that is, a participant observer known personally to the research subject, as opposed to an unknown pollster – has not really been tested.

Generally, this technique is reliable and requires relatively little field time. Where the community is a neighbourhood, village, or other cluster of residences, it is possible to visit a great many people in the course of an hour, and observe and record their activities. If care is taken to randomize the visits so that the time of day and the order of visits is unpredictable, then rather accurate and complete descriptions of time-allocation patterns for all members of the community for periods of one year or more are obtained with a few hours of work each week, leaving the field-worker free to pursue the other goals of participant observation research.

The main shortcomings of this technique are, first, that the night hours are not covered. Usually, the hours between 8 p.m. and 6 a.m. must be described through interviews and general ethnographic observations, as when the researcher spends a few nights in a family dwelling. Second, direct observation certainly introduces observer effects on the behaviour of the research subjects. This latter problem varies in intensity from one ethnographic setting to another. For example, among the Machiguenga Indians of the Peruvian Amazon (Johnson, 1975), casual, short visits to see what someone is doing are not only allowed, but are a regular part of daily life. Spot checks fit in the most natural way. We can imagine settings where the disruption created by such visits might be massive, as in a male researcher trying to visit a group of Muslim wives, or an outside visitor calling at a Chinese village home, where everyone immediately scurries to make the guest feel welcome. None the less, such failures of the method have not actually been reported, and we may imagine more difficulties than actually would arise in field situations.

Methods Depending on Self-report

Three styles of time-allocation research depend on informant self-reports. Specific methods are even more variable, but the diversity in costs and benefits of self-report methods are illustrated by these three styles of research.

Global Self-reports

In this technique, informants are asked only once to describe the overall pattern of their time allocation. They may be asked to estimate the hours per week they devote to a checklist of activities, or to assign their time to activities as a percentage of the whole. For example, the University of California periodically asks its faculty to describe their time use: how many hours per week are spent in teaching, how many in research, administrative work, and so on. These data are then compiled and reported as averages, which are then compared to patterns of time use in previous years or used to draw contrasts between different campuses of the university.

Such data must be viewed with the greatest caution. Global patterns of time use are very difficult for informants to report with accuracy, even (or perhaps especially) about themselves. Variations over the course of a year will be missed, and informants are likely to forget about the amount of time spent in idle chatter, daydreaming unrelated to work, and other less-esteemed activities.

Above all, in this example, it is very clear to the informant that these data will be used in the state government to make the case for university funding, including academic salaries, in future years. It is not surprising, therefore, that professors in the University of California system regularly report themselves as working on university business more than 60 hours per week throughout the year. Some no doubt do work this many hours per week, especially at times of peak load, but we are entitled to be sceptical until some kind of behavioural confirmation has been supplied (i.e. by direct observation). It is noteworthy that these data are used in a number of university publications and documents without questions ever being raised concerning their reliability.

Ethnographic research experience in a community can help compensate for some of the distortion inherent in global estimates, because the knowledgeable ethnographer can identify areas in which informants are not adequate reporters and then can devise strategies to obtain compensatory data. For example, in their study of rural women's work, Deere and de Leal (1979) found that women's global self-reports virtually ignored agricultural labour. Knowing that women were indeed part of the agricultural workforce from their previous ethnographic field-work, the researchers developed a specific questionnaire concerning who performed what tasks in each agricultural plot in the sample, and did obtain good evidence of the real extent of women's labour in agriculture.

In this vein, Rogers (1984) has suggested that asking householders to list the tasks for which they normally are responsible in their family division of labour may be a useful shorthand method to estimate patterns of time allocation. Although such a method, used alone, would be vulnerable to the same criticisms as global self-reports (i.e. that we are obtaining a description of the informants' cognitive maps of "appropriate behaviour" rather than a description of actual behaviour), this does suggest the possibility of combining such shorthand methods with behavioural methods to develop ways of estimating time-allocation patterns. For example, in a region where a certain similarity in households may be observed (a rice-growing region or a coastline of fishing communities), random spot checks might be used during repeated visits to a selected range of villages to establish common patterns of time use. Such a baseline study could develop a set of reliable predictors of time allocation. Task allocation might be one of these, as might occupation, household structure, ethnicity, and many other variables which can be determined through household surveys. Then relatively simple interviews of large numbers of households could be used to determine their relevant characteristics, in conjunction with the time-allocation study, to estimate probable patterns of time use throughout the entire region at much lower cost than a full-scale regional time-allocation study.

Twenty-four-hour Recall Interviews

A definite gain in accuracy is achieved by not expecting informants to know the global patterns of their behaviour, but instead asking them to report their activities over the previous 24-hour period. Informants can generally remember bedtimes, mealtimes, and the approximate times spent in major activities such as going to work or watching TV. By careful probing, an interviewer can help the informant go back over the previous day thoroughly, retrieving smaller, forgotten pieces of behaviour.

The limits to this method are set by the human propensity to forget routine activities and the many small activities that momentarily interrupt the more salient activities. Hence, conversations with family and friends, helping a child tie his shoes, eating a snack while watching television, and so on may well be lost to the research. Where the researcher is a stranger to the informant, there is also an unwillingness to admit to embarrassing or prohibited activities. Certain activities may be over- or underestimated, again reflecting the cultural bias of the informant or his or her wish to appear in a certain light to the researcher.

But, done with careful probing, perhaps with a checklist to remind both the researcher and the subject of behaviours that may have been forgotten, this method produces reliable data, as far as we know, and it is a widely practised technique (e.g. Sanjek, 1972; White, 1976). It is probably most successful when an interviewer who is already known and trusted by the informant collects the data, rather than asking informants to fill out a questionnaire by themselves. Recall instruments can be carefully constructed to preserve simultaneity and organizational or chronological relationships between activities (cf. Schlossman, 1986, for details). These instruments have been successfully used and can provide reliable and accurate results even by telephone (Schlossman, 1986; Zeitlin et al., in preparation).

Informant Diaries

In this method, informants are asked to keep records of their own activities (e.g. Bergman, 1980). The reliability of the data can be very high or very low, depending entirely on how well-prepared the informants are, and how committed to the research goals they are. Obviously, if the informants view the task with suspicion or boredom, the results will be poor; but if they can be motivated to keep careful records of their activities at frequent intervals throughout the day, this method overcomes many of the lacunae due to forgetfulness that afflict the global self-report and even the 24-hour recall methods.

DISCUSSION

The ideal of a time-allocation study is a "god's-eye view" of everything everyone in the research population does. That this is completely unfeasible should not deflect us from recognizing that it is the ideal. When we compromise this ideal for practical reasons, we should do so reluctantly and self-reflectively, with the knowledge that too many compromises may result in collecting masses of misleading or useless data. In designing a time-allocation study, evaluation of alternative methods should incorporate the following four rules of thumb.

Coding Rules Must Be Explicit

At the present stage of research, when standards for describing human behaviour are neither rigorously developed nor widely shared, the best that researchers can hope for is to develop explicit descriptions of how they recorded particular behaviours and how they coded them into higher-order categories. Each study should, as a matter of course, produce a code-book that other researchers may obtain and use when comparing one study with another. Then it will not matter so much if one baseball-playing father is coded as "child-caretaking" while in another study such a father is coded as enjoying "recreation," because, by referring to the separate code-books for each study, comparative researchers can recode the behaviours to correspond.

This problem is among the most serious confronting time-allocation research. It was the single most time-consuming and difficult aspect of developing a standardized coding scheme for cross-cultural comparisons in the UCLA Time Allocation Project. In a co-ordinated field study, such as that of Gross and his co-workers in Central Brazil (1979), a team of researchers can achieve intercoder reliability through pre-field-work training. But such projects are rare, and the prevailing pattern of individualistic, and to a degree idiosyncratic, coding schemes means that some ambiguity in exactly how observed behaviour comes to be coded as this or that "activity" is inevitable whenever we are trying to interpret another researcher's time-allocation data.

For those responsible for making and implementing policy, this implies both a need for caution and an opportunity. Time-allocation data, being numerical, can be presented in decimal-point precision, but, given the limitations of data-collection techniques, must not be regarded as more than estimates of the general pattern of time allocation in a community. On the other hand, by designing their own time-allocation component into new research, planners can carefully define coding rules, train for intercoder reliability, and feel suitably confident of the accuracy of their findings (see, for example, Neumann and Bwibo, 1987). This is a case where careful planning well in advance of field research can pay large dividends in the quality of data obtained.

Samples Must Be Representative

One of the compromises with the god's-eye view ideal is that we can only observe or interview a fraction of the population a fraction of the time. Thus, all time-allocation research is done on samples. This means that the rules of statistical inference apply, and the basic requirement for *representative* sampling must be met. To the greatest possible extent, the individual subjects should be randomly drawn from the population, and the times for which their behaviour is recorded should be random moments drawn from the stream of time. When this is impossible, a researcher must pause and give careful thought to what is being lost in terms of the generalizability of the data, and should devise compensatory methods wherever possible. For example, Baksh and Paolisso (1986), in collecting a very large set of time-allocation observations among the Embu of Kenya, found that observing individuals at random throughout a large region of scattered homesteads was prohibitively costly in researchers' travel time. Instead, they devised a roundabout route through the territory that passed each homestead, and proceeded to move along that route making spot checks at each house along the way, resuming each day where the previous day's observations left off (a team of researchers took turns). Since each household visit involved certain unpredictable delays, the day's observations never ended at the same house, and over time an essentially random pattern of household visits resulted. This compromise allowed for a highly efficient use of researchers' time without seriously compromising representativeness.

Short-term Memory Is More Reliable than Long-term Memory

It has been demonstrated that reports of behaviour made immediately (within 2–3 minutes) after an observed event are much more accurate than reports made after several minutes have elapsed, when short-term memory retention gives way to the distortion of information in long-term memory, which is dominated by pattern-seeking. Thus, long-term memory conforms much more to "cognitive maps" of what behaviour *should* be like than does short-term memory. While fresh, it retains a fairly clear and objective image of what actually happened. These cognitive maps are partly cultural, so that long-term recall tends to conform to implicit, shared ethnocentric preconceptions, and partly personal, which may lead to the recollection of selected behaviours that confirm biases and support personal theories while failing to capture those that do not. It is especially important to keep in mind that this is done completely unconsciously. In fact, people are strongly inclined to doubt that they even do this, though the experimental evidence is overwhelming (Bernard et al., 1984).

150

Methodologically, this implies that direct observations will be most effective when the observer immediately records the behaviour as it happens. Similarly, for informant self-reports, greater accuracy will be achieved if the informant immediately records his or her behaviour. How to do this without totally disrupting the flow of behaviour will require some ingenuity. For example, researchers are beginning to experiment with beeper-type systems, whereby the subject is "beeped" at a random moment, and complies by quickly noting in a pocket notebook the time and a description of the activity in which he or she is engaged and then proceeding with the activity. This method, if it is successful, will combine some of the strongest features of both the direct observation and informant self-report methods.

Direct Observation Generates Unexpected New Information

Researchers who specialize in direct observations rather than informant self-reports often comment on the serendipity of unexpected insights provided by the first-hand observation (Johnson, 1978b; Gillespie, 1979). Direct observation of behaviour on a random schedule forces the researcher out of routines, landing him or her in unexpected places at unexpected times. It enhances the participant observer aspect of the field-work, and generally strengthens and extends the field-worker's personal relations among the study population. It can help the investigator overcome some timidity or reluctance about being in certain situations, and, just as a picture is worth a thousand words, it gives the researcher the wealth of data and sense impressions which only direct apprehension of an event can provide, but which cannot be achieved by asking an informant to tell about it.

SUMMARY

Time-allocation data are valuable means for describing the behaviour of people in the full range of their activities. Incorporated during the planning stages, studying time allocation in the proposed project area can provide a wide range of information for project development. Integrated into project implementation, it can help monitor changes as they occur. For example, are members of a targeted group increasing their participation in income-generating activities? All methods of time-allocation research, however, involve compromises with the ideal of obtaining complete and accurate information. Researchers must select from a variety of possible approaches those which achieve their specific research goals most fully.

It is important to maintain the clear distinction between methods based on direct observation by a trained researcher and those based on informant self-report. Direct observation tends to be expensive of a researcher's time and may be perceived as intrusive by the subjects, whereas informant self-reports depend on the documented frailty of human memory and may suffer greatly if informants are indifferent or secretly hostile to the research project and its personnel.

Four rules of thumb can help strengthen any time-allocation project: coding rules and categories must be made explicit and available to other researchers; observations must be representative of the population to which they will be generalized; observations recorded immediately after the event has occurred (short-term memory) are much more reliable than observations recorded more than a few minutes after the event (long-term memory); and direct observation of the event, by placing the researcher in the fullness of the context of behaviour, generates unexpected new data and insights beyond the mere quantitative description of time use.

Obviously, descriptions of patterns of time allocation can be useful in a wide variety of ways, complementing (not replacing) data on economic behaviour, household structure, socio-economic status, ethnicity, and so on. Perhaps the most significant limitation from the policy standpoint is that, like many essentially ethnographic methods, the data are most complete when collected over a period of at least a year, in a fairly small community. How can such a method be of use in a real world where a research team may have only two weeks to survey a region and develop policy recommendations?

In cases of extreme urgency, collection of valid time-allocation data is probably impractical. But, with some foresight, several possibilities suggest themselves on how to include such data in many projects. First, as mentioned above, if one time-allocation study can be done in a region, future short-term research projects can make inferences of time use based on that study. Such projects might include household surveys measuring useful predictors of time-use patterns (as established in the study). Second, in many world areas it is practical to train local researchers to conduct time-allocation studies over the long term; an expert team of researchers may actually need to visit the area only for a short period. If the study is done in advance of the team visit, the team can use the data to develop more precise questions and to formulate their recommendations.

Finally, even if time-allocation data are only collected over a short period, they can be very useful. True, we cannot use such data to construct a model of time use for an entire year. But they can give a rich picture of the daily round, of where and how people spend their time, and in whose company. Particularly when the preferred methods (spot checks, informant diaries, and 24-hour recall) are used, it is much better to have such data than not to have it, for it provides insights and opens avenues of inquiry that no other kinds of information can offer.

NOTE

1. Support for this seven-year project, Standardized Cross-cultural Time Allocation Database, comes from National Science Foundation (NSF) grants BN84-19033 and BN87-04604.

REFERENCES

As, D. 1978. Studies of Time-use: Problems and Prospects. *Acta Sociologica*, 21(2): 125–141.

Andorka, R., I. Harcsa, and I. Niemi. 1983. *Use of Time in Hungary and in Finland*. Central Statistical Office of Finland, Helsinki.

Baksh, M. 1984. Cultural Ecology and Change of the Machinguenga Indians of the Peruvian Amazon. Unpublished doctoral dissertation. Department of Anthropology, University of California, Los Angeles, Calif.

——. 1985. Faunal Food as a "Limiting Factor" on Amazonian Cultural Behavior: A Machiguenga Example. *Res. Econ. Anthropol.*, 7: 145–175.

Baksh, M., and M. Paolisso. 1986. Time Allocation Methods. Unpublished MS. School of Public Health, University of California, Los Angeles, Calif.

Becker, G.S. 1965. A Theory of the Allocation of Time. *Econ. J.*, 75(2): 493–518.

——.1981. *A Treatise on the Family.* Harvard University Press, Cambridge, Mass.

Behrens, C. 1981. Time Allocation and Meat Procurement among the Shipibo Indians of Eastern Peru. *Human Ecol.*, 92(2): 189–220.

——. 1984. Shipibo Ecology and Economy: A Mathematical Approach to Understanding Human Adaptation. Unpublished doctoral dissertation. Department of Anthropology, University of California, Los Angeles, Calif.

Bergman, R. 1980. *Amazonian Economics: The Simplicity of Shipibo Wealth.* Dellplain/University Microfilms, Syracuse, N.Y.

Bernard, H.R., P. Killworth, D. Kronenfeld, L. Sailer. 1984. The Problem of Informant Accuracy: The Validity of Retrospective Data. *Ann. Rev. Anthropol.*, 13: 495–517.

Bevans, G. 1913. *How Working Men Spend Their Time.* Columbia University Press, New York.

Boserup, E. 1965. *The Conditions of Agricultural Growth: Economics of Agrarian Change.* Aldine, New York.

Carlstein, T. 1982. *Time Resources, Society and Ecology.* George Allen & Unwin, London.

Carneiro, R.L. 1979a. Forest Clearance among the Yanomamo: Observations and Implications. *Anthropologica*, 52: 39–76.

——. 1979b. Tree Felling with the Stone Ax: An Experiment Carried out among the Yanomamo Indians of Southern Venezuela. In: C. Kramer, ed., *Ethnoarcheology*, pp. 21–58. Columbia University Press, New York.

Clark, C., and H. Haswell. 1970. *The Economics of Subsistence Agriculture.* Macmillan, London.

D'Andrade, R.G. 1974. Memory and the Assessment of Behavior. In: H. Blalock, ed., *Measurement in the Social Sciences.* Aldine, Chicago.

Deere, C.D., and M.L. de Leal. 1979. Measuring Women's Work and Class Position. *Stud. Fam. Plan.*, 10: 370–374.

Dufour, D. 1983. Nutrition in the Northwest: Household Dietary Intake and Time-energy Expenditure. In: R.B. Hames and W.T. Vickers, eds., *Adaptive Responses of Native Amazonians*, pp. 329–355. Academic Press, New York.

Edmundson, W. 1977. Individual Variations in Work Output per Unit Energy Intake in East Java. *Ecol. Fd. Nutr.*, 6: 147–151.

Ember, C.R. 1983. The Relative Decline in Women's Contribution to Agriculture with Intensification. *Am. Anthropologist*, 85(2): 285–304.

Erasmus, C.J. 1955. Work Patterns in a Mayo Village. *Am. Anthropologist*, 57(2): 322–333.

Foster, G.M. 1948. *Empire's Children: The People of Tzintzuntzan.* Publication 6. Institute of Social Anthropology, Smithsonian Institution, Washington, D.C.

Fox, R.H. 1953. A Study of the Energy Expenditure of Africans Engaged in Various Rural Tasks. Unpublished doctoral dissertation. London University.

Gillespie, V.H. 1979. Rural Women's Time Use. *Stud. Fam. Plan.*, 10: 383–384.

Gross, D.R. 1984. Time Allocation: A Tool for the Study of Cultural Behavior. *Ann. Rev. Anthropol.*, 13: 519–558.

Gross, D.R., G. Eiten, N. Flowers, F. Leoi, M. Ritter, and D. Werner. 1979. Ecology and Acculturation among Native Peoples of Central Brazil. *Science*, 206(4422): 1043–1050.

Grossman, L.S. 1981. The Cultural Ecology of Economic Development. *Ann. Assoc. Am. Geographers*, 71(2): 220–236.

Grossman, L.S. 1984. Collecting Time-use Data in Third World Rural Communities. Department of Geography, Virginia Polytechnic Institute and State University.

Hames, R.B. 1979. A Comparison of the Efficiencies of the Shotgun and the Bow in Neotropical Forest Hunting. *Human Ecol.*, 7(3): 219–252.

Hames, R.B., and W. Vickers. 1982. Optimal Foraging Theory as a Model to Explain Variability in Amazonian Hunting. *Am. Ethnologist*, 9(2): 358–378.

Hames, R.B., and W. Vickers, eds. 1983. *Adaptive Responses to Native Amazonians.* Academic Press, New York.

Hawkes, K., K. Hill, and J.F. O'Connell. 1982. Why Hunters Gather: Optimal Foraging and the Ache of Eastern Paraguay. *Am. Ethnologist*, 9: 379–398.

Hipsley, E.H., and N.E. Kirk. 1965. *Studies of Dietary Intake and the Expenditure of Energy by New Guineans.* South Pacific Commission Technical Paper 147. Noumea, New Caledonia.

Johnson, A. 1975. Time Allocation in a Machiguenga Community. *Ethnology*, 14(2): 301–310.

——. 1978a. In Search of the Affluent Society. *Human Nature*, 1(9): 50–59.

——. 1978b. *Quantification in Cultural Anthropology.* Stanford University Press, Stanford, Calif.

153

Johnson, A., and M. Baksh. 1987. Ecological and Structural Influences on the Proportions of Wild Foods in the Diets of Two Machiguenga Communities. In: M. Harris and E.B. Ross, eds., *Food and Evolution: Toward a Theory of Human Food Habits*, pp. 387–405. Temple University Press, Philadelphia, PA.

Johnson, A., and C. Behrens. 1982. Nutritional Criteria in Machiguenga Food Production Decisions: A Linear Programming Analysis. *Human Ecol.*, 10(2): 167–189.

Johnson, A., and O.R. Johnson. 1988. Time Allocation among the Machiguenga of Shimaa. In: A. Johnson, ed., *Cross Cultural Studies in Time Allocation.* Vol. I. Human Relations Area Files, New Haven, Conn.

Lee, R.B. 1969. !Kung Bushmen Subsistence: An Input–Output Analysis. In: A.P. Vayda, ed., *Environment and Cultural Behavior*, pp. 47–79. Natural History Press, New York.

——. 1979. *The !Kung San.* Cambridge University Press, Cambridge.

Lewis, O. 1951. *Life in a Mexican Village: Tepotzlan Revisited.* University of Illinois Press, Urbana, Ill.

Linder, S.B. 1970. *The Harried Leisure Class.* Columbia University Press, New York.

Lizot, J. 1977. Population, Resources and Warfare among the Yanomami. *Man*, 12: 497–517.

Lundberg, G., M. Komarovsky, and M.A. McInery. 1934. *Leisure: A Suburban Study.* Columbia University Press, New York.

McCarthy, F., and M. McArthur. *The Food Quest and Time Factor in Aboriginal Economic Life.* Melbourne University Press, Melbourne.

McSweeney, B.G. 1979. Collection and Analysis of Data on Rural Women's Time Use. *Stud. Fam. Plan.*, 10: 379–383.

Minge-Klevana, W. 1980. Does Labor Decrease with Industrialization? A Survey of Time Allocation Studies. *Curr. Anthropol.*, 21(3): 279–298.

Montgomery, E., and A. Johnson. 1977. Machiguenga Energy Expenditure. *Ecol. Fd. Nutr.*, 6: 97–105.

Munroe, R., and R.H. Munroe. 1971. Household Density and Infant Care in an East African Society. *J. Soc. Psychol.*, 83: 3–13.

Munroe, R.L., R.H. Munroe, C. Michelson, A. Koel, R. Bolton, and C. Bolton. 1983. Time Allocation in Four Societies. *Ethnology*, 22(4): 355–370.

Nag, M., B. White, and R.C. Peet. 1978. Anthropological Approach to the Study of Economic Value of Children in Java and Nepal. *Curr. Anthropol.*, 19(2): 293–306.

Neumann, C., and N. Bwibo. 1987. The Collaborative Research Support Program on Food Intake and Human Function, Kenya Project: Final Report. Report submitted to USAID under grant DAN-1309-G-1070-00. School of Public Health, University of California, Los Angeles, Calif.

Norgan, N.G., A. Ferro-Luzzi, and J.V.G.A. Durnin. 1974. The Nutrient and Energy Expenditure of 204 New Guinea Adults. *Trans. R. Soc.* (Ser. B), 268: 309–348.

Paolisso, M., and R. Sackett. 1985. Traditional Meat Procurement Strategies among the Irapa-Yukpa of the Venezuelan–Colombian Border Area. *Res. Econ. Anthropol.*, 7: 177–199.

Pimentel, D., and M. Pimentel. 1979. *Food, Energy and Society.* John Wiley & Sons, New York.

Pospisil, L. 1963. *Kapauku Papuan Economy.* Publications in Anthropology, 67. Yale University, New Haven, Conn.

Rappaport, R.A. 1971. Energy Flow in an Agricultural Society. *Sci. Amer.*, 224(3): 116–132.

Reiss, A. 1959. Rural–Urban and Status Differences in Interpersonal Contacts. *Am. J. Soc.*, 65(2): 182–195.

Richards, A. 1939. *Land, Labour and Diet in Northern Rhodesia: An Economic Study of the Bemba Tribe.* Oxford University Press, London.

Robinson, J.P. 1977. *How Americans Use Time: Sociopsychological Analysis of Everyday Behavior.* Praeger, New York.

Rogers, B. 1984. Personal communication.

Rogoff, B. 1978. Spot Observations: An Introduction and Examination. *Quart. Newsl. Inst. Compar. Human Devel.* (Rockefeller University), 2(2C): 21–26.

Ruthenberg, H. 1980. *Farming Systems in the Tropics.* Clarendon Press, Oxford.

Sahlins, M. 1972. *Stone Age Economics.* Tavistock, London.

Salisbury, R.F. 1962. *From Stone to Steel: Economic Consequences of Technological Change in New Guinea.* Melbourne University Press, Melbourne.

Sanjek, R. 1972. Ghanaian Networks. Unpublished doctoral dissertation. Columbia University, New York.

Schlossman, N.P. 1986. Work Resumption, Breast-feeding, and Time Allocation of Mothers in Boston, Massachusetts: The First Half-year Postpartum. Unpublished doctoral dissertation. Tufts University School of Nutrition, Medford, Mass.

Sillitoe, P. 1979. Stone versus Steel. *Mankind*, 12: 151–161.

Sorokin, P., and C. Berger. 1939. *Time-budgets of Human Behavior*. Harvard University Press, Cambridge, Mass.

Szalai, A., P.E. Converse, P. Feldheim, E.K. Schevich, and P.E. Stone. 1972. *The Use of Time: Daily Activities of Urban and Suburban Populations in Twelve Countries*. Mouton, The Hague.

Tanaka, J. 1980. *The San Hunter-gatherers of the Kalahari*. Trans. D.W. Hughes. University of Tokyo Press, Tokyo.

Thomas, R.B. 1976. Energy Flow at High Altitude. In: P.T. Baker and M.A. Little, eds., *Man in the Andes: A Multidisciplinary Study of High Altitude Quechua*. Academy Press, Chicago, Ill.

Townsend, W.H. 1969. Stone and Steel Tool Use in a New Guinea Society. *Ethnology*, 8: 199–205.

Tripp, R.B. 1982. Time Allocation in Northern Ghana: An Example of the Random Visit Method. *J. Devel. Areas*, 16: 391–400.

Van Arsdale, P. 1978. Activity Patterns of Asmat Hunter-gatherers: A Time Budget Analysis. *Mankind*, 4: 453–460.

Waddell, E. 1972. *The Mound Builders*. University of Washington Press, Seattle, Wash.

White, B. 1976. *Production and Reproduction in a Javanese Village*. Agricultural Development Council, Bogor, Indonesia.

Whiting, B., and C.P. Edwards. 1974. A Cross-cultural Analysis of Sex Differences in the Behavior of Children Aged Three and Eleven. In: R.A. LeVine, ed., *Culture and Personality*, pp. 188–201. Aldine, Chicago.

Yost, J.A., and P.M. Kelley. 1983. Shotguns, Blowguns and Spears: The Analysis of Technological Efficiency. In: R.B. Hames and W.T. Vickers, eds., *Adaptive Responses of Native Amazonians*, pp. 189–224. Academic Press, New York.

Zeitlin, M.F., N.P. Schlossman, and A.S. Beiser. 1988. Validation of a Telephone Time Use Recall Instrument. In preparation.

Zelkind, I., and J. Sprug. 1974. *Time Research: 1172 Studies*. Scarecrow Press, Metchuen, N.J.

11
Use of Emic Units for Time-use Recall

MARIAN FRANK ZEITLIN

Tufts University School of Nutrition, Medford, Massachusetts, USA

INTRODUCTION

It is effective to use emic units of time, that is, units constructed from culturally familiar reference events such as work tasks, to collect time-use recall information when studying cultures that do not customarily use timepieces. The term emic refers to the definition of concepts according to the explanatory system of the culture that is the object of study. It is used in contrast to the term etic, which refers to definition according to the terms of the culture conducting the research (cf. Messer; Scrimshaw, this volume, for other uses of these terms). The case for the use of emic units rests on five arguments:

1. People who do not have modern timepieces mentally represent their activities in terms of tasks or activities having relatively standardized times of performance; moreover, these modes of representation enable them to provide meaningful time-use recall information to an interviewer. This premise challenges the common statement, "they do not think in terms of time."
2. It is possible either to use existing emic units or to construct meaningful units from local time reference points and to use these measurement units in survey research.
3. There are purposes for which information from time-use recall is inherently more useful than information obtained using observational approaches.
4. An emic approach to the recall process may enhance rather than detract from the value of time-use information, and may in fact independently shed light on aspects of resource allocation and on time-sensitive processes within a given culture.
5. The amount of error inherent in measurement of timed events in general, and in the use of recall methods in particular, is so great that the imprecision introduced by using emic units does not substantially compromise precision of the data.

TIME REPRESENTATION IN CULTURES WITHOUT WATCHES

All languages have words for the times of day, but not all cultures represent time in the same way. The angle of the sun as an indicator of time appears to be one common

156

human approach that does not require a formal sundial. Brearley (1919) made the distinction between natural sundials, which were naturally occurring rocks or trees whose shadows were used for making and keeping appointments and timing events, and artificial sundials specially constructed or placed for this purpose. He chronicles the gradual improvements in the technology of sundials through the ages. These time-pieces were universally used until clocks and watches became widely available about 300 years ago.

Even today, natural sundials such as familiar trees are commonly used by villagers in Swaziland. During work designing the Swaziland Nutrition Survey (Government of Swaziland, 1983) for instance, one mother commented that her baby had no appetite, because it had not eaten since "the shadow was at this point" (Aphane, 1984). Another mother was heard scolding her child for lateness, saying, "You always come home from school when the shadow is here." Members of the same household commonly used the same nearby tree for keeping track of time (Aphane, 1984).

Swazi villagers were found to keep track of time in at least two additional ways. They had specific terms for 12 times of day: dawn, early morning, mid-morning, late morning, midday, early afternoon, mid-afternoon, late afternoon, sunset, early evening (just after sunset when people could still walk about freely), night (lasting until about 3 a.m.), and very early morning (before dawn). The use of the number 12 in time computation is ancient and tends to be widespread (Brearley, 1919). Swazi villagers appear to be more attuned to the angle of the rays of the sun than people accustomed to using timepieces. Moreover, these times consistently refer to the same sun angles. This hypothesis could be tested empirically. To the extent that this holds true, major bias would be introduced into estimates based on these time units only by seasonal changes in the timing of dawn and sunset.

Finally, villagers measure time by events and tasks. A specific time during the morning is "when boys take the cows out." If the village is on a bus route, the first, second, third, etc., buses passing through could be used as time references.

ON USING EMIC REFERENCE POINTS

Field researchers have long used local events calendars with individualized protocols for measuring the passage of years and months to pinpoint ages and dates. The same approach can be used to measure time within daily or weekly activity cycles. This approach was taken in my work on a health and nutrition baseline survey conducted among the Dinka in Sudan (Zeitlin, 1977). We used emic time units to estimate the study population's walking distance from resources. This survey estimated distances from the household to the water source, the market, and to health services. The emic units were developed through discussions with informants in Abyei (Sudan) and by timing the sun. Informants were the town's two elementary-school teachers, who had grown up in rural homes but who possessed watches and were accustomed to measuring time in hours and minutes. As in the construction of a local events calendar, the assistance of interested individuals who were thoroughly familiar with both traditional and modern approaches to time computation was essential to the derivation of a normative schedule of times when familiar events occurred. Focus groups and semi-structured interviews with members of rural households provided additional information to fill in gaps in this schedule and helped describe its variability.

At the time of the survey, dawn to sunrise was timed to be exactly one hour. Milking

157

time was claimed by the informants and the chief to be about 9 a.m. We accepted this and used it to represent 9 a.m. Since the nature of the information required by the survey was approximate, we did not validate this representation, although we easily could have. While we did not conduct validity checks on responses to these questions, the apparent speed and ease with which the respondents replied suggested that they were being questioned in terms that were familiar to them. This familiarity also appeared to facilitate rapport between the Arab Sudanese and American interviewers and the Dinka households they visited.

In another example, Marlett (1988) studied the manner in which the work burden of Gambian mothers influenced their choice of treatment for their children's diarrhoea. From her own experience living for two years in Gambian village compounds, she was able to estimate the average number of hours required for the mothers' basic work activities. By asking the mothers in a cross-sectional survey how many times per week they performed these activities and how many helpers they had per activity, she was able to estimate a total time burden per mother. The time required per activity was multiplied by the number of times the activity was performed, under the simplifying assumption that the tasks were not overlapping. In this case, Marlett did not abstract emic concepts of time from the work tasks in which they were embedded. Questions measuring time use were then developed. The survey respondents easily answered these questions because they understood that the intent of the study was to investigate the mothers' time/work burden.

ADVANTAGES OF TIME-USE RECALL OVER OBSERVATION

In spite of certain limitations (see Johnson, this volume), recall methods have several major advantages over observational techniques in special circumstances. First, they require much less labour and less time to collect. Second, recalled activities are not biased by the presence of an outside observer while the activity is performed. Third, they can be collected in situations where privacy is valued too highly to permit the presence of an observer. This last feature is important in societies where the most basic of observational procedures for studying traditional households, the spot observation, is not feasible (see Johnson's paper in this volume for a description of this procedure). For example, accurate spot observations would have been impossible to collect in the Mexican squatter community outside Cuernevaca that was the site of a recent micro-behavioural study of infant feeding (Zeitlin et al., in preparation). Much of family life occurs inside one- or two-room cement blockhouses located inside walled compounds. Before an observer (even an acquaintance from the community itself) can gain entry, the household will rearrange itself.

Finally, recall captures the passage of time as people remember it, or, in other words, framed in the mental constructs that people use in planning and evaluating the use of time as a resource. Recall methods, therefore, have the advantage of eliciting information that is potentially more intuitively understandable to the study population than time sampling or other observational data and hence is more readily usable as the basis for planning and action. Expressing time-use information in emic terms should enhance its relevance to the life-styles of the study community. This feature should be particularly effective in applied research conducted for the purpose of designing development programmes.

EMIC TIME-USE INFORMATION AND RESOURCE
OR TASK ALLOCATION

Time tends to be quantified when the conscious and public measurement of time, as a commodity, yields social or economic benefits. Disputes over time allocation may need to arise in order to stimulate the quantification of time. Control of the labour of others is a major arena for time disputes. In the simplest case, a mother in a traditional agricultural society who sends one child for water and the other to collect firewood knows very well how long it should take to complete each task. The culprit who spends too much time playing along the way is also in trouble. The wife who does not have food ready for her husband is in trouble, as is the husband if he does not arrive home to eat it. It does not take a clock to tell that "Johnny is too long at the fair."

Developing an inventory of the types of time-use concerns that arise in a culture, and the types of events that are closely time-monitored, should yield insight into disputed resources and the intra-household decision-making processes for the allocation of these resources. More basically, time-use concerns reveal time-dependent agricultural, food-processing, biological, manufacturing, and other cycles.

ERROR INHERENT IN THE MEASUREMENT OF TIMED EVENTS

Two types of error inherent in the measurement of timed events cause so much imprecision in the measurement process that any additional error caused by the use of emic units is small by comparison. The first type is error caused by imprecise definition of the study variables. The second will be termed fragmentation error.

Imprecise Definition of Variables

Basic problems of validity occur when interviewers, observers, and respondents mean different things by the words they use to represent their study variables. Such error commonly occurs (although it is preventable) when survey instruments are translated in an ad hoc manner from one language to another, without careful back-translation. It is possible to minimize this type of error when dealing with simple concepts such as numbers of children born, years of education, presence of a radio, or type of roofing material.

The words used to label events, however, are intrinsically much less precise than the words used to label objects. The label "housework," for example, is much less specific than the label "car" or even the label "vehicle." The vehicle is a visible object. Housework consists of a sequence of movements that not only vary from individual to individual, but also may be automatic (and thus unconscious) to the persons performing them. Both familiar and unfamiliar activities may not consciously be recognized and reported as events either by the persons who perform them or by persons sent to observe them. A further problem is that activities commonly are classified according to function. Moreover, the functions of familiar activities may not be consciously recognizable or may be defined in general rather than specific terms.

At the micro-behavioural level, psychologists insist on using videotapes of behavioural sequences (Dehavenon, 1978) in order to operationalize the definitions of behaviours and to train observers to recognize and record them reliably. Most time-use studies are concerned with macro-level events and therefore do not aspire to this degree of precision. The danger is that definitions of events may be based on very specific micro-level assumptions that vary subjectively from individual to individual. Without descending to the micro-level to specify these assumptions, time-use research may be limited in its validity.

As an example of such problems of definition, a validation study of maternal time-use recall in the Boston area in the United States found that mothers' recall of time spent bottle-feeding their babies was particularly unreliable when compared to time recorded by an observer in the home (Zeitlin et al., 1988). A major reason for this apparent lack of reliability was that the time-use protocol had not specified whether time spent preparing bottles should be included in the record of time spent in bottle-feeding. Some mothers classified it in their memories as part of the feeding while others did not.

Another example of such lack of validity comes from a recent observational study of infant feeding in Bangladesh (Zeitlin and Guldan, 1987). Based on dietary-recall data, it has long been accepted in the infant-feeding literature that Bangladeshis delay the introduction of weaning foods to their infants until the children are between 1 and 2 years of age (Israel and Tighe, 1983). In the cross-sectional baseline survey conducted prior to the observational study cited above, mothers reported that they introduced rice to their infants on average at the age of 12 months (Zeitlin et al., 1985). Event observations conducted by local observers over a period of six months, however, revealed that infants received supplementary foods on average every three hours by 4–6 months of age, increasing to every two hours by 12 months and 1.5 hours by about 21 months. Rice feedings started on average once per day by a year, and increased to every four hours by 18 months and every three hours by 24 months. Discrepancy between reported and observed events in this case probably arose more from a difference in definition than from errors of recall. The mothers apparently did not consciously define placing small amounts of food into the child's mouth as "feeding" the baby, in part because there were cultural sanctions against feeding infants before a certain age (Israel and Tighe, 1983).

The same study (Zeitlin et al., 1985) investigated the speed with which the mothers cleaned up their infants after they defecated. In the baseline survey for this research (Zeitlin et al., 1985), 50 per cent of mothers had asserted that they cleaned their babies "when they saw it." The observational study, currently being analysed, which timed the delay in clean-up found, however, that only 5 per cent of mothers started to clean their infants within the first three minutes after the defecation occurred, and that median time from defecation to start of clean-up was six minutes. In this case, the mothers' and the interviewers' definitions of rapid action appeared to differ.

An example of lack of awareness of performing an activity comes from a cross-cultural study of infant development comparing Yoruba mothers in Nigeria with mothers in Scotland (Agiobu-Kemmer, 1981). As compared with Scottish mothers, the Yoruba mothers were observed systematically to stimulate their infant's motor development by such activities as repeatedly placing play objects just beyond the reach of the infant who was learning to crawl, for example, and praising the child when (s)he reached the object. When asked whether they tried to help their children to develop motor skills, however, these mothers denied that they did so and asserted that the child's development was up to God.

160

Errors of Fragmentation

The term fragmentation (Schlossman, 1986) refers to the degree to which an activity is fragmented into subunits of time. Housework, for example, can be done in a single long stretch, in several shorter stretches punctuated by breaks or other activities, or intermittently interspersed with other activities such as cooking, phone calls, etc. Two observers watching the same woman engage in housework may very likely report different numbers of house-cleaning episodes, and their reports might differ from the woman's own recalled activities. The reporting of any event that is made up of repeated actions with pauses between them is by definition vulnerable to such fragmentation error. Housework is an example of an activity for which the number of discrete episodes might be less important to the researcher than the total time spent on the task.

Yet imprecise reporting of fragmentation introduces error into counts of events where the number of events is of greater intrinsic interest, as for example numbers of breast-feedings, or number of snacks or meals in nutrition studies. Older infants commonly detach and reattach to the breast while nursing. If every reattachment is counted as a separate breast-feeding, a ten-minute feeding for a distractable baby may be recorded as ten feedings. Konner and Worthman (1980), in studying the !Kung, for example, reported that the 17 babies (ages 3–34 months) they observed for six hours each breast-fed on average every 14.8 minutes for an average of 1.92 minutes per feed. In the Bangladesh study noted above in which 185 babies, ages 4–27 months, were observed for eight hours each (Guldan et al., 1989), the duration per feeding ranged from 1 to 14 minutes and averaged 8.3 minutes, while the average number of detachments and reattachments from the breast per feeding was 2.3. The average frequency of feeding decreased from one per 52 minutes at 4–6 months to one per 73 minutes at 13–15 months and one every 2.5 hours at 22–24 months. If fragmentation had been computed differently (i.e. if each recorded reattachment had been counted as a separate feeding), the computed duration per feed would have been 3.6 minutes and the frequency would have gone down to one per 22.6 minutes at the younger age period.

In the Bangladesh study only detachments and reattachments that the observer could distinguish were recorded. Because the Bangladeshi mothers wore saris, the baby's mouth could be obscured from view during the feeding, in contrast to the !Kung mother-infant pairs. In observational studies of this nature, it would be possible to specify that a certain number of minutes between reattachments would differentiate between separate feedings. More generally, observational researchers should specify the time interval between recurrences of an activity that differentiates between recorded events (just as epidemiologists specify the number of symptom-free days needed to differentiate between illness episodes).

The two problems with such specification are that: (1) any given fixed interval is unlikely to capture the boundaries between events that are perceived by the various actors – two different mothers could easily count the same breast-feeding behaviour differently; and (2) the definition of episodes or events that describes the behaviour of some groups of individuals breaks down for others: as an example, the !Kung babies who are constantly held next to their mothers' uncovered breasts may nurse off and on in a continuous fashion, whereas Bangladeshi babies, whose mothers' breasts are covered by saris and who are frequently held by other family members, may exhibit less fragmented nursing behaviour.

It is precisely distinctions of this nature that the concept of fragmentation is designed to capture and study. The problem arises that policy-relevant research on time use tends not to be interested in this level of distinction. Adequately resolving the problem of fragmentation requires more expensive research procedures than applied researchers need to use to obtain the bulk of the information that they need. Therefore, major fragmentation errors persistently flaw their results.

CONCLUSIONS

Time-use recall information in emic units potentially provides insight into the manner in which cultures conceptualize the allocation of time-dependent resources as well as information regarding time use. Given the degree of imprecision inherent in most time-use research, it is concluded that researchers should not hesitate to obtain time-use recall data based on timed tasks and other emic units. Such data should ideally complement more objectively collected information.

REFERENCES

Agiobu-Kemmer, J.S. 1981. Infant Development in Two Cultures: Nigeria and Britain. Unpublished doctoral dissertation. University of St. Andrews.

Aphane, J. 1984. Personal communication.

Brearley, H.C. 1919. *Time Telling through the Ages*. Doubleday, Page & Co., New York.

Dehavenon, A.L. 1978. Superordinate Behavior in Urban Homes: A Video Analysis of Request-compliance and Food Control Behavior in Two Black and Two White Families Living in New York City. Unpublished doctoral dissertation. Columbia University, New York.

Government of Swaziland. 1983. Swaziland National Nutrition Status Survey. Full report AID/IHF, Chevy Chase, Maryland.

Guldan, G.S., M.F. Zeitlin, and J. Zeitlin. 1989. Breastfeeding Practices and Behaviours. In: M. Zeitlin, C. Super, A. Beiser, G. Guldan, N. Ahmed, and J. Zeitlin, *A Behavioural Study of Positive Deviance in Young Child Nutrition and Health in Rural Bangladesh*. Report to the Asia and Near East Bureau, US Agency for International Development, and the US Office of International Health, October 1989.

Israel, R., and J.N. Tighe, eds. 1983. *Maternal and Infant Nutrition Reviews, Bangladesh*. An International Nutrition Communication Service Publication. Education Development Center, Newton, Mass.

Konner, M., and C. Worthman. 1980. Nursing Frequency, Gonadal Function, and Birth Spacing, among !Kung Hunter Gatherers. *Science*, 107: 788–791.

Marlett, M.J. 1988. The Effect of Time and Resource Availability on Mothers' Use of Oral Rehydration Therapy in the Gambia, West Africa. Unpublished doctoral dissertation. Tufts University School of Nutrition, Medford, Mass.

Schlossman, N.P. 1986. Work Resumption, Breast-feeding, and Time Allocation of Mothers in Boston, Massachusetts: The First Half-year Postpartum. Unpublished doctoral dissertation. Tufts University School of Nutrition, Medford, Mass.

Zeitlin, M.F. 1977. Report of a Nutrition Survey Conducted in Abyei District, S. Kordofan Province, Sudan, by the Nutrition Division of the Ministry of Health, Government of the Sudan, and by the Harvard Institute for International Development, Cambridge, Mass., in November and December 1977.

Zeitlin, M.F., and G. Guldan. 1987. Bangladesh Infant Feeding Observations. Preliminary report submitted to the Office of International Health and the Asia and Near East Bureau of the United States Agency for International Development, Washington, D.C., 7 September 1987.

Zeitlin, M.F., G. Guldan, and N. Ahmad. 1985. Sanitary Conditions of Crawling Infants in Rural Bangladesh. Report to the USAID Asia and Near East Bureau, Washington, D.C., November 1985.

Zeitlin, M.F., F.C. Johnson, and K. Houser. In preparation. Active Maternal Feeding and Nutritional Status of 8–20 Month Old Low Income Mexican Children.

Zeitlin, M.F., N.P. Schlossman, and A.S. Beiser. In preparation. Validation of a Telephone Time Use Recall Instrument.

12

Data on Food Consumption by High-risk Family Members: Its Utility for Identifying Target Households for Food and Nutrition Programmes

PER PINSTRUP-ANDERSEN

Cornell Food and Nutrition Policy Project, Cornell University, Ithaca, New York, USA

MARITO GARCIA

International Food Policy Research Institute, Washington, D.C., USA

INTRODUCTION

Efforts to target and assess the nutritional effects of food and nutrition programmes suffer from the lack of a unique or commonly agreed-upon indicator of nutrition impact. Anthropometric measures such as weight- and height-for-age are frequently used in evaluations of nutrition or food distribution programmes, while the impact on the food acquisition of calorie-deficient households is more often used as a proxy for the nutritional effects of food and agricultural policies and programmes. The impact on the food consumption of malnourished individuals is used in some cases, but much less frequently because it is more difficult and costly to obtain reliable data on an individual's food consumption than to obtain his or her anthropometric measurements, or data on household food acquisition.

Attempts to establish a direct causal link between individual anthropometric measures and the effects of nutrition programmes have been disappointing because the intermediate steps and relationships influencing or determining the nutrition effects often are ignored. Results of the evaluations of many nutrition programmes have thus been inconclusive. It is quite possible that in many cases the actual impact on nutrition went undetected but could have been detected if the most important intermediate relationships, such as the impact of the programme on household and/or individual food consumption, had been taken into account. Changes in household food acquisition, similarly, may be a poor proxy for the impact on an individual member's nutritional status. This is because the intra-household food distribution patterns are ignored, as is the impact of changes in an individual's food consumption on his or her nutritional status.

This paper addresses the question of whether or not collecting data on individual household members' food consumption is likely to greatly enhance the reliability of efforts to target food and nutrition programmes to households with malnourished individuals, when malnutrition is measured in terms of calorie intake relative to requirements. The paper specifically seeks to answer three related questions:

164

1. How efficient are estimates of household-level calorie adequacy as a proxy for the calorie adequacy of pre-schoolers and pregnant or lactating women? The answer to this question is crucial to the effective targeting of programmes to households with malnourished members. Can such targeting be based on household-level food consumption data, or must food consumption data be collected on individual high-risk household members?
2. How efficient is weight-for-age as a proxy for the calorie adequacy of pre-schoolers? This is of particular importance in efforts to target programmes to households including calorie-deficient pre-schoolers, because weight data are far easier to collect than data on individual pre-schoolers' calorie consumption.
3. Is the calorie adequacy of individual pre-schoolers and pregnant or lactating women closely correlated with other variables for which data are easier to collect, such as household calorie consumption, household income, and individual anthropometric measures? A high correlation with one of these variables would indicate that collection of data on individual food consumption might not be essential.

Answers to these questions should assist in assessing whether the increased cost of collecting data on individual food consumption can be justified as part of efforts to target nutrition programmes more effectively. This paper should contribute to a better understanding of the trade-offs between cost and reliability of the collection of household- versus individual-level food-consumption data.

SAMPLE DESCRIPTION

The analysis presented here is based on data collected as part of a consumer food-price subsidy scheme in three regions of the Philippines[1] (Garcia and Pinstrup-Andersen, 1987). Data on household-level variables were collected twice during 1983 from a cross-section of 840 households. Anthropometric data on pre-school children were collected monthly from the same households over a 12-month period. Data on the food consumption of individual household members were also obtained twice, but only from a subsample of 134 households (table 1).

The sample was selected from a population of low-income households with a high probability of malnutrition. The overall calorie adequacy for the sample was 70 per cent, as compared to 89 per cent for the Philippines as a whole. About one-third of the sample pre-schoolers had second- or third-degree malnutrition, as compared to 17 per

Table 1. Sample size by region

Region	Total sample households		Households in subsample with individual consumption	
	Round 1[a]	Round 2	Round 1	Round 2
Abra	240	228	40	38
Antique	360	352	60	60
South Cotabato	240	220	40	36
Total	840	800	140	134

a. The first survey round took place during May–June 1983 and the second during September–October 1983.

165

Table 2. Percentage of sample pre-schoolers falling into second- and third-degree malnutrition on the basis of weight-for-age

Region	Percentage second and third degree
Abra	25.5
Antique	34.4
South Cotabato	37.2
Total sample	32.5
Philippines (FNRI, 1982)	17.2

Sources: IFPRI/National Nutrition Council Survey, 1983; Food and Nutrition Research Institute, *Second Nationwide Nutrition Survey of the Philippines* (NSTA, Manila, 1982).

Table 3. Estimated calorie adequacy (in percentage of RDA) of various sex- and age-groups of sample by region[a]

Population group	Abra	Antique	South Cotabato
Fathers	75.5	83.9	86.8
Pregnant women	70.1	63.3	46.4
Lactating women	67.1	71.1	62.9
Adults			
Male	75.8	81.3	83.7
Female	77.6	81.9	71.5
Adolescents			
Male	62.2	65.0	57.2
Female	53.6	64.9	50.4
Schoolers			
Male	56.4	72.4	66.3
Female	56.8	66.6	62.7
Pre-schoolers			
Male	57.2	69.7	63.7
Female	49.5	62.3	61.8
Average, household	65.7	73.6	70.1
Overall average		70.4	
The Philippines (FNRI)		88.6	

a. See Appendix to chapter for RDA for calories for Filipinos.
Sources: IFPRI/National Nutrition Council Survey, 1983; Food and Nutrition Research Institute, *Second Nationwide Nutrition Survey of the Philippines* (NSTA, Manila, 1982).

cent for the Philippines as a whole (table 2). Estimated calorie adequacy was low among sample individuals regardless of age, sex, and region. Calorie adequacy was calculated as actual consumption relative to recommended daily allowances. The latter are shown in the Appendix to this chapter. Severe calorie deficiencies were found among pre-schoolers, particularly girls. Other population groups, including adolescent girls and pregnant or lactating women, were also seriously affected (table 3). This table indicates unequal food distribution within the household. Two independent studies, one in rural Laguna (Valenzuela, 1977), and the other in urban Manila (Aligaen and Florencio, 1980), also reveal inequality in food adequacy between adults and children.

166

HOUSEHOLD ADEQUACY AS A PROXY FOR ADEQUACY AMONG HIGH-RISK INDIVIDUALS

The efficiency of estimates of household-level calorie adequacy as a proxy for the calorie adequacy of high-risk household members, as shown in tables 4 and 5, will be discussed in an attempt to answer question 1 above. Reliance on household calorie adequacy as an indicator of the degree of calorie adequacy of pre-schoolers introduces large errors. Only 39 per cent of the households with pre-schoolers consuming less than one-half of their calorie requirements would be captured by a programme targeted on households below 50 per cent calorie adequacy (24 per cent of all households). A programme targeted on households consuming 60 per cent of requirements or less would leave out 61 per cent of the pre-schoolers who consume 60 per cent or less, including 29 per cent who consume less than 50 per cent of their requirements (table 4).

Table 4. Relationship between calorie adequacy of households and those of pre-schoolers within the households

Calorie adequacy of pre-schoolers (%)[a]		Household calorie adequacy (%)[b]					
		0–50	51–60	61–80	81–100	Above 100	Total
0–50	Number of households	43	17	42	7	2	111
	Percentage of sample	15.69	6.20	15.33	2.55	0.73	40.51
	Row percentage	38.74	15.32	37.84	6.31	1.80	
	Column percentage	64.18	34.69	40.00	16.28	20.00	
1–60	Number of households	14	10	18	1	1	44
	Percentage of sample	5.11	3.65	6.57	0.36	0.36	16.06
	Row percentage	31.82	22.73	40.91	2.27	2.27	
	Column percentage	20.89	20.41	17.14	2.33	10.00	
61–80	Number of households	8	17	31	16	1	73
	Percentage of sample	2.92	6.20	11.31	5.84	0.36	26.64
	Row percentage	10.96	23.28	42.46	21.92	1.37	
	Column percentage	11.94	34.69	29.52	37.21	10.00	
81–100	Number of households	2	4	11	12	3	32
	Percentage of sample	0.73	1.46	4.02	4.38	1.09	11.68
	Row percentage	6.25	12.50	34.37	37.50	9.37	
	Column percentage	2.98	8.16	10.48	27.91	30.00	
Above 100	Number of households	0	1	3	7	3	14
	Percentage of sample	0.00	0.36	1.09	2.55	1.09	5.11
	Row percentage	0.00	7.14	21.43	50.00	21.43	
	Column percentage	0.00	2.05	2.86	16.28	30.00	
Total	Number of households	67	49	105	43	43	274
	Percentage of sample	24.45	17.88	38.32	15.69	3.65	100.00

a. Calorie consumption by household members between 12 and 84 months of age divided by the sum of the RDAs for these household members and multiplied by 100.
b. Total household calorie consumption divided by the sum of the RDAs for all household members and multiplied by 100.
Source: IFPRI/National Nutrition Council Survey in Abra, Antique, and South Cotabato, the Philippines, 1983.

Table 5. Relationship between calorie adequacy of households and those of pregnant and lactating women within the households

Calorie adequacy of pregnant and lactating women (%)[a]		Household calorie adequacy (%)[b]					
		0–50	51–60	61–80	81–100	Above 100	Total
0–50	Number of households	17	2	2	1	0	22
	Percentage of sample	11.72	1.38	1.38	0.69	0.00	15.22
	Row percentage	77.30	9.10	9.10	4.50	0.00	
	Column percentage	39.50	6.90	3.60	5.60	0.00	
51–60	Number of households	10	10	16	0	0	36
	Percentage of sample	6.90	6.90	11.03	0.00	0.00	24.80
	Row percentage	27.80	27.80	44.40	0.00	0.00	
	Column percentage	23.30	34.50	29.10	0.00	0.00	
61–80	Number of households	12	14	23	4	0	53
	Percentage of sample	8.27	9.66	15.86	2.76	0.00	36.60
	Row percentage	22.60	26.40	43.40	7.50	0.00	
	Column percentage	27.90	48.30	41.80	22.20	0.00	
81–100	Number of households	3	2	10	8	0	23
	Percentage of sample	2.07	1.38	6.90	5.52	0.00	15.80
	Row percentage	13.00	8.70	43.50	34.80	0.00	
	Column percentage	7.00	6.90	18.20	44.40	0.00	
Above 100	Number of households	1	1	4	5	0	11
	Percentage of sample	0.69	0.69	2.76	3.45	0.00	7.60
	Row percentage	9.10	9.10	36.40	45.50	0.00	
	Column percentage	2.30	3.40	7.30	27.80	0.00	
Total	Number of households	43	29	55	18	0	145
	Percentage of sample	29.60	20.00	37.90	12.40	0.00	100.00

a. Calorie consumption by pregnant and lactating household members divided by their RDAs and multiplied by 100.
b. Total household calorie consumption divided by the sum of the RDAs for all household members and multiplied by 100.
Source: IFPRI/National Nutrition Council Survey in Abra, Antique, and South Cotabato, the Philippines, 1983.

Household-level calorie adequacy is a more efficient indicator of the calorie adequacy level of pregnant and lactating women (table 5). Thus, a programme targeting households with at-risk women and calorie adequacy levels of 50 per cent or less would capture 77 per cent of the pregnant and/or lactating women whose calorie adequacy levels are 50 per cent or lower.

The problem of excluding such a large number of target households through a targeting approach based on household-level calorie adequacy is compounded by the inclusion of a correspondingly large number of non-target households. Thus, 28 per cent of the households benefiting from a programme targeting households with pre-schoolers and with a household-level calorie adequacy of 60 per cent or lower do not include any pre-schoolers whose calorie adequacy is this low. Similarly, in more than half of the households with pregnant and/or lactating women which would be included on the basis of household-level criteria, these women's calorie adequacy would be actually higher than 60 per cent.

WEIGHT- AND HEIGHT-FOR-AGE AS PROXIES FOR CALORIE ADEQUACY AMONG HIGH-RISK PRE-SCHOOLERS

Tables 6–9 address question 2. They present results of comparisons between anthropometric measures of pre-schoolers and their calorie adequacy or the calorie adequacy of their households. As table 6 shows, targeting households with 60 per cent calorie adequacy or lower (41 per cent of households) would capture one-half of the pre-schoolers whose weight-for-height was 60 per cent or less of standard and 37 per cent of those whose weight-for-height was 61–75 per cent of standard. But 33 per cent of the pre-schoolers who showed no sign of malnutrition (over 90 per cent of weight-for-height standard) would also be covered. Thus, the targeting efficiency is low (table 6). If calorie adequacy of pre-schoolers is used instead of household adequacy, as shown in table 7, two-thirds of the pre-schoolers with third-degree and 54 per cent with second-degree malnutrition would be covered. However, 52 per cent of all households would fall into the target group (table 7), as compared to 40 per cent (table 6) when targeting is based on household adequacy. Furthermore, 46 per cent of the pre-schoolers showing no sign of malnutrition would be included in the target group. In this case, the targeting efficiency is even lower. If, on the other hand, targeting is based on the weight-for-age of pre-schoolers (table 7), and households with pre-schoolers whose weight-for-age is less than 75 per cent of standard are defined as the target group (27 per cent of all households), 28 per cent of the pre-schoolers with a calorie adequacy of 60 per cent or below will be covered, along with the same percentage of those with calorie adequacy of between 60 and 75 per cent. But 22 per cent of the

Table 6. Relationship between weight-for-age of pre-schoolers and household calorie adequacy

Household calorie adequacy (%)		Weight-for-age (in % of standard)				
		0–60	61–75	76–90	Above 90	Total
0–60	Number of households	3	25	65	18	111
	Percentage of sample	1.1	9.1	23.7	6.6	40.5
	Row percentage	2.7	22.5	58.6	16.2	
	Column percentage	50.0	37.3	44.5	32.7	
61–75	Number of households	2	23	40	22	87
	Percentage of sample	0.7	8.4	14.6	8.0	31.8
	Row percentage	2.3	26.4	46.0	25.3	
	Column percentage	33.3	34.3	27.4	40.0	
76–90	Number of households	1	12	19	9	41
	Percentage of sample	0.4	4.4	6.9	3.3	15.0
	Row percentage	2.4	29.3	46.3	22.0	
	Column percentage	16.7	17.9	13.0	16.4	
Above 90	Number of households	0	7	22	6	35
	Percentage of sample	0.0	2.6	8.0	2.2	12.8
	Row percentage	0.0	20.0	62.9	17.1	
	Column percentage	0.0	10.4	15.1	10.9	
Total	Number of households	6	67	146	55	274
	Percentage of sample	2.2	24.5	53.3	20.1	100.0

Source: IFPRI/National Nutrition Council Survey in Abra, Antique, and South Cotabato, the Philippines, 1983.

Table 7. Relationship between weight-for-age and calorie adequacy of pre-schoolers

Pre-schooler calorie adequacy (%)		Weight-for-age (in % of standard)				
		0–60	61–75	76–90	Above 90	Total
0–60	Number of households	4	36	76	25	141
	Percentage of sample	1.5	13.1	27.7	9.1	51.5
	Row percentage	2.8	25.5	53.9	17.7	
	Column percentage	66.7	53.7	52.1	45.5	
61–75	Number of households	1	16	31	13	61
	Percentage of sample	0.4	5.8	11.3	4.7	22.3
	Row percentage	1.6	26.2	50.8	21.3	
	Column percentage	16.7	23.9	21.2	23.6	
76–90	Number of households	1	9	18	11	39
	Percentage of sample	0.4	3.3	6.6	4.0	14.2
	Row percentage	2.6	23.1	46.2	28.2	
	Column percentage	16.7	13.4	12.3	20.0	
Above 90	Number of households	0	6	21	6	33
	Percentage of sample	0.0	2.2	7.7	2.2	12.0
	Row percentage	0.0	18.2	63.6	18.2	
	Column percentage	0.0	9.0	14.4	10.9	
Total	Number of households	6	67	146	55	274
	Percentage of sample	2.2	24.5	53.3	20.1	100.0

Source: IFPRI/National Nutrition Council Survey in Abra, Antique, and South Cotabato, the Philippines, 1983.

Table 8. Relationship between weight-for-height of pre-schoolers and household calorie adequacy

Household calorie adequacy (%)		Weight-for-height (in % of standard)				
		0–60	61–75	76–90	Above 90	Total
0–60	Number of households	1	2	35	73	111
	Percentage of sample	0.4	0.7	12.8	26.6	40.5
	Row percentage	1.9	1.8	31.5	65.8	
	Column percentage	100.0	25.0	44.9	39.0	
61–75	Number of households	0	4	19	64	87
	Percentage of sample	0.0	1.5	6.9	23.4	31.8
	Row percentage	0.0	4.6	21.8	73.6	
	Column percentage	0.0	50.0	24.4	34.2	
76–90	Number of households	0	2	13	20	35
	Percentage of sample	0.0	0.7	4.7	7.3	12.8
	Row percentage	0.0	5.7	37.1	57.1	
	Column percentage	0.0	25.0	16.7	10.7	
Above 90	Number of households	0	2	13	20	35
	Percentage of sample	0.0	0.7	4.7	7.3	12.8
	Row percentage	0.0	5.7	37.1	57.1	
	Column percentage	0.0	25.0	16.7	10.7	
Total	Number of households	1	8	78	187	274
	Percentage of sample	0.4	2.9	28.5	68.2	100.0

Source: IFPRI/National Nutrition Council Survey in Abra, Antique, and South Cotabato, the Philippines, 1983.

170

Table 9. Relationship between weight-for-height and calorie adequacy for pre-schoolers

Pre-schooler calorie adequacy (%)		Weight-for-height (in % of standard)				Total
		0–60	61–75	76–90	Above 90	
0–60	Number of households	1	6	41	93	141
	Percentage of sample	0.4	2.2	15.0	33.9	57.5
	Row percentage	0.7	4.3	29.1	66.0	
	Column percentage	100.0	75.0	52.6	49.7	
61–75	Number of households	0	1	19	41	61
	Percentage of sample	0.0	0.4	6.9	15.0	22.3
	Row percentage	0.0	1.6	31.1	67.2	
	Column percentage	0.0	12.5	24.4	21.9	
76–90	Number of households	0	0	10	29	39
	Percentage of sample	0.0	0.0	3.6	10.6	14.2
	Row percentage	0.0	0.0	25.6	74.4	
	Column percentage	0.0	0.0	12.8	15.5	
Above 90	Number of households	0	1	8	24	33
	Percentage of sample	0.0	0.4	2.9	8.6	12.0
	Row percentage	0.0	3.0	24.2	72.7	
	Column percentage	0.0	12.5	10.3	12.8	
Total	Number of households	1	8	78	187	274
	Percentage of sample	0.4	2.9	28.5	68.2	100.0

Source: IFPRI/National Nutrition Council Survey in Abra, Antique, and South Cotabato, the Philippines, 1983.

pre-schoolers with calorie adequacy levels above 75 per cent will also be included in the target group.

The weight-for-height of about one-third (31.8 per cent) of the sample pre-schoolers was 90 per cent of standard or below. Forty-four per cent of these would be covered by a programme targeting households with 60 per cent or lower calorie adequacy. However, 39 per cent of the children with weight-for-height above 90 per cent of standard would also be covered (table 8). Targeting households with children weighing 90 per cent or less of standard for their height would cover about 34 per cent of all households and also 32 per cent of pre-schoolers with calorie adequacy of 60 per cent or less (table 9).

CORRELATION BETWEEN CALORIE ADEQUACY OF HIGH-RISK INDIVIDUALS AND SELECTED INDICATORS

Tables 10 and 11 address the third question, i.e. the correlation between individual calorie adequacy and other potential nutrition indicators. The correlations are low, indicating that none of the selected variables are good proxies for the calorie adequacy of individual high-risk household members. Household calorie adequacy, however, is a much better proxy for the calorie adequacy of pregnant and lactating women than for the calorie adequacy of pre-schoolers. This may be due in part to the greater relative importance of the quantity of food consumed by pregnant and lactating women in relation to overall household food consumption. The implication of this finding, if it is of general validity, is that it is more important to collect data on the individual con-

171

Table 10. Simple correlation between calorie adequacy of pre-schoolers and selected proxies (sample size = 375)

Proxy measure	Correlation coefficient
Household calorie consumption/capita	0.42
Household calorie consumption	0.30
Household calorie adequacy	0.27
Household food acquisition (expenditures)	0.12
Household food acquisition/capita (expenditures/capita)	0.11
Household income/capita	0.04
Weight of pre-schooler relative to standard	0.03

Table 11. Simple correlation between calorie adequacy of pregnant and lactating women and selected proxies (sample size = 124)

Proxy measure	Correlation coefficient
Household calorie adequacy	0.52
Household calorie consumption	0.35
Household calorie acquisition/capita (expenditures/capita)	0.17
Household food acquisition (expenditures)	0.12
Household income/capita	0.09
Household food acquisition/capita (calories/capita)	0.09
Household food acquisition (calories)	0.05

Table 12. Simple correlation between weight of pre-schoolers relative to standard and selected proxies (sample size = 2,526)

Proxy measure	Correlation coefficient
Household income/capita	0.22
Household food acquisition/capita (expenditures/capita)	0.17
Household calorie consumption/capita	0.16
Household calorie adequacy	0.15
Household food acquisition (expenditures)	0.12
Household calorie consumption	0.08

sumption of pre-schoolers, while household-level data may suffice to target and assess the impact of policies and programmes for pregnant and lactating women.

Table 12 shows that the correlation between the weight of pre-schoolers relative to standard weights and household-level variables is generally low. It is noteworthy that household incomes per capita appear to be a better proxy for the weight of pre-schoolers than household calorie variables. This is probably because incomes fluctuate less than calorie consumption and thus are a better long-term indicator of the well-being of the household.

CONCLUSIONS

The results presented in this paper lead to the following conclusions:
1. If weight-for-age and weight-for-height of pre-schoolers are deemed to be the most appropriate nutrition indicators, then collection of data on the calorie consumption

of individual household members does not appear to be justified for targeting purposes.

2. If the calorie adequacy of pre-schoolers is the indicator chosen to assess their nutritional status and thus is used as the basis for targeting, data should be collected on the calories consumed by these children. In our study, neither household-level variables nor anthropometric measures were found to provide acceptable proxies for the calorie adequacy of individual pre-schoolers.

3. Household calorie adequacy appears to be an acceptable indicator for targeting if the goal of the project is to improve the nutritional status of pregnant and lactating women with large calorie deficits.

Thus, collection of data on the food consumption of individual high-risk household members for the purpose of programme targeting does not appear to be justified if the identification of target households is based on anthropometric measures of pre-schoolers or calorie adequacy of pregnant and/or lactating women. On the other hand, no acceptable proxy was found for calorie adequacy of pre-schoolers. Efforts to target programmes on households with pre-schoolers showing a large deficit in calorie intakes, therefore, should be based on consumption data for those individuals.

The conclusions we have drawn appear to be valid for our data from the Philippines. Caution should be exercised, however, in interpreting the results and in generalizing the findings beyond the scope of this study. The collection of reliable data on the food consumption of individual household members is extremely difficult, time-consuming, and expensive.[2] In our study, for instance, household and individual consumption were measured (by food weighing) for only one 24-hour period in each survey round. Thus, day-to-day variations may have introduced errors in the estimates, although the consumption of high-risk members relative to total household consumption may not show a large day-to-day variation. To ensure more reliable data, one would have to expand data collection beyond one 24-hour period to seven or more consecutive days. This would greatly increase costs and reduce the feasible sample size.[3] Furthermore, efforts to weigh all foods consumed by individual household members are likely to influence their actual consumption and considerably reduce the reliability of the data. The presence of the researcher during meals would also be likely to interfere in the normal table behaviour during a family meal. Dietary recall, aided by food models, is a less intrusive method. Adequate social preparation must take place, as was done in this survey, in order to ensure accuracy and representativeness of the usual intakes.

In addition to the difficulties of obtaining reasonably accurate measures of calorie consumption, there are also problems with respect to the measurement of calorie requirements. In this analysis, average RDAs for each population subgroup for the Philippines was used (see Appendix to this chapter). However, variation in requirements among individuals within a subgroup may be large and is not reflected in the estimated adequacy levels.

This paper has not addressed the question of whether calorie adequacy or anthropometric measures of high-risk individuals are the most appropriate indicator of nutritional status. Because anthropometric measures reflect the impact of both food and health factors, poor growth performance detected by anthropometric assessment may not be caused by lack of food. Thus, targeting food transfers to households with children with, say, low weight-for-age will only be appropriate if the food and nutrient intake of these children is insufficient as reflected in their calorie or nutrient adequacy. Therefore, food transfer programmes should be targeted on the basis of the degree of calorie deficiency rather than individual anthropometrics.

This study did not identify acceptable proxies for the calorie adequacy of pre-schoolers. Thus, in spite of the high cost, data must be collected on the food consumption of individual pre-schoolers if programmes are to be targeted on households with pre-schoolers suffering from a high level of calorie or nutrient deficiency.

NOTES

1. This study was jointly supported by grants from the United Nations Development Programme (UNDP) and the National Nutrition Council (NNC) of the Government of the Philippines.
2. It was estimated that the cost of collecting consumption data through food-weighing during one 24-hour period was two-and-a-half times the cost of collecting the data from seven-day recall of food acquisition if the total household consumption was weighed, and four times if foods consumed by each individual were weighed.
3. Food-weighing for each individual household member for each of seven consecutive days was estimated to cost about ten times the cost of obtaining the data from seven-day recall, or, conversely, for a given cost, the relative size of the samples that could be included under each of the two approaches would be 1 to 10.

REFERENCES

Aligaen, M., and C. Florencio. 1980. Intrahousehold Nutrient Distribution and Adequacy of Food and Nutrition Intake of Filipino Urban Households. *Phil. J. Nutr.*, 1: 11–19.

Food and Nutrition Research Institute. 1977. *Recommended Dietary Allowances for Filipinos*. Publication 75. FNRI, Manila.

Food and Nutrition Research Institute. 1982. *The Second Nationwide Nutrition Survey*. NSTA, Manila.

Garcia, M., and P. Pinstrup-Andersen. 1987. The Pilot Food Price Subsidy Scheme in the Philippines: Its Impact on Income, Food Consumption, and Nutritional Status. Research Report 61. International Food Policy Research Institute, Washington, D.C.

Valenzuela, R. 1977. A Study of Nutrient Distribution within the Family and Factors Affecting Nutrient Intake. Mimeo. University of the Philippines, Quezon City.

APPENDIX. RDA for Energy for Filipinos (Kcal/Day)

Men		Girls	
20–39 years	2,580	10–12 years	2,170
40–49 years	2,450	13–15 years	2,200
50–59 years	2,320	16–19 years	2,060
60–69 years	2,060		
70 and over	1,810	*Pregnant*	
		13–15 years	2,630
Women		16–19 years	2,490
20–39 years	1,920	20–39 years	2,350
40–49 years	1,820	40–49 years	2,250
50–59 years	1,730		
60–69 years	1,540	*Lactating (1–6 months)*	
70 and over	1,340	13–15 years	2,750
		16–19 years	2,610
Infants (6–11 months)	970	20–39 years	2,470
		40–49 years	2,370
Children			
1–3 years	1,310	*Lactating (6–12 months)*	
4–6 years	1,640	13–15 years	2,640
7–9 years	1,870	16–19 years	2,500
		20–39 years	2,360
Boys		40–49 years	2,260
10–12 years	2,270		
13–15 years	2,510		
16–19 years	2,700		

Source: Recommended Dietary Allowances for Filipinos, FNRI Publication No. 75 (FNRI, Manila, May 1977). 1977).

13
Determinants of the Ability of Household Members to Adapt to Social and Economic Changes

CONSTANTINA SAFILIOS-ROTHSCHILD

Department of Women's Studies, Agricultural University, De Leeuwenborch, Wageningen, The Netherlands

The determinants of the ability of household members to adapt to social and economic changes can be best examined within the theoretical framework of a social and sex-stratification model, supplemented by the conflict theory of family dynamics (Collins, 1975). While the social stratification theory is quite well known, it is important to spell out the nature of the sex-stratification theoretical model. The sex-stratification system has been defined as follows (Safilios-Rothschild, 1982a):

The sex-stratification system ranks the one gender, practically always the male gender, higher than the other – the female gender – and determines that men only will occupy major decision-making positions and will control the valued resources in the society. Such valued resources include a wide range of resources such as: wealth, income, credit, knowledge (in terms of literacy and education as well as information), technology, valued skills, valued income-generating activities, food, health, power, and prestige. The sex-stratification system, that is, men's superior status leading to power over women and control of valued resources, is supported by laws and policies that spell out and legitimise men's privileged and dominant status and is justified by religious, traditional, moral, and/or pseudo-scientific ideologies and beliefs.

Moreover, it has been documented that sex stratification is institutionalized and pervasive and is being maintained and supported by widespread institutional mechanisms and sets of beliefs. Such mechanisms and beliefs help perpetuate the sex-stratification system even in the face of structural changes that ought to diminish, if not completely undermine, the strength of its operation. A striking example can be found in Lesotho, where about half (47.7 per cent) of the men are absent from the country working in South African mines at any time (and the percentage is much higher in mountainous rural areas). Even so. several mechanisms and beliefs aiming to diminish the impact of this absence are responsible for only a delayed and at best partial definition of the persisting pattern of male absence as a long-term manpower shortage necessitating structural dedifferentiation in many sectors. As a consequence, the process of structural dedifferentiation has taken a very long time and is by no means complete so as to allow especially rural women greater access to all types of services and resources, including political participation (Safilios-Rothschild, 1985).

176

The combined framework of the two stratification systems helps to predict some important trends at the societal and the household level. The theoretical model predicts, for example, that in countries in which the class system tends to be closed and rigid, with few institutionalized avenues for social mobility, membership of a social class represents such an important status that it can neutralize the negative effects of the female (low) sex status (Safilios-Rothschild, 1980). A study in rural Kenya, for example, showed that élite women farm managers were visited as often by agricultural extension officers as were male farmers in élite jointly managed farms. Low-income women farm managers, on the other hand, were visited much less often than low-income male farmers in jointly managed farms and less often than were élite women farm managers. The same trends, though even more accentuated, held true with regard to loans and access to agricultural training (Staudt, 1979). Thus, low-income women's access to resources is doubly curtailed by the compound effect of being a low-status member in both stratification systems.

The theoretical model can be used to make predictions for society at large and within the household. The more scarce the valued resources, the more the patterns of allocating these resources represent "rational" investment strategies that are thought to maximize the short- and long-term survival chances of the institution (i.e. society or household). The pervasiveness of a powerful sex-stratification system operating in practically all developing countries, coupled with an equally powerful social stratification system, is responsible for the fact that such rational investment strategies are usually male-biased. At the societal level, traditional patriarchal values assign to men the economic responsibility for women and children.[1] Men are thus given priority over women in terms of preferential access to paid employment, income-generating productive activities, and credit, in addition to better education and training opportunities. Such a pattern is clearly discerned in developing countries in which rapid rates of population growth are making scarce such key resources as paid employment, credit, training facilities, teachers, and land.

Similarly, gender (along with age) is a key distributional criterion at the household level. It can be used as a proxy for income-earning capacity, since women usually have lesser access to paid employment and income in general than do men. In many instances, women have no job or income-earning opportunities at all. Poor households, in which food and access to health care and education are scarce, allocate these resources on the basis of gender and age priorities (Safilios-Rothschild, 1980). By systematically favouring over women and girls (in descending order) adult men, young men, adolescent boys, and infant boys, all of whom have greater actual or potential access to income than do female household members, the chances for household survival are maximized. Alternatively, in households which are not constrained by scarcity of these resources, there is no need to make difficult allocation decisions: male and female members of all ages tend to have a greater probability of equal access to resources than in poorer households (Safilios-Rothschild, 1979, 1980).

The sex-stratification theory predicts the important determinants of flexibility or rigidity a society, community, or household experiences in the face of important social and economic changes. The key determinant of the extent of flexibility or rigidity in response to these changes is *the visibility* of the changes in terms of their accurate documentation and the availability of the facts to policy-makers and programme designers and implementers. Institutional mechanisms and sets of beliefs play crucial roles in keeping "undesirable" changes *invisible* and, thus, in maintaining the sex-stratification system intact (Safilios-Rothschild, 1985). Examples of significant changes that have remained invisible for a long time (and in a number of countries are still invisible) are the increasing incidence of female-headed households (legal and de facto), the feminization of smallholder agriculture, and the existence and importance of wives' incomes.

The sex-stratification system rests on the premise that women are economically dependent on men. The increased prevalence of female-headed households in many developing countries has been viewed as a challenge to this basic premise and a threat to the very fabric of patriarchal society. Sex-role stereotypes espoused by statisticians and interviewers, as well as male and female respondents, have led to methodologies and datasets that underestimate the prevalence of female-headed households, particularly of de facto rural female-headed households created by male migration (Safilios-Rothschild, 1982a, 1982b, 1982c; Youssef and Hetler, 1983). In Lesotho, for example, the official statistics have enumerated only the legal female-headed households (35 per cent) and not the other half (35 per cent) of de facto female-headed households (Safilios-Rothschild, 1985). Research undertaken in rural Kakamega, Kenya, showed that women whose husbands worked in Nairobi, and only visited for about one month per year, had diffculty admitting that they made all agricultural decisions by themselves. Such an admission would indicate that husbands no longer played a dominant role in the family and would shake the established sex-stratified order.

In addition, even when the appropriate data are collected, they are often not analysed and disseminated to policy-makers and programme designers and implementers. Through these mechanisms, the true prevalence of female-headed households remains underestimated and no structural changes are brought about to help these households become integrated into the development process on the same basis as male-headed households. Finally, even when the statistics concerning the prevalence of such households are collected and disseminated, the impact on policies and programmes is often negligible because of the existence of sex-stereotypic beliefs that tend to diminish the significance of the statistical trends. In Lesotho, for example, it is believed that men make all important agricultural decisions and do most of the heavy work in agriculture, despite the fact that they are present at home only for about one month in twelve, after a year's hard work in the South African mines. These beliefs are responsible for the fact that the women heads of 75 per cent of the households in most rural areas are not integrated into the mainstream of agricultural planning and programmes (Safilios-Rothschild, 1985).

In many areas of sub-Saharan Africa, male migration has led to the feminization of smallholder agriculture. The lack of societal adaptation to these changes, in terms of reorientation and redirection of agricultural services and resources towards women farmers, and the failure to provide women farmers with incentives, however, carries the heavy price of low agricultural productivity, lack of interest in adopting long-term land improvements and agricultural investments, and lack of food self-sufficiency for the household.

Women's income can also play a crucial role in the dynamics of intra-household allocation of resources. The *visibility* of this key variable is an especially important factor. In the context of low-income households (particularly of rural households), women's income, although usually very low, often represents as much as 40 to 50 per cent of the total household income. In-depth studies in various developing countries (e.g. Honduras) have revealed that, despite the crucial role that women's income

178

often plays for family survival, in the traditional context of low-income households the size and importance of this income is usually not acknowledged by husbands. This is because such an acknowledgement would constitute an admission of the husband's inadequacy as a breadwinner, and would tend to undermine his unquestioned dominance (Safilios-Rothschild, 1988).

The maintenance of invisibility in this case is facilitated by the characteristics of women's income, particularly of rural women's income, and a number of mechanisms women (and men) use to minimize the significance of women's economic contributions. Their income is usually earned in very small sums from a variety of sources (such as selling eggs and chicken, foodstuffs, straw mats, or small quantities of crops). Moreover, it is unpredictable in that there is no regular amount and no set time when it is earned, as there would be with a regular pay cheque. Finally, since women in low-income households often use these small sums almost immediately to buy food or other needed household items, they do not always have the chance to develop the concept of an income that they earn and control. Interviewed rural women sometimes report that they do not earn an income, or that they earn less than is the case. This perception reduces the threat that a wife's earnings may represent to a husband with marginal income-earning capacity (Safilios-Rothschild, 1983, 1988). The combined class and sex theoretical model predicts that increases in women's income will tend to remain invisible if they are perceived as threatening to the image of men as breadwinners. Indeed, in-depth studies in rural Honduras have shown that when husbands do not earn a sufficient income to support their families properly, and when their wives earn almost as much as they do, the threat is diminished through a variety of mechanisms which minimize the importance of their wives' incomes. Although it is difficult to achieve the total invisibility of women's earnings, men grossly underestimate this income and thus are able more comfortably to retain power and authority. This distorted perception is reinforced by the characteristics of the income and by the women themselves, who understate what they earn partly in order not to threaten their husbands (Safilios-Rothschild, 1988).

Under these circumstances, women's income can easily remain invisible. Its characteristics in low-income rural households (e.g. irregularity, unpredictability, and small amounts from different sources) explain not only the fact that increases in women's earnings often pass totally unnoticed, but also such increases do not in any way affect the allocation of women's labour, time (especially for leisure), or decision-making power within the household. It is only when women earn a visible, stable, and substantial income from agricultural and market activities or from wages, and when husbands earn a secure income, larger than their wives', that the distribution of labour, time, and decision-making power is shifted according to the importance of the wives' economic contributions (Safilios-Rothschild and Dijkers, 1978; Safilios-Rothschild, 1988). What is unknown within this type of household context and needs to be researched is the extent to which invisible increases in women's income lead to positive changes in the intra-household allocation of food and/or health care, even when there is no reallocation of other inputs such as power or time and tasks.

When, on the other hand women's income becomes visible as a result of the shared earnings from a women's co-operative or group, or from participation in the formal employment sector, and the sums of money earned are both more regular and more substantial, the usual mechanisms for minimizing women's monetary contribution and maintaining its invisibility are no longer effective. In areas in which social structural conditions make it very difficult for men to be adequate breadwinners, women's access to income generated through such visible means is even more of a threat to men's status and identity. Powerful mechanisms are called into play to maintain the sex-stratification bias. In some cases, men have taken over the control of development projects that exclusively benefit women as soon as they show some potential for generating a substantial income (Bekele, 1982; Noble and Nolan, 1983; Sundar, 1981). In Mombasa, Kenya, for instance, it was found that in areas in which men had poorly paid, marginal occupations, the incomes women earned through group projects were controlled by the men, and the women were not able to acquire prestige or decision-making power as a function of such income (McCormack et al., 1986).

Within the context of a powerful and pervasive sex-stratification system, men cannot adapt to social and economic changes that significantly increase women's access to income, the key resource. Instead, under these circumstances, they usually resort to mechanisms that neutralize the impact of ongoing changes, and thus preserve the sex-stratification status quo. The degree of potential rigidity of adult male household members in response to women's increased and visible access to income becomes even more accentuated when all these mechanisms fail to bring about the desired outcome. Men have been found to resort then to force and violence: they may usurp the women's earnings, even if they have to beat them up, or they may become more domineering, authoritarian, repressive, and violent at home than before in order to ensure that the integrity of the existing patriarchal power structure is not in any way challenged by women's changing status (de Graft-Johnson, 1984).

This type of rigidity explains why women-focused income-generating projects in low-income communities, where men have few opportunities to increase their own incomes, are usually doomed to failure; it also accounts for the fact that, even when women are able to substantially increase their own incomes, this change sometimes has little, if any, impact on the intra-household allocation of resources or power. It must be noted, however, that when men are able adequately to support their families, there is also considerable evidence of substantial male adaptability to women's increased income-earning. The men's willingness to change the intra-household allocation of resources under these circumstances is high. The more secure men are in their breadwinner role, the more adaptable they are to women's income-earning ability, probably because women's income does not represent a threat to their superior position as males (Safilios-Rothschild and Dijkers, 1978; Safilios-Rothschild, 1985). In Mombasa, Kenya, it was found that only in one community, in which husbands had a stable and sufficient economic base, were women able to translate their economic contributions into a valuable resource that earned them more decision-making power and more equality in the division of labour (McCormack et al., 1986).

The degree of rigidity or adaptability on the part of household members to social and economic changes may, in fact, differ according to the type of resource allocated and to the generation of the recipient. It is therefore possible that under the conditions specified above, wives' increased access to income and/or paid employment would promote rigidity with respect to changes in intra-household power allocation, but considerable flexibility and adaptation in terms of time allocation. Or, more importantly, these changes in wives' income-earning potential might prompt intra-household redistribution of resources such as food, health care, and education and training in favour of young girls, even if they do not favour adult women, or specifically wives. This pattern might be explained by the logic that women's increased access to income increases the rationality of investments in daughters, in addition to sons, for maximizing household welfare (cf. Rosenzweig, this volume). Such an intergenerational reallocation in investment priorities does not pose as big a potential threat to adult males as do changes that may affect their power relationships with adult women.

The class- and sex-stratification theoretical model must be supplemented by a conflict theory of family dynamics (Collins, 1975) in order to derive predictions and explanations of what determines the degree of rigidity or adaptability household members experience when faced with social and economic changes. An important premise of such a conflict theory is that families and households cannot be viewed as monolithic institutions in which the members all agree on the strategies and means to be used to maximize family or household welfare. Instead, individual household members have different interests and needs which are often incongruent and conflict. Household welfare is thus the balance achieved through a series of compromises and accommodations among individual household members according to their interests and needs, as determined by their bargaining power. This is a function of members' personal characteristics (cf. Engle, this volume), their access to economic resources, the availability of alternatives, prevailing cultural norms, influential institutions, and macro-policies (Folbre, 1984; Jones, 1983; Fapohunda, 1987; Safilios-Rothschild, 1987). This reality of household dynamics is central to the understanding of rigidity and adaptability patterns.

The addition of a second wife to a household illustrates how conflicting interests between household members can lead to rigidity in some cases and adaptability in others, depending on the perceived costs and benefits to individual household members. Evidence from several sub-Saharan African countries in which polygamy is still widespread shows that first wives tend to accept the second or third wife because they perceive several advantages and not only disadvantages. This adaptability is predicated on the fact that first wives (particularly in rural areas) have a very heavy workload, and they welcome labour-sharing with the second or third wife (McSweeney, 1979). This is especially true when wives' land plots are large and productive enough to feed their own children and to yield a potential surplus. Thus, first wives adapt to a structural change that decreases their access to their husbands' love, sexual favours, labour, and income contribution because they gain in terms of time for their own sleep, labour, and a certain degree of autonomy in terms of being able to control the money they earn and to get involved in marketing away from home (Safilios-Rothschild, 1983). In some provinces and countries in sub-Saharan Africa, on the other hand, land is a scarce resource, and it is possible that additional wives become more threatening and less acceptable to first wives.

Macro-policies such as agrarian reform, population, and producer pricing policies have significant potential social and economic consequences for households and may have a differential impact on household members. Probably the least recognized and studied macro-policies in terms of their impact on household members are the producer pricing policies. In several sub-Saharan African countries (e.g. Zambia), such policies have been adopted, often favouring "men's crops," and thus creating considerable intra-household conflict regarding the mode of allocation of different household members' time and labour to agricultural production, as well as the allocation of resulting profits. Under these conditions, husbands may attempt to increase the size of land on which the favoured crop is cultivated, but are quite dependent on their wives' (and children's) labour for the successful outcome of this expansion. Wives, on the other hand, have little or no motivation to reallocate their labour so as to give their husbands more time at the expense of time for their own crops, the profits of which they control (Jones, 1983). There is, therefore, a source of built-in rigidity on the part of wives to adapt to macro-policies having potentially substantial social and economic consequences for intra-household allocation of time, labour, and income when their own status as independent farmers and producers is threatened. They are reluctant to change their status to that of unpaid or poorly paid family workers on their husbands' plots. The situation becomes even more complicated when official producer pricing policies encourage the cultivation of "men's" crops (cash crops) and also of "women's" crops such as sorghum, millet, and cassava. This is true in Zambia, where wives have an even greater vested interest in allocating their labour inputs to their own crops. The extent of women's rigidity or adaptability, as evidenced by their resistance or willingness to compromise and achieve a balance of labour-sharing between their *own* crops and their husbands', depends on several things.

A first important factor is the nature of the cost-benefit balance perceived by men and women as a result of changes in labour requirements, prices, and market demand for "men's" and "women's" crops and women's ability to control their crops and the resulting income. The types of incentives available for women's labour investment play a crucial role in the way conflicts are resolved. These incentives depend, on the one hand, on men's willingness to reward women's labour inputs to their crop production and, on the other hand, on women's ability to take advantage of formal markets and prices for their products without losing control over their own crops or income as they did in Cameroon (Jones, 1983; Guyer, 1978). Women's ability to take advantage of formal markets and prices may be curtailed by their not being members of the co-operatives which buy the crops, and, even more importantly, by their husbands, who may take over the formal market transactions of their wives' crops because now they involve greater sums of money. Husbands may be able to do so because they themselves are members of co-operatives.

Second, women's access to land and other assets independently of men and/or access to reliable income-generating activities can also influence considerably the extent to which wives are willing to adapt to the agro-policy changes. The lesser the women's access to land, assets, and income-generating activities, the greater their willingness to compromise by apportioning their labour between their husbands' crops and their own. On the other hand, in several sub-Saharan countries where women own their own land (via inheritance or outright purchase) on which they cultivate cash crops in addition to food crops, they may be under no obligation to provide their husbands with labour (Vellenga, 1977).

Finally, since marital dissolution is the limiting factor in this type of marital conflict (this is especially true in sub-Saharan countries), the degree of social acceptability of divorce, the probability of remarriage for women, and the viability of female-headed households, which in turn is determined by access to significant income-earning opportunities, further conditions wives' (and husbands') degree of rigidity or adaptability.

In conclusion, adaptability to social and economic changes on the part of household members generally appears to be determined by the extent to which these changes threaten their access to valued resources, especially those of power and prestige. Household members, therefore, tend not to perceive threatening changes or to minimize them as long as possible. Alternatively, they may react with rigidity to changes they cannot minimize or make invisible. For development policies and programmes it is crucial to determine what facilitates household members' adaptability to social and economic changes affecting their access to resources. This is particularly important since development interventions cannot directly interfere with household dynamics in order to obtain desirable outcomes in terms of intra-household resource allocation: they can only alter household members' access to resources, and thus indirectly affect such outcomes. Intra-household dynamics determine whether or not and to what extent changes in household members' *access* to resources lead to changes in intra-household *allocation* of resources.

The theoretical frameworks presented in this paper and illustrated with concrete examples from developing countries provide some important clues as to how development policies and programmes can increase household members' access to key resources and thus promote a more equitable distribution of resources within the household. The following findings seem to be the most important for development interventions.

1. In areas where men and women have very few opportunities to earn a regular income, development interventions that increase women's without increasing men's access to income are a threat to the basis of the sex-stratification system. For a variety of reasons, therefore, they may not lead to changes in terms of intra-household resource allocation or even in terms of access to the income. Hence, development interventions need to increase men's and women's income in a balanced manner in order to achieve desirable outcomes in terms of intra-household reallocation of food, health care, time, labour, and power.

2. Social and macro-economic policies, as well as development programmes, need to take into consideration the fact that households are not monolithic institutions within which all members have the same interests and needs and decide together how to maximize household welfare. Instead, policy-makers need to obtain solid information about the conflicting interests and needs of different household members, according to their gender and generation, in order to be able to predict the differential impact that policies and programmes will have on these members and their reactions to changes. The understanding of the interests and needs of different household members is the key to understanding intra-household dynamics.

3. It is essential to monitor and evaluate both the short- and long-term impacts of development policies and programmes on the household. More specifically, the focus should be directed on the effects of policies and programmes on individuals within the household, in order to improve predictions and the likelihood of attaining desirable outcomes (cf. Engle, this volume).

NOTES

1. The strength of these patriarchal values is demonstrated by the fact that they persist even in societies – as in most sub-Saharan African countries – in which women traditionally are responsible for feeding the family, and in which, as is the norm especially in the rural areas of some districts and provinces, 40–50 per cent of the households are headed by women.

REFERENCES

Bekele, F. 1982. Report of Mission to DANA and Golgotta Settlement Schemes. Mimeo. Addis Ababa.

Collins, R. 1975. *Conflict Sociology*. Academic Press, New York.

Fapohunda, E.P. 1987. The Nuclear Household Model in Nigerian Public and Private Sector Policy: Colonial Legacy and Socio-political Implications. *Devel. Change*, 18: 281–294.

Folbre, N. 1984. Household Production in the Philippines: A Non-neoclassical Approach. *Econ. Devel. Cult. Change*, 32: 303–430.

de Graft-Johnson, K.E. 1984. Oral Presentation at the Inter-regional United Nations Seminar on Changing Families: Relevant Social Welfare Strategies, Moscow, USSR, 1984.

Guyer, J.I. 1978. Women's Work in the Food Economy of the Cocoa Belt: A Comparison. Working Paper 7. Boston University African Studies Center, Boston, Mass.

Jones, C. 1983. The Mobilisation of Women's Labor for Cash Crop Production: A Game Theoretical Approach. *Am. J. Agric. Econ.*, 65(5): 1049–1054.

McCormack, J., M. Walsh, and C. Nelson. 1986. *Women's Group Enterprises: A Study of the Structure of Opportunity on the Kenya Coast*. World Education, Inc., Boston.

McSweeney, B.G. 1979. An Approach to Collecting and Examining Data on Rural Women's Time Use and Some Tentative Findings: The Case of Upper Volta. Working paper prepared for the Seminar on Rural Women and the Sexual Division of Labor of the Population Council, New York, 30 March 1979.

Noble, A.L., and M.F. Nolan. 1983. Sociological Constraints and Social Possibilities for Production of Goats in Western Kenya. Department of Rural Sociology, University of Columbia, Columbia, Mo.

Safilios-Rothschild, C. 1979. *Access of Rural Girls to Primary Education in the Third World: State of Art, Obstacles and Policy Recommendations*. Agency for International Development, Office of Women in Development, Washington, D.C.

——. 1980. The Role of the Family: A Neglected Aspect of Poverty. In: P. Knight, ed., *Implementing Programs of Human Development*, pp. 311–372. Staff Working Paper 403. World Bank, Washington, D.C.

——. 1982a. A Class and Sex Stratification Model and Its Relevance for Fertility Trends in the Developing World. In: C. Hohn and R. Mackensen, eds., *Determinants of Fertility Trends: Theories Re-examined*, pp. 191–202. Ordina Editions, Liège.

——. 1982b. Adequacy of Socio-economic Indicators for Monitoring and Evaluation of the Impact of Agrarian Reform and Rural Development on Low-income and Disadvantaged Groups. Background document for the Expert Consultation on Socio-economic Indicators for the North African and Middle Eastern Region, organized by FAO in Tunis, Tunisia, 1982.

——. 1982c. Pertinencia de los indicadores socioeconómicos para el seguimiento y la evaluación de los grupos de bajos ingresos y desfavorecidos. Background document for the Expert Consultation on Socio-economic Indicators for the Latin American and Caribbean Region, organized by FAO in La Paz, Bolivia (ESH/ESS:ARRD/LA/4), 1982.

——. 1983. Family and Development in Sub-Saharan Africa. Paper commissioned by the Centre for Social Development and Humanitarian Affairs, Social Integration and Social Welfare Section, Vienna International Centre.

——. 1985. The Persistence of Women's Invisibility in Agriculture: Theoretical and Policy Lessons from Lesotho and Sierra Leone. *Econ. Devel. Cult. Change*, 33(2): 299–317.

——. 1987. *Farming Systems and Gender Issues*. Ministry of Agriculture and Fisheries of the Netherlands, The Hague.

——. 1988. The Impact of Agrarian Reform on Men's and Women's Incomes in Rural Honduras. In: D. Dwyer and J. Bruce, eds., *A Home Divided: Women and Income in the Third World*. Stanford University Press, Stanford, Calif.

Safilios-Rothschild, C., and M. Dijkers. 1978. Handling Unconventional Asymmetries. In: R. Rapaport and R.N. Rapaport, eds., *Working Couples*, pp. 62–73, Routledge & Kegan Paul, London.

Staudt, K.A. 1979. Class and Sex in the Politics of Women Farmers. *J. Politics*, 41(2): 492–512.

Sundar, P. 1981. Khadgodhra: A Case Study of a Women's Milk Cooperative. *Soc. Action*, 31: 79–88.

Vellenga, D.D. 1977. Differentiation among Women Farmers in Two Rural Areas in Ghana. *Labour and Society*, 2(2): 197–208.

Youssef, N.H. and C.B. Hetler. 1983. Establishing the Economic Condition of Woman-headed Households in the Third World: A New Approach. In: M. Buvinic, M.A. Lycette, and W.P. McGreevey, eds., *Women and Poverty in the Third World*, pp. 216–243. Johns Hopkins University Press, Baltimore, Md.

Conclusions

BEATRICE LORGE ROGERS AND NINA P. SCHLOSSMAN

The underlying goal of economic development is to improve the welfare of disadvantaged people. The individual is the ultimate target of development efforts, be they undertaken at the household, community, or national level. A successful programme or policy improves human welfare. It benefits the intended target group and achieves the desired result without any unforeseen negative side-effects on other groups. Understanding current patterns of resource distribution and the factors which determine them is necessary in order to design programmes effectively, as new projects or policies may alter the determining factors and thereby change the patterns of allocation.

The effects of projects on intra-household dynamics may be subtle and complex, but they are absolutely central to the successful outcome, and even to the successful implementation of development interventions. This is because development projects are based on certain assumptions about how households will behave in the face of the change they intend to bring about.

For example, a new technology which increases productivity may change the value of an individual's time, with consequences for the time spent on other tasks he or she performs. An immunization programme which alters the probabilities of child survival may change the strategies by which households decide to invest in certain children. A paved road may open new opportunities for wage employment, altering the opportunity cost of time devoted to unpaid household production.

Understanding intra-household decision-making is important in order to predict who in the household is likely to gain and lose (in both the short and long run) as a result of an intervention. Projects which place unacceptable burdens on some individuals without compensation may find themselves compromised by lack of participation. Projects which attempt to target consumption goods to particular household members often find that the household's own preferences in allocation supersede those of the programme planners.

The papers in this volume describe the wide variety of linkages between programme interventions and individual outcomes. They spell out a set of issues which, in turn, suggest the need for obtaining information on some specific variables, including household composition, income and assets, task allocation and time use, and individual consumption and welfare. Neither income, capital, nor the time of given members is necessarily interchangeable with that of other household members, so that these variables need to be measured for each individual.

The papers discuss alternative approaches to collecting data on the internal processes by which households allocate resources and responsibilities among their members. The authors make it clear that both information gleaned from secondary sources and primary data obtained using a wide range of qualitative and quantitative methods are needed to investigate intra-household processes. None of these methods is novel, although their application to household dynamics is relatively untried. The important message is that the combination of methods is stronger than any single methodological approach, because analysis of the household draws on the concepts of a variety of disciplines.

Many measurement problems have not been satisfactorily resolved. The household and its internal dynamics have only relatively recently become a focus for research, and one result of this work has been to identify new areas of investigation, requiring the development of new measurement techniques.

The search for inexpensive and quick methods of measurement has not always been successful, and in many cases short-cuts simply cannot be taken. Collecting data on individuals is necessarily more time-consuming than collecting aggregate data. It makes sense to seek proxy variables and easily accessible indicators for some of the more difficult-to-measure concepts in household-level studies, but it will not always be possible to find them.

These papers taken together clearly demonstrate that information on intra-household allocation and its determinants is central to effective development planning. Including this level of analysis in the planning process certainly requires more resources, both in time and money. But the return on these additional costs should be more than compensated by the greater likelihood of project success.

Appendix

INTRODUCTION

These tables present, in summary form, an approach for incorporating intra-household analysis into development planning. They are taken from a methodological guideline prepared for the United States Agency for International Development and other donor agencies which implement development projects abroad. The guideline, *Incorporating the Intrahousehold Dimension into Development Projects: A Guide* (Rogers, 1988), can be obtained from USAID/Bureau of Policy and Program Coordination/Human Resources Division, in Washington, D.C.

The papers in this volume underscore the importance of including intra-household issues in the design, monitoring, and assessment of projects and programmes. The tables include a list of key variables, methods of measurement, and the comparative advantages of various approaches, as they pertain to each stage of project implementation.

REFERENCE

Rogers, B.L. 1988. *Incorporating the Household Dimension into Development Projects: A Guide.* Office of Policy Development and Program Review, Bureau of Policy and Program Coordination, US Agency for International Development, Washington, D.C.

Table A. Data to be collected: variables, uses, methods

Type of data	Variables	Uses of the information	Methods
Household composition, structure, and function			
Members living under one roof or in one compound (co-residential unit)	a. Number of members, age and sex	Measure level of need in relation to resources (vars. a, e, f)	Secondary data is often available on common household structures
	b. Common household structures (nuclear, extended, multi-generational, other)	Assess possibilities for task-sharing within household (vars. a, b, e, f)	Key informant interviews can cover common household structures
	c. Number of unrelated individuals		Small-scale surveys of households should start with a listing of all members (in table form) including age, sex, relation to household head, educational level, occupation(s) for each
	d. Number of members tied by blood, by marriage, to household head	Indicate vulnerable groups at risk of low (relative) levels of consumption (vars. c, g)	
	e. Ratio of children to adults (age depends on local definition)	Identify possible sources of resistance to change (var. b)	
	f. Ratio of non-working to working members (depending ratio)		Seasonal variation may be addressed by questions on the household list ("Is this person usually present all year? During what season is she absent?") or by covering several seasons
	g. Sex of household head		
	h. Seasonal changes in co-residential household size and composition due to in- and outmigration		Servants or other unrelated individuals may be defined as members for some purposes and not others, e.g. if they eat with the household they may be members; if they are paid by the household rather than contributing to it, they may be considered separate

188

Group eating from a common food supply (commensal unit)	a. Degree of overlap of this group with the co-residential unit	Identify possibility for leakage of benefits	If servants are considered a separate unit, any study of households should include them in the sample
	b. Frequency of food gifts sent and received	Identify possible paths for dispersion of benefits	Secondary data on social organization may include information on sharing and gift-giving
	c. Rules governing exchanges of food		Direct observation of households at mealtimes to determine whether members are usually absent or guests are present
	d. Frequency of members eating away from home	Define level of need. Co-residential unit may not accurately define need if much sharing occurs	In small-scale surveys, a question in the household list may be added for some or all members: "How many meals are taken at home/away from home?"
Group pooling its income and resources for common support (income-pooling unit)	a. Degree of overlap of this group with co-residential and commensal units	Identify possibility for leakage of benefits	Information on income/resource pooling is very difficult to obtain in a short-cut manner. Food-sharing may be a proxy in some cases
	b. Degree of pooling by different members: male head, female head, young adult children, elderly relatives, unrelated members	Identify possible paths for dispersion of benefits	Secondary data on pooling is not commonly available
	c. Degree of pooling with persons not living in the household: relatives living elsewhere, foster children	Define level of need	Direct observation of pooling is not possible
	d. Frequency and source of gifts in cash and kind		Informal questioning of key informants may give idealized rather than actual picture but should indicate how to pose survey questions

189

Table A (*continued*)

Type of data	Variables	Uses of the information	Methods
			In small-scale surveys, may ask individual members: "What categories of expenditure do you spend *your* income on?" "How frequently do you receive (give) gifts of cash, of goods?" "Does anyone outside the household depend on your income?" "How much of your income is reserved for your personal (as opposed to household) use?"
Labour-sharing unit	a. Degree of overlap with co-residential, commensal, or income-pooling group	Identify possible conflicts with time and labour requirements resulting from development projects or policies, and possible means of accommodating to them	Studies on labour obligations may exist in the anthropological or sociological literature
	b. Nature of labour obligation (type of work, whether mutual or one-way)		Informal direct questioning of local informants can reveal rules for labour-sharing and the nature of the shared tasks
	c. Whether labour obligations are determined by blood, affinal, or other ties	Identify possible sources of resistance to change, or barriers to individuals taking advantage of new programmes or policies	
	d. Seasonality of obligations		
	e. Whether there are several different labour-sharing units with different obligations and tasks	Identify possible paths for dispersion of benefits, especially of productive assets and training	
	f. Degree of overlap among the different labour-sharing units	Identify possible detrimental effects from disruption of the labour-sharing units or possible shifts in membership (due to introduction of new technology, for example)	

Income

a. Agriculture

Issues / Questions	What can be estimated or predicted	Sources of information
a. Agriculture		
– Degree of dependence on agricultural wage labour, subsistence farming, and farming for sale (proportion of households which earn income from each source; proportion of each household's income from each source)	Estimate level of income adequacy and security of households	Information on the nature of the economy (types of employment, types of production) will certainly be available from either published studies or internal government or donor agency reports
– Are certain types of agricultural labour performed by women, men, children (whether for pay or for own production)?	Estimate returns to different kinds of human capital (wage rates) based on education, age, sex, to predict incentives for investment in particular individuals; to estimate relative value of individuals' time in home and market activities	Direct observation of workplaces (fields, markets, factories) can indicate by whom certain jobs are done and the types of work performed
– Who in the household – owns land; – controls the uses of its products; – markets the products?	Identify likely degree of control (by individuals) of income as a whole; of income from different sources	Key informant interviews can provide information on: – association of crops, tasks with certain individuals; – seasonality of employment; – labour shortage/surplus; – types of work available
– Are certain crops or types of crops the responsibility of certain members (women, men)?	Predict changes in returns to different kinds of human capital; possibly predict changes in household's investment in different individuals	Focus group methods may be used to obtain information on: – general pattern of income-earning (number of earners, their sex, age, type of jobs); – perceived association of individuals' income with specific expenditures; – perceived association of individual income with control over income uses
– Seasonality of income from different crops and labour	Predict changes in returns to physical assets and possible consequences for access	Small-scale surveys can identify: – individual income streams within households: approximate amount, frequency, reliability of income;
– Rates of pay for different kinds of work	Predict changes in individuals' incomes (amount, reliability, frequency)	
– Form of pay (cash, in-kind)	Predict changes in household income (amount, reliability, frequency)	
b. Formal sector employment: – Types of jobs available – Full-time, part-time, seasonal – Skill or educational level required – Rate of pay	Predict possible changes in control over assets and income, and in their uses	

Table A (*continued*)

Type of data	Variables	Uses of the information	Methods
	– Period of pay (piece, day, week, etc.) – Form of pay (cash, in-kind) – Are the jobs for men, women, children, or no restriction? – Is labour in surplus, or scarce in different kinds of jobs? – Seasonality of labour demand c. Informal sector employment: – Types of jobs available – Level and reliability of income – Done by men, women, children – Seasonality	Identify possible sources of resistance to change Identify possible change in how food is acquired (purchased, home-grown), and possible consequences for food adequacy and security Predict who might gain and lose from altered employment opportunities	– categories of expenditure associated with individual income streams (subjective perception of respondents)
Assets and wealth Productive assets	a. What major productive assets are owned by households? (Proportion type of household) b. Is ownership joint or individual? c. How is access obtained? Distinguish use rights (rights to the product) from ownership (right to allocate). Are rights obtained by purchase, inheritance, through blood or marriage ties, etc.?	Predict changes in ownership or access to the use of resources Identify possible sources of resistance to change Predict who will and will not benefit from changes in the productivity of assets Predict who may be displaced from use of assets	Existing studies Key informant interviews Small-scale surveys of households, asking about ownership and use of resources (e.g. a checklist format covering, for each listed asset, ownership, use, how obtained) Previous studies might exist in the anthropological literature

192

Category	Variables	Analysis	Methods
Publicly owned assets	a. What resources are freely available to all?	Identify possible changes in availability of free goods (e.g. food, water, fuel, other goods) Predict consequences for consumption and time use	Direct observation Key informant interviews
Ownership of consumption goods	a. Quality of housing (roof, walls, floor) b. Utilities (electricity, water, waste disposal available to household) c. Ownership of goods indicating wealth (e.g. bicycles, automobiles, radios, televisions, cows, goats)	Estimate general economic level of households Identify vulnerable population Predict project or policy effects which may vary depending on total resource level of household	Direct observation In small-scale surveys, include questions about ownership of resources Note that choice of which specific goods are accurate indicators of wealth depends on local knowledge
Task allocation and time use Inventory of tasks	a. Major taks of – household maintenance; – home-board production; – work outside home b. Range of time required for each task	Use to collect and organize information from subsequent sections	Existing studies (including anthropological and sociological research) Key informant interviews Direct observation of tasks that can be publicly viewed
Organization of tasks	a. Which tasks can be done together b. Which tasks *must* be done together or in a fixed sequence c. Time restrictions on tasks (e.g. done only at certain times of day, week, year) d. Location restrictions on tasks	Predict possible conflicts with new tasks required as result of a policy change Predict shifts in the time spent on certain tasks or their frequency	Existing studies Key informant interviews Direct observation Focus groups

Table A (*continued*)

Type of data	Variables	Uses of the information	Methods
Task allocation	a. Which tasks are performed by individuals of particular age, sex, status, what proportion of the time	Predict possible conflicts of current tasks with new tasks required as a result of a project or a policy change	Existing studies may be available for some tasks
		Predict which tasks are likely to shift and from/to which individuals	Key informants may be useful but may provide idealized rather than accurate information
		Predict consequences for quality of the work performed	Direct observation of the performance of tasks is necessary to determine actual distribution of tasks
		Predict changes in total work burden of individuals	
Social norms regarding work	a. Restrictions on types of work or place of work based on sex, age, status, religion	Predict which individuals will take advantage of changing work and income-earning opportunities	Previous studies
	b. Degree to which these restrictions are observed	Identify possible sources of resistance to changes resulting from project	Key informants most useful for information on norms
	c. Social norms governing earnings by age, sex	Identify possible sources of social stress, family disruption, and violence as a result of changes due to a project or policy	Focus groups may be useful to determine which restrictions are followed in practice, especially for activities which are difficult for an outsider to observe
Time burden of individuals	a. Amount of time spent in each of various tasks identified by methods in previous four sections	Identify possible conflicts with project-related tasks	Previous studies of time-use patterns may exist in a few cases only; check UCLA database of time-allocation studies (see Johnson's chapter in this volume)
	b. Time constraints on individuals (available leisure; amount of time spent sleeping; working;	Predict possible changes in the performance of tasks (who does them; how well; how much time is spent)	Information from direct observation of tasks, the time they re-

in recreation; flexibility in allocation of time) c. Work burden of individual	Assess whether time will be shifted, reduced, increased, for a given task as a result of the time requirements of the project; or whether the task will be displaced to another person altogether	quire, how they are organized, and their allocation among individuals can be combined with information on household size and composition to estimate work burden on particular individuals
	Predict changes in the work burden of certain individuals; consequences for their welfare; the welfare of children	Small-scale surveys can ask questions on: - the frequency of performance of certain tasks; - the frequency of available help, or number of helpers, for the task; - age and sex of helpers, to estimate work load; - the range of time different activities take; - how tasks are organized (sequence steps; are they done alone or always in conjunction with other tasks?)
	Assess available leisure, amount of sleep, as a measure of welfare of individuals	24-hour activity recall or spot checks
		Direct observation of time use of individuals
Consumption Food a. Growth outcomes, growth rates of children by age and sex b. Specific foods or types of foods allocated to certain individuals (by age, sex, work or pregnancy status, kinship status in household)	Identify vulnerable groups, groups at risk of inadequate food intake Predict who will benefit in food availability at household level	Growth outcomes can be measured in a small-scale survey measuring height, weight, and age of children and comparing height/age and weight/height with a standard. This the best measure of adequacy of food consumption

Table A. (*continued*)

Type of data	Variables	Uses of the information	Methods
	c. Specific foods or type of foods allocated or withheld during illness, pregnancy, lactation	Anticipate possible changes in access to food if consumption pattern changes	Key informant interviews and focus groups can indicate whether specific foods or types of food are preferentially given to certain types of individuals, and what foods are given or withheld in illness, pregnancy, etc.
	d. Meal patterns of individuals: frequency of formal meals at home, away, and informal consumption (wild food, street food, snacks at neighbours'); illness	Assess degree to which household food availability is a proxy for food available to each member	In a survey, questions may be included on allocation of foods to individuals and on allocation in sickness. For example, a checklist of local foods may be presented with questions like "Is this food mainly given to children? babies? boys? girls? adults? men? women?" "If your child is sick, do you increase feeding of any foods? Which? Decrease? Which?"
	e. Food intake (quantity) of specific individuals		A food-frequency questionnaire may be administered to certain individuals in a sample of households; principal caretaker may answer for younger children
			Meal pattern information may be obtained from local informants and from direct observation inside households
			Note that household food consumption cannot be used as a proxy for adequacy of consumption by individuals.

196

Health care			
a. Morbidity of individuals by age, sex	Identify vulnerable groups	Previous studies and government or agency reports may exist on available types of health care (but reliability may be questionable)	
b. Infant and child mortality by age and sex	Predict likely pattern of use if available services are changed	Direct observation at health-service locations can indicate who uses the services; how much time is required; and what services, personnel, and supplies are available	
c. Frequency of use of different categories of health-care services	Predict who is likely to benefit first from changed services; who in long-term	Focus groups and local informants can provide information on what services are used for what complaints; who is responsible for providing the care; time costs and other constraints to use. Information on sex bias will probably not emerge from this method	
d. Time and cash costs of services	For what kinds of problems are services likely to be used	In a small-scale survey, questions may be included on:	
e. Number of hours services are open; who staffs them during which hours (doctor; nurse; lay health worker); sex of staff members	For which members	– morbidity of children and adults (accurate retrospection probably limited to 2–4 weeks; may distinguish diarrhoea, fever, respiratory problems);	
f. What medicines/vitamins are dispensed; under which circumstances		– use of services: accuracy is probably better if questions refer to the last illness episode of the individual rather than "usual practice"; it is helpful to distinguish first source of care, second source of care (if applicable), etc.	

Table A (*continued*)

Type of data	Variables	Uses of the information	Methods
Education	a. Educational levels of household members by age, sex b. Current school enrolment of individuals by age, sex c. Proportion of girls and boys in school by age/grade level	Indicate preference for investment in certain individuals Identify groups not receiving services Predict who will benefit first from changes in availability of services or access to them Predict who will benefit from a change in the returns to education of specific individuals	Information may be available in government or other agency reports Direct observation of schools can indicate relative attendance of boys and girls, members of different ethnic classes Direct observation of communities can suggest degree of non-attendance (in some circumstances) Focus groups can address questions of who is sent to school and why, and what barriers to attendance exist In a small-scale survey, questions on educational level, literacy, and current enrolment can be included in the household listing

Table B. Intrahousehold analysis procedures

Steps	Outputs	Approximate time required
Review of project idea or plan		
1. Project or policy idea is presented		1–2 weeks
2. Objectives of the project or policy change are specified		
3. Linkages between inputs of project or policy and expected individual outcomes are spelled out in detail, using the following questions regarding intra-household issues. A detailed scheme or model of these links between the project inputs or policy-induced changes and individual outcomes is prepared	A flow chart or other framework specifying the linkages between project (or policy) inputs and expected outcomes	

4. Missing information needed to complete the model is identified
   – Who will participate in project activities?
   – Will the project require or cause a change in household structure, composition, or function?
   – Will the project change any person's access to productive resources, or any person's control over what is produced (including control over income from his/her labour)?
   – Will the project affect any person's wage rate (returns to labour) or the rate of return to assets under any person's control?
   – Will the project require changes in the inventory of tasks performed by household members, or in the organization of tasks?
   – Will the project change the allocation of tasks among members or the time use of members?
   – Will the project change any person's access to consumption goods (food, health care, education, etc.) which affect welfare?
	Written specification of a model of expected effects on individual income, command over resources, task performance, time burden, and consumption
	
	Written identification of gaps in knowledge, necessary to assess these effects	

Table B (*continued*)

Steps	Outputs	Approximate time required
Integrating information from existing sources		1–6 weeks
5. Published and unpublished literature is reviewed to fill in missing information on projects' or policies' effect on individuals		
6. Literature review is used to identify people who have worked in the area of the proposed project or policy		
7. These people are contacted for the information they can provide. Additional written information and personal contacts may be identified		
8. The written model for project effects on individuals is updated, and the remaining areas of missing information are identified	Updated written specification of model of expected effects Updated written indication of missing information	
Planning for field-work		1–2 weeks
9. These are used to prepare a set of topic guidelines (questions appropriate to direct observation and to different categories of informants) to be followed during on-site data collection	Topic guides Data collection plan	
Preparations are made for on-site data collection		1 month
10. Geographic area(s) for on-site data collection are identified; government and agency concurrence obtained if necessary	List of geographic areas for data collection, with reasons for selection	
11. Identify skill areas required for data collection; identify person or team to conduct the field-work	List of people, qualifications and availability	
12. Identify persons in-country who may help with data collection effort		
13. Select team; prepare contracts; deploy in field	Administrative paperwork required to field team	
Field-work		1–2 weeks
14. Contact with local sources of		

200

Table B (*continued*)

Steps	Outputs	Approximate time required
information: team visits knowledgeable social scientists, programme administrators, government officials to obtain opinions and information required to complete intra-household analysis of proposed project. Hiring of additional team members		
15. Field data collection – Team travels to area of proposed project (repeated in several areas if appropriate to nature of project). Hiring of local assistants – Data collected using topic guides, updated as needed. – Direct observation of representative sample of households, schools, clinics, markets, shops, or other locations as appropriate to the proposed project or policy. Observations used to obtain data and to verify the accuracy of verbal reports – Informal interviews with local informants chosen to represent varying perspectives and points of view – Focus groups of local population conducted as appropriate – Model of project is updated and remaining knowledge gaps identified	Updated written specification of model of expected project or policy effects	Minimum 4 weeks in most cases
16. Survey research: if necessary, a small-scale household survey may be undertaken, using the results of the previous data-collection effects as a basis for designing a survey instrument		Minimum 2–4 additional weeks in most cases
17. Integration of data into project plan – Proposed project or policy plan is reviewed and elaborated or modified as needed – Completed model of expected effects is prepared	Completed written model of predicted effects Project or policy implementation plan	1–3 weeks

201

Table B (*continued*)

Steps	Outputs	Approximate time required
– A plan for the timing and date requirements for monitoring of the intra-household effects of the project is developed	Written project-monitoring plan	

Participants

Similolu Afonja
University of Ife
Department of Sociology and
  Anthropology
PO Box 1052
Ile-Ife, Nigeria

Jere Behrman
Economics Department
University of Pennsylvania
3718 Locust Walk
Philadelphia, PA 19104-6297, USA

Patrice Engle
Psychology and Human Development
  Department
California Polytechnic State University
San Luis Obispo, CA 93407, USA

David Franklin
Sigma One Corporation
PO Box 12425
Raleigh, NC 27605, USA

Marito Garcia
International Food Policy Research
  Institute
1776 Massachusetts Avenue, NW
Suite 400
Washington, DC 20036, USA

Peter Heywood
Papua New Guinea Institute of Medical
  Research
PO Box 378
Madang, Papua New Guinea

Elizabeth Jelín
Centro de Estudios de Estado y
  Sociedad (CEDES)
Avenida Pueyrredon 510-Fe
1032 Buenos Aires
Argentina

Allen Johnson, Chairman
Department of Anthropology
University of California
Los Angeles, CA 90024, USA

Shubh Kumar
International Food Policy Research
  Institute
1776 Massachusetts Avenue, NW
Washington, DC 20036, USA

Judith McGuire
The World Bank
1818 H Street NW
Washington, DC 20433, USA

Ellen Messer
Alan Shawn Feinstein World Hunger
   Program
Brown University
Providence, RI 02912, USA

Isabel Nieves
Instituto Nutricional de Centro
   América y Panamá (INCAP)
Guatemala City, Guatemala

Patricia O'Brien-Place
US Agency for International
   Development Africa Bureau
Washington, DC 20520, USA

Per Pinstrup-Andersen
Director of Cornell Food and Nutrition
   Policy Project
Division of Nutrition Sciences
Savage Hall
Cornell University
Ithaca, NY 14853, USA

Ellen Piwoz
Pan American Health Organization
525 Twenty-third Street, NW
Washington, DC 20037, USA

Najma Rizvi
International Centre for Diarrhoeal
   Disease Research (ICDDR)
GPO Box 128
Dhaka–2
Bangladesh

Beatrice Lorge Rogers
Tufts University School of Nutrition
126 Curtis Street
Medford, MA 02155, USA

Mark Rosenzweig
Department of Economics
1035 Business Administration
271 19th Avenue South
University of Minnesota
St Paul, MN 55455, USA

Constantina Safilios-Rothschild
Population Council
1 Dag Hammerskjold Plaza
New York, NY 10017, USA

Susan Scrimshaw
School of Public Health
University of California
Los Angeles, CA 90024, USA

John Strauss
Economics and Statistics Department
RAND Corporation
1700 Main Street
Santa Monica, CA 90406, USA